D0987397

THE MUSICIAN

Mike Shaw

For permissions, email: blueroombooks@outlook.com
Blue Room Books | Subject: The Musician

Cover design and interior layout: Angela K. Durden
Editor: Tom Whitfield

THE MUSICIAN
MIKE SHAW
BLUEROOMBOOKS.COM
978-1-950729-09-8

To the hundreds of thousands who
strum, blow, beat, pluck, or sing
impressively enough to
make a living making music.

"It is the truth:
Comedians and jazz musicians have been more comforting
and enlightening to me than preachers or politicians or
philosophers or poets or painters or novelists of my time.
Historians in the future, in my opinion, will congratulate us
on very little other than
our clowning and our jazz."
Kurt Vonnegut

"If I skip practice for one day, I notice.
If I skip practice for two days, my wife notices. If I skip for
three days, the world notices."
Vladimir Horowitz

"Music, the combiner, nothing more spiritual,
nothing more sensuous, a god, yet completely human,
advances, prevails, holds highest place;
supplying in certain wants and quarters
what nothing else could supply."
Walt Whitman

"Fiction is not fact, but fiction is fact selected and
understood, fiction is fact arranged
and charged with purpose."
Thomas Wolfe

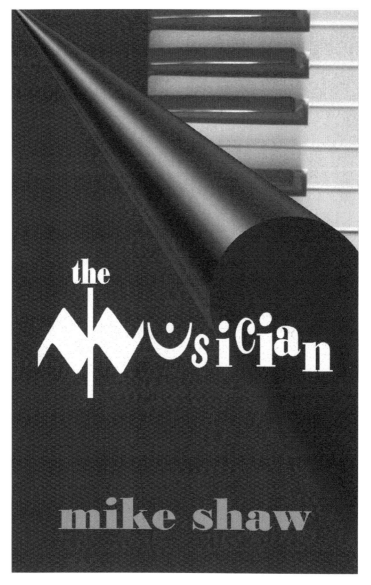

If you were a singer in the decade of discontent, you probably sang folk songs. And if you sang folk songs, a coffee house gig was as good as it got. In Kansas City, on the Missouri side, that would've been the Village.

I didn't set out to protest the war or campaign for free love. Just wanted to sing. I'd been in a college talent show, a medley of Sinatra tunes concluding with a toe-tapping, finger-snapping, horn-punctuated version of "Learnin' The Blues." Not than anyone would mistake me for someone who'd learned the blues.

Pure white boy, raised in comfort, privately educated. Still, I must have done justice to Ol' Blue Eyes' songs because I got a standing ovation. And that was all I needed to set me on my way to more crowds, applause, stardom.

I'd been fantasizing about singing in front of an audience forever. While most of my high school buddies were in their hot-rod Chevys going for free feelies in the dark corners of the Springfield Steak 'n Shake parking lot, I was in my basement with LPs — those long-playing vinyl records that have made quite a comeback these decades later — mimicking Sinatra, Mathis, and Bennett, their intonation and breathing, the way they attacked and held notes, how they told songs' stories.

But the standing O was proof of talent, that I could do this. And the very next weekend I was on the prowl, from downtown dive bars to fussy hotel lounges with peach-colored sofas and waiters in tuxedoes balancing drink trays on their fingertips.

Most places with live music were restaurant-bars. They were many with all kinds of music, from Elvis Presley imitations to twangy Ventures' licks to florid piano solos. People came for a steak, or a bourbon or two, the music mostly an afterthought. Guitarists and pianists and singers finished songs to light applause, if any. They were wallpaper, by design, the most common request: "Turn it down!" The musicians didn't seem to object to being ignored; they looked as indifferent as their audiences.

Well, none of that for me.

I wound up late that Saturday night at Jimmy's, a converted barn a couple miles on the Kansas side of town. The large square room glowed orange under fixtures mounted on vertical timbers that appeared to be all that kept the roof off the drinkers. Canoe oars, football pennants, a tricycle, and a hodge-podge of objects and gadgets were draped over, attached to, and hung from the crossbeams.

I sat at a high-top table listening to a copper-haired kid on an acoustic guitar. Despite the chatter and the clatter of dinner plates and whiskey glasses, he was hard at it. He ended his set with an arrangement of "The Girl from Ipanema" tagged with a few lines from another song I recognized only as not from Ipanema. He rested his instrument on its stand and hopped off the stool.

I approached. "That last tune?"

The kid was about my age, slight in stature like me, but with redder hair and even more freckles.

"Is that yours?"

"Ipanema?" He grunted. "Wish it was. Wouldn't be playing this dump."

"No, I meant the other one, the last eight bars."

Eight bars at least got an answer. "It's 'Scotch and Soda.' You haven't heard it?"

I shook my head.

"As big a folk hit as ever was."

Folk. Hmmmm. "I'm not exactly into folk music."

He pursed his lips and exhaled slowly. Maybe he couldn't believe someone his age wasn't a folkie.

"Then I guess you haven't been to the Village. One of the singers I play for over there does that tune most every night." He started toward the bar. "Too bad she can't sing."

I stopped him and stuck out my hand. "I'm Tom Cliffe. I'm a singer. And that melody? That's my kind of song. Maybe I could come here one night and sing it with you?"

He looked at my hand like I might have been to the bathroom and forgot to wash. "This ain't my gig. Just filling in for the regular guy who got something better for tonight." He raised his head and met my eyes. "Where you gigging?"

"Well, nowhere now. I...I'm out looking."

The kid flashed a deprecatory grin and continued toward the bar.

Okay, I'd get another chance at him. He was going back on...and wasn't going anywhere without his guitar.

About fifteen minutes later he appeared at my table jiggling ice cubes in what was left of a dark brown drink. "If you're *looking*, Tom Cliffe" — he was ragging me, but in a friendly sort of way — "it's the Village. There're lots of singers there, at least people who think they can sing, but you can go and try out. Eddie'll give you a shot."

* * *

A college classmate had been to the Village. "Those cats are serious. Their music isn't just good, it's *important*. It's about *things that matter*, things in this country that *need changing*." It was the prevailing sentiment of the day.

I decided I'd go. The very next weekend, Friday night, I drove to midtown in a '53 Plymouth I'd bought against the advice of several upperclassmen from a used car lot neighboring the campus. The decade had been unkind to the once brilliantly toreador red Belvedere, rusting its fender skirts and imposing a life-threatening oil leak.

I parked on a side street in a residential neighborhood several blocks from the Village and its Troost Avenue pay-to-park meters. The brief Kansas City fall was already hinting a long, damp winter.

The Village was so unlike the restaurants and barrooms I'd been prospecting. The room was bright, a street-side bay window open to a setting sun that gave way to the blue-green incandescent Troost Avenue street-lamps. White cinder block walls were nearly hidden by artwork: painted portraits and Midwestern scenes, and photography of folk musicians performing in front of huge audiences. The aroma was church incense.

[10]

The club sold some food, but no alcohol, just coffee. Patrons, mostly college students and recent grads, moved around the room conversing like they all knew each other well. A Burl Ives replica climbed on stage and plopped onto a wooden chair. He pulled a polished red acoustic guitar from its cradle and rested it in his lap. The crowd hushed and settled in.

"Friends, I do protest!" He strummed an open chord. "Do you know what they call this war in Vietnam? They call it 'The American War.'" A second open chord. "*I* call it McNamara's war!" Back to the first chord. "And if we don't stop him and the compromised president who's lining his pockets with the spoils of this so-called conflict…" A third chord. "We're all gonna go…and we're all gonna die."

For nearly an hour the tie-dyed crowd remained focused on the music, breaking silence only as a song ended to snap their fingers in appreciation. Performers crowded the stage: choruses of guitarists behind singers belting out songs celebrating freedom and individuality, chastising politicians and corporations for their callous disregards. And one or two sensitive ballads. In those, I saw myself. I was one with the audience in appreciating the music as relevant, but also apart. I belonged on that stage, not at a table.

Among the performers was the copper-haired guitarist, introduced to the audience as Dave Hartwell. As he and the singers he was accompanying finished the final song of the set, he found me in a corner under an oil of Woody Guthrie.

"I see you fell in to check us out. Groovy, eh?" his vocabulary markedly different from our first meeting.

"It's not like the Sinatra and Mathis tunes I've been singing." I stood and offered my hand. He didn't take it. "But Dave, I could own those ballads. Seriously."

It sounded like begging, but I had to get a shot at this, the one chance I'd found; I knew I could sing as well as, even better than, anyone who'd just stepped down from that riser.

"I'll hook you up with Eddie, but don't be spouting jive about Sinatra. That's way uncool. Just tell him you dig the place and would like to jump stage with us for a chance at a gig."

I'd read *Naked Lunch* — or started it; what male college student in the '60s hadn't at least pretended to have read it? The nearer we got to the coffee bar where Eddie was fingering the cash register, the more he resembled the writer: the thin, long face, the frowning eyes, the black-rimmed glasses.

"Man, he's a dead ringer for William Burroughs."

Hartwell chuckled. "Everybody tells him that. Eddie himself is a beat generation survivor. Read his poetry here when it was a beatnik hangout. Nice cat. Shitty poet. A bit off the cob. Got the manager's gig 'cause the owner didn't want to hurt his feelings, so asked him to trade proselytizing for running the joint. Like I say, nice enough cat."

Nice enough, for sure. Dave asked and Eddie agreed to let me join the evening's concluding hootenanny sing.

There must have been ten singers on that little wooden riser. And the songs, so simple and popular I knew them before I sang them. To our left and right and behind, an orchestra of guitars. And my voice, so strong back then, and so sure — and so naïve.

Hartwell found me as the stage unloaded. "Hey, man, you *can* sing. If you still want to do 'Scotch and Soda,' we can try it here."

Then from Eddie a nod; a nickname, "Silvertone"; and an offer of a weekend spot: my first paid gig, a regular at Kansas City's Village Coffee House.

* * *

Optimistically named after Max Gordon's Village Vanguard in New York, the Village occasionally featured touring acts but mainly showcased local folk musicians: singers and guitarists railing against war and hypocrisy, exposing a full slate of conditions ripe for outrage and repair. Hartwell and Cliffe, now a fixture on the Village roster, were performing the most popular music of the time in the city's hippest and hottest club. While my college classmates were restacking library shelves or bussing tables, I was earning money living my dream.

For more than a year we played the Village every weekend, and were enthusiastically applauded, in the mode of the era, by an audience absorbed in the sincerity of our songs and the commitment in our delivery.

I was the featured vocalist, but Dave also sang, agile with harmonies and hitting notes with precision. We covered the hits: Dylan's "The Times They Are A Changin'" and "Don't Think Twice It's Alright"; The Kingston Trio's "Greenback Dollar"; and the Weavers' sing-along, "Wimoweh." The arrangements, they were ours.

We unearthed a few traditionals our counterparts had yet to frazzle, like "Ja-Da," a bone-simple, sixteen-bar melody sung in rounds, like "Three Blind Mice." *Ja-da, ja-da jing jing jing.*

But our signature tune became "Until It's Time for You to Go," a tender if somewhat obscure ballad from Canadian folksinger Buffy Sainte-Marie. It was perfect for my voice. Dave sang a third above on the choruses. It was the song audiences, especially the women, requested again and again.

The night of my college talent show, the pianist had told me I *connected* more than other singers he'd accompanied. "There's something special there, kid," he'd said. His words gave me confidence; I'd remind myself of them over the years on nights when I wasn't connecting.

But at the Village, when we performed "Until It's Time for You to Go," I could always find a girl in the audience with a tissue dabbing an eye.

* * *

"You play guitar?" Eddie asked as we completed a Saturday night's final set. "If you could accompany yourself, I might have a slot for you as a single now and then."

I'd considered taking up guitar. How difficult could it be? I'd seen several of the Village performers fingering the simplest of chords behind their singing.

"Guitar? Way cool," Dave agreed. So he didn't object to me working alone?

"Not the code, Cliffe. When you get a chance, take it. Nobody's got the right to hold you back." Instead, he talked about how it would fatten our sound and free him up to do more lead work.

"And now for your first axe." Dave rubbed his palms together, clearly relishing the idea. "The place to get it is Big Daddy's," a downtown pawnshop, he added, where many a hungry guitarist had abandoned his instrument.

* * *

[14]

Big Daddy's neighborhood, legendary for its "corner of 12th Street and Vine," was now broken and angry, crumbling and dissonant with neglect and preoccupation with that "bottle of Kansas City wine." The shop was a box, one small room, but with a diversity of merchandise that could have challenged the buyers for Sears, including a row of guitars strung across the wall behind the glass case separating Big Daddy from his clientele.

"Big Daddy, this here's my partner, Tom Cliffe. Need to fix him up with one of your special deals on one of your finest six-strings."

Big Daddy, who looked exactly as I'd imagined except for the scar on the left side of his head where an ear should have been, sat motionless on his metal stool. We might be irritating him just by being there, maybe more just by being two red-headed, freckled-faced white boys. Still, we were able to get him to pull down several instruments when we pointed them out.

Within an hour we'd chosen my inaugural guitar, a Goya classical, the nylon strings and wide fretboard so much easier to play than steel-string Martins and Gibsons Dave and other accomplished Village players preferred. It was light as air, beautifully blond, smelling of polish, and only slightly scarred by a few belt-buckle scratches on the back that Dave honored as experience. And I paid for it with wages from my Village gig.

Dave taught me enough major and minor chords to play most folk songs, and showed me how to fingerpick, just the style for the ballads that had earned me my Silvertone moniker. And so, on occasion, mainly weeknights when the

Village crowds were insufficient to support a full slate, I performed solo.

The Village audiences so respectful and attentive, the music and musicians so serious and relevant, my part so singular and central, that first gig might have been my best.

* * *

One sweltering July 1965 evening, Dave and I arrived earlier than usual to huddle in the Village kitchen and rehearse one more time a song we'd introduce as our first original: Dave as composer and, he insisted, me as lyricist.

"You're a lit major, right? You ought to be able to come up with something. Think about all the bad shit going on in the world and make it rhyme."

I'd labored over the verses for weeks. My first thought was to create a vision of a better world. Unable to imagine one, I decided instead to issue a challenge to work toward one, a call to action to those committed to the cause, to hope and peace and universal love and understanding.

Is this a new revolution,
A world as yet undefined?
Is this the end of democracy?
Is it the end of our time?

Opening with a series of questions seemed a good idea. Wouldn't that be a way to rouse the believers? Then take it to another level.

Do you believe times are changing?
Are you excited or afraid?

[16]

Will you be part of the movement?
Or will you turn and walk away?

Not exactly Dylanesque, but solid enough in meter that Dave should be able to work with it.

I see a future up and coming
Something oh so natural
A truly modern revolution
One people, one united world

I rewrote that verse a hundred times before landing on "modern revolution." Aha! That was the hook, the earworm playing over and over in the heads of our admirers.

Yes, a modern revolution
A world as yet undefined
The end of politics and borders
A new and better time

That last line, a couple of beats shorter than the others, gave Dave space for something musically distinctive, some rhythmic twist.

We'd practiced the song relentlessly, and as we prepared for its debut in the Village kitchen, we played it flawlessly. "Modern Revolution" was to be the signal of our transition from singers to songwriters, launching us toward the fame so conspicuously portrayed in those photos on the Village walls.

We emerged from the kitchen to a house full but nothing like itself. There was a palpable pall, a shared distress, dour faces, and plangent sighs.

The musicians seemed the most distraught. Had someone died? One guitarist, a flamenco specialist who boasted a rare Martin D-28 and was the uncontested master among the Village's players, sat in the bay window seat, his back to the room, stroking his goatee and mumbling.

"It's over." He spoke to me but just kept staring across Troost into a setting sun. "Dylan's gone electric."

Robert Allen Zimmerman, who'd rung in the revival, was ringing its death knell, violating the sanctity of the genre and everything it represented by shelving his acoustic guitar for an electric. In true poetic nuance, he'd used the Newport Folk Festival, the terra firma of folk purity, to flaunt the transition in the face of the era's archetypal voice, Pete Seeger, sparking the galled composer of "If I Had a Hammer" to comment, "If I had an ax, I'd chop that cable."

Indeed, the ax fell. Record sales plummeted; the era's idols faded. The Kingston Trio disbanded in 1967 after a final performance at San Francisco's Hungry I followed by Peter, Paul, and Mary a couple years later, Peter in jail for overtures to a fourteen-year-old. Significance and understanding surrendered to a beat, and substance and harmony to bass and drums. A next generation, unwilling to sit and listen, preferred to drink and dance.

The denouement felled the Village. Audiences thinned, as they did at folk houses across the country. The more capable of the Village guitarists announced their departures for destinations like Denver, Nashville, or Austin, where an acoustic guitarist could find work if willing to do his picking behind a country singer.

Hartwell and Cliffe were among the last Village performers, some weekends the only act to a handful of faithful as reluctant to give up on folk music as the musicians who couldn't imagine playing anything else.

One fall evening shortly before the Village shuttered its bay window forever, Dave and I sat a few minutes before taking the stage to play for an audience comprised principally of empty chairs.

"So much for our careers as songwriters," I chuckled. We'd never performed our original. In the wake of folk music's demise, it now seemed a bit contrived.

"You could come with me." Dave's hip lingo had gone the way of our music. "There's work on the road for guys like us. We could update our repertoire, replace folk with some of the new tunes from The Byrds and Stephen Stills."

I'd yet to consider options, dulled as I was by how our limelight had been so suddenly and thoroughly extinguished.

Dave leaned in. "I didn't want to tell you until I had more time to look into it, but a booking agent from Chicago was here and heard us. He said he'll put us on the road. Just let him know when we're ready. Eddie says he's legit."

There was a knot in my throat that was hard to talk around. "But…I've got to finish college."

Dave's eyes narrowed. "I thought you wanted to be a musician, man. No club owner's going to ask to see your fucking degree. No concert promoter or record company executive will give a shit that you didn't do all four years."

He was right, but that wasn't the point — or couldn't be. "I've got too much invested in it. And my parents…"

"Your parents? You told me you want to play music more than anything. And now you have a chance to get a real career started and you're going to turn it down because you're afraid to tell Mommy and Daddy?"

Fear wasn't the issue. There was something ignoble and wasteful, maybe even mean about abandoning the course they'd provided for, paid for, something more careless than carefree.

"Damnit, Dave, I'd love to do it. But I don't know that I can uproot myself like that and just go. At least give me some time to think about it."

"Sure. But don't take too long. I'll find another golden throat if I have to, 'cause I'm outta here."

The night proved to be our last performance — and the last time I'd see or even talk with Dave Hartwell. It wasn't the last time I thought about going with him. Thought about little else for days, weeks. But couldn't bring myself to commit, or to call Dave to tell him. Instead, I figured folk music's fate had decided my own. I'd found myself in those ballads, that music, that culture.

But they were gone, and all I could feel was lost.

Post-Village performances were sporadic: an occasional weekend night in a bar singing tunes I could fingerpick on my Goya, a few gigs with a female vocalist, fronting a band for a party. The less I performed, the more I craved it. Music was all that mattered. Songs were my religion, lyrics my beliefs, and an audience my society.

"How about dropping by my office later this afternoon and I'll fill you in on what the glee club is doing these days?" Dr. Johnathon Phillips stopped me as we passed in a hallway in Immaculata's Liberal Arts building. He was shorter than me, barely five feet tall and stocky, but with thick, muscular arms. The pinstriped Bermuda shorts he wore exposed heavy, bowed legs coated with long, twisted black hairs. A full black beard was stark contrast to the crown of his head, bald but for a thin line of hair around the back from ear to ear.

Phillips taught Understanding Classical Music. The course was known as an easy A and fought over at registration, including by a substantial contingent of tone deaf students who despite acing the class would never understand or appreciate classical music. He also directed the college's glee club and had pitched me following my debut performance in Talent Night '63, and then at the beginning of each new school year.

Now he was upping his ante.

"I'd like to talk to you about doing the solos for our Christmas program."

The idea of joining a "gentlemen's singing club" and performing archaic compositions *a cappella* in a blue blazer and starched white pants didn't appeal to me.

"It'll be a huge crowd and I need a strong voice like yours to lead us."

Christmas mass was a major event at Immaculata. The holiday ceremony drew hundreds of Catholics from both sides of the state line. I might, after all, look rather smart in a sharp blue blazer and creased white slacks.

As a bright, brisk fall surrendered to the onset of gray, slushy winter, I attended glee club rehearsals. I made no friends — the club appeared reserved for the most sheepish of students, what the Village crowd called pussies.

I was to sing lead on "The First Noel" and "I Wonder As I Wander," a folk hymn I liked much more than the Christmas staple.

Midway through the first week of December the school announced the dorms were closing for Christmas week, the expressed intent being to encourage students to spend the holidays with their families.

More likely, administrators wanted to ward off a repeat of the previous year's seasonal celebrations, when, with no classes or other disciplines to keep us in check, the midnights clear were marked by several unCatholic-like incidents and a few arrests.

"Looks like we'll be performing our Christmas program this year with a smaller group," Dr. Phillips addressed the club at its next rehearsal. "I hope those of you from the dorms who want to perform will be able to find places to stay. Perhaps some of you locals will offer shelter to your fellow clubmen."

He corralled me after he dismissed the group. "We'll have to cancel without you, Tom," he pressed. "No one else can handle the solos. If you'll stay, you can bunk in with me at my place."

I'd phoned home to say, much to Mom's displeasure, that I'd miss Christmas with the family, then with the announcement of the dorm closing, had cheered her with a call saying I'd be coming after all. Now a difficult third call, reversing the charges as usual, explaining that I must remain in Kansas City to "fulfill my commitment to school and church."

On Friday afternoon before Christmas, as the dorms were closing I stuffed my Dopp kit and a few clothes, including my neatly folded blue blazer and white slacks, into a duffel bag, grabbed my guitar and descended to the lobby to wait for Dr. Phillips, who in addition to a bunk had offered a ride, suggesting I leave my ailing Plymouth bent over its oil puddle in the college's student parking lot.

He arrived in a brilliant red Corvette, top down despite the cold.

"What a ride, Dr. Phillips!" I threw my duffel into the backseat and wedged the guitar case into the narrow space behind the front bucket seats. "I've never been in one of these before."

"Tell you what, Tom. Tomorrow morning you can take it for a spin. Drive it around town. Visit some friends."

"Way cool, Dr. Phillips. I'll buzz some of the old Village gang. Can't wait to see the looks on their faces."

Dr. Phillips lived alone in a small apartment in the middle of the city. "I like being around all the hustle and bustle," he explained. "I direct two choirs and the churches are within ten blocks, so I can walk to rehearsals and services. And there're several good restaurants just outside my door. Do you like Kansas City, Tom?"

"Sure, I guess. People are friendly. Met a lot of nice people at the Village."

"Are you dating anyone?"

"Not really. There's this girl, Penny, from the Village. She's really pretty… and sweet. But frankly, I'd rather be playing somewhere than on a date."

"Just throw your stuff over there by the couch."

The front room of the apartment was what I figured a bachelor's pad would look like, except nicer and a lot cleaner. A couch and two leather chairs in what you might call the living room gave way to a space just large enough for a dining table then to a small, narrow kitchen. Dr. Phillips' walls were covered with what I took for modern art, mostly shapes and colors in forms I couldn't identify, no matter how I tilted my head. Dividing the kitchen from the front room and dining area was a counter just high and long enough to support two barstools. I tossed my duffel on the couch and leaned the Goya against a wall where it couldn't get stepped on.

"You want a soda? Or how about a beer or glass of wine? You're twenty-one now, right?"

Well, close enough. I sat at a kitchen stool and we talked while Dr. Phillips prepared steaks, the thickest filet mignons I'd ever seen, and tossed a salad. He'd pre-cooked two huge baked potatoes and added them to the oven as the steaks broiled. He asked about my family and school, and showed particular interest when I told him I hoped to make a career of singing.

I drank two or three beers as we talked and red wine with my steak, then joined him in an after-dinner liqueur. "Baileys," he said, "better than dessert."

"Time to hit the hay, eh?" Dr. Phillips had cleared the dining table and was rinsing the dishes in the sink with his back to me. "Sorry about how small this place is, Tom, but there's only one bedroom and only one bed. You don't mind sharing my space, do you?"

I'd packed a pair of pajamas Mom had sent with me to college that had never been slept in. I pulled them from my bag and changed in the bathroom.

"You can have that side," Dr. Phillips directed. I got in, faced away from him, and settled my head into a cushy pillow. Just as I relaxed, a heavy, hairy leg lapped me knee high. Not a second elapsed before I was on my feet.

"What are you…What do you think…" I was breathing in bursts, half angry, half stunned.

"I'm sorry, Tom." He sat up in the bed, bedsheet pulled to his waist. He spoke calmly. "You said you wanted to stay with me. And then you got in bed with me. I assumed…"

I was pulling on my street clothes over my pajamas. "Oh, God, no. I just thought you wanted me to sing those solos. I mean, if you thought I was… well, I'm not. I'm definitely not." There was nothing in my life I was surer of.

Dr. Phillips was on his feet, pulling on the boxer undershorts I now realized with horror he'd shed before climbing into bed.

"Tom, where are you going?" His was the professor's voice, measured and authoritative. "It's too late. You'll sleep on the couch."

I'd never been one to defy authority. A respectable Catholic kid who never sassed the nuns. I'd have been thrashed, had my mouth washed out with soap, and sent to bed without dinner.

But though I had no idea where I was going, I was leaving. "I'll be fine, sir. It's not that late. I'll catch a cab to a, my, a…"

I could think of nothing to explain where I might go at eleven o'clock on a Friday night with the dorm closed.

"Tom. My apologies. I was mistaken. You can't leave at this hour."

I was not going to stay, couldn't. And when his plea changed from concern for me so obviously to concern for himself, I knew he realized it.

"I hope you won't go telling people about this. You might not know it or see it, but there are many homosexuals at the school, students and faculty. Several of the priests. We don't broadcast it. Hell, I could get caught screwing the dean's secretary in the sacristy and get away with it. But if my relationship with another male faculty member got out, it would be the end of both our jobs at Immaculata — and probably any other school in the Midwest."

"I won't say anything." I just wanted out.

Homosexuality common? Ridiculous. I'd never met a homosexual. And priests? Impossible. They don't even have sex with women.

"I won't tell anyone," I promised again, zipping the duffel and grabbing the Goya. I escaped into a December drizzle and spoke into the night. "But I also won't be singing at Christmas — or ever coming back to glee club."

He stood at the apartment door watching me scurry down three flights of steps to the street below.

"Oh, Tom." He was on his landing, his barrel chest black with hair pressed into the railing, leaning over to yell at me. "About that career? If you want to be a musician you better think about becoming a little more open-minded."

Was he trying to embarrass me into not telling anyone his dirty little secret? I hailed a cab easily enough and directed the driver to the Greyhound station. I slid a dime into a payphone and asked the operator to reverse charges.

"What is it, Tom? Are you okay? What's happened?"

"I'm fine, Mom." I hoped I sounded so. "Just calling to tell you my plans have changed again. I'm coming home for Christmas after all. In fact, I'm at the bus station."

"Why in God's name are you getting on a bus at this ungodly hour?"

"It's just that things didn't quite work out here as planned." Then to head off further investigation, "I was promised the solos, but he gave them to somebody else."

"Oh, Thomas, Thomas. So naïve. Will you be forever naïve." It wasn't a question.

"But don't be getting on a bus at this hour. I'll get you a train ticket in the morning. Stay in a hotel if you have to, but your father's finally asleep — thank God the phone didn't wake him — and your getting here in the middle of the night would put him in such a state. He's so delicate these days. Everything has to be just so. It'll ruin him for the holidays."

* * *

"Penny?"

A reluctant, sleepy voice on the other end was as much as I could have hoped for — and such a relief to hear.

"Tom? Cliffe? Is that you, Tommy?"

"Yeah. I'm sorry, I know it's really late, but…well…I'm in kind of a pickle."

"It's okay. We're still up."

"Could I, well, maybe, sleep on your couch tonight? It's a long story but I'm kind of stuck in town in a way I didn't think I'd be."

"Where are you?"

"Actually, the Greyhound bus station."

A long pause and my hopes were slipping. Please, I thought, please have pity on me.

"I know where that is. I'll pick you up as soon as I can get dressed and get down there."

"Penny, oh God, thanks. You're so sweet. I can't believe that I called you at this hour and you're…"

But she'd already hung up.

* * *

"He didn't."

"He did."

"Without letting you know up front, I mean, *before* you went to his place?"

[28]

"Can you believe it? And then he has the nerve to tell me there are homosexuals all over the campus, including priests. How about that?"

Up an elevator to the fourth floor, then over brown cushy carpeting to a door marked 413. She dug a key out of her purse and let us in.

A girl with a rugged, athletic complexion suggesting years of outdoor sports was curled up on a white couch. She nodded over a paperback but said nothing. I recognized her as Penny's companion most nights at the Village, a roommate, most likely. Her leathery skin and coarse, untamed hair marked her as a stark contrast to Penny: that creamy coloring around her vibrant eyes, those glimmering black strands that fell past her waist, the prominent nose that made her look smart and determined.

"What a nice apartment, Penny." How clean and orderly everything looked, like they'd been getting ready for a parental visit.

"The fruits of a capitalist pig — actually two capitalist pigs." She nodded toward the girl on the couch. "Captains of industry."

The roommate closed her book and grinned in agreement, then unfolded herself from the couch; she was taller than I'd remembered, and skinnier. Still without a word, she left the room.

It hadn't struck me that someone I'd met at the Village, someone in our audience almost every night we played, wasn't as disillusioned with the world as we were — or at least as our songs portrayed. But how could I have missed it? The nice clothes, the almost new Volvo, and here, unmistakable signs of wealth: leather sofa, glass-top table over wooden legs carved into the shape of lions' paws, real artwork, and shelf racks crowded with tiny figures of glass and wood and maybe porcelain, which I later learned the two girls had brought back from trips to Europe and Africa and India.

"Surely, Tommy," Penny shook her head, "all those CPAs in their plaid button-down shirts, and the students from your private school in their ironed jeans? Did you really think you were singing to the oppressed?"

"No, just that everybody *cared* about the oppressed."

She put her arms around my waist, then her lips to mine. We'd been on dates, and kissed goodnight, but nothing like this. I felt her whole body against me. "I care that you called me when you needed help. And that you're going to spend the night with me."

Maybe I wasn't going home for Christmas after all.

* * *

I awoke, head pounding. We'd drunk a whole bottle of Lancer's and, counting the drinks I'd had at Dr. Phillips' apartment, it amounted to more alcohol than I'd ever before consumed in one night.

I rolled over from the unfamiliar pillow to see Penny standing at the bedside in a snow-white silk robe.

"You are one sleepy boy. I've been up for an hour. Want some coffee?"

She was so pretty standing there, black hair draped over a shoulder and down the front of that white robe. The throbbing in my head was changing locations.

"Coffee. Well, okay. But can I talk you into getting back in bed?" A humbled and humiliated college kid just a night ago, now a confident man of experience.

She opened her robe and let it fall. The first time I'd seen a girl naked, in real life, in the light of day, and it was as magnificent as I had imagined — so much better than the dormitory magazines.

She slid under the covers, snuggled up beside me and kissed my neck.

"Tommy. You did fine."

It took a few seconds to sink in. Manliness gained, manliness lost.

"Was it that obvious?"

"It was sweet…and good."

She sat up, her nipples pink and round as the tips of a baby's fingers, prettier than any *Playboy* photo I'd ever hovered over.

Still, I was hardly her first. How many men before me? How many in this bed? How many this week?

"Maybe I should go."

She moved from me to the edge of the bed, then pulled her robe over her shoulders. "Because I'm not a virgin?"

"No, no. It's just that I always thought the girl, I mean, a girl…shit." Her eyes widened with disappointment. It was so like me at that age not to think before I said something stupid. She'd get up and leave now — or more likely, ask me to leave. I was about to apologize, almost said please, but just reached to try to pull her back to me.

"Tommy." She took my hand and wound her delicate fingers through mine, but stayed at the edge of the bed. "I'm twenty-four. I married when I was nineteen. I have a three-year-old girl."

Not only was she not a virgin, but she had a husband and a kid.

"Maybe I should go." A bit more anxious than the first time I'd said it.

She leaned into me and twirled one of my curls around her finger. "Tommy, I'm divorced. Janice is with my mother this weekend. And I haven't slept with another man since my divorce."

We locked eyes. It might have been the first time that morning.

"Feel better?" There was a bit of tease in her voice.

But I did, even if it resolved something that never should have needed resolution. She let me pull her back into the bed and we kissed. And when she pressed against me in that way she had of letting me feel every part of her body, I began making love for the second time in my life.

Compliments of a half-hearted application and a good score on the Graduate Record Exam, I received an offer to attend graduate school at the University of Miami on a teaching assistantship. It provided tuition and a small allowance for teaching underclassman the rudiments of grammar.

My commitment to music would be delayed for more years of academics, the choice of someone who has trouble making choices.

Breaking the news to Penny was going to be more difficult than acing the GRE. She wanted me to find Dave and put our duo back together. Get out on the road and get my singing career started. She would visit me from time to time, the doting grandmother always available for as long as Penny would leave little Janice with her.

"Teaching's an honorable profession, but it's not you." Penny and I bent over our dinners at one of Kansas City's many white-tablecloth steakhouses. "You're just putting off the inevitable."

"I'm not going to stop singing. I'm going to do it on the side. But teaching is something I could always do if I don't make it, something I could fall back on."

"Fall back on? Sounds like you're already giving up." She pointed a steak knife at me. "Damn it, Tommy, you're going to make it. You'll be a star."

She sliced a piece of steak and feathered it at me on the edge of a fork. "You won't have to worry about money. I'll help out. And if we ever...well, there's enough for the three of us — and any more — for the rest of our lives."

I had pride, even if she was paying for the bone-in ribeyes. "The last thing I'd do is live off your dough."

"Don't be silly. It's only money."

"Money matters," I said, sounding just like my father.

"Only to people who don't have it." She smiled at her peas as she stirred them into her mashed potatoes. God, I was going to miss my Penny.

"Well, I'm not going to be the kind of guy who takes money from his girl," and slid another slice of ribeye into my mouth then reached for more wine. "Say, maybe you and Janice should come to Miami with me. I'm being paid to teach. There are lots of places to sing there. It's a big music town. Have you seen the Jackie Gleason show? Hell, he's got some local musician on every week."

"Sorry, Tommy. Janice and I, and my mom, live in Kansas City."

She put down her fork and used both hands to sweep hair from those brandy-colored eyes, their golden rays unrestrained with affection. "I'm in love with you, you know." Those eyes, staring right into me; their warmth, leaving me in a cold shiver.

THE MUSICIAN

* * *

"Hey, roomie, not good news," my roommate greeted me as I returned to the dorm from a final exam. "I, unfortunately, am familiar with that envelope. Your ass is headed to Vietnam."

In addition to averaging more than twenty points a game for Immaculata's otherwise inept basketball team, Al Jackson was on an academic scholarship. I'd met him in freshman chemistry over a Bunsen burner and an Erlenmeyer flask where we discovered our common interest in singing.

It was Al who suggested I try out for Talent Night '63. Soon thereafter, I moved in with him when we learned we both wanted to escape the roommates we'd been paired with at registration. It had raised more than a few eyebrows, including my mother's whose take was — to be fair, it was not an uncommon sentiment in those days — "It's fine to be friends with a Negro, but do you have to live with him?"

I admired Al, first for his athletic prowess, then for how easily he handled the lead in "Two Silhouettes on the Shade," then for acing chemistry and every other subject he took. But as I got to know him better, I was most impressed, more like amazed, by his unfailing, unflagging common sense, always able to get to the heart of a matter.

Al handed me the envelope, clearly marked: Selective Service System.

The country had been involved in Vietnam since the mid-1950s, but reports, later determined to be contrived, of confrontations between a U.S. destroyer and North Vietnamese torpedo boats led to open warfare. The draft and deployment of large numbers of American boys followed, all to save Southeast Asia from communism.

That year, 1966, was the mother draft of them all.

I tore open the envelope.

"Fuck! You're right. I'm drafted. Man, I can't do this. I'll go to Canada with the protesters. Or marry Penny. Or just hide out in the middle of Kansas somewhere. I can't do this. No fucking way I can do this."

"Yeah, you and the rest of us graduating this year. No, we'll go down there like the good American boys we are and report as instructed. And they'll be so impressed with our college degrees they'll make us officers. Before we know where we are, we'll be yelling at a hundred rubes behind us, 'Let's take this hill.'"

"Man, there's got to be something we can do."

"Ask the sergeant when we report tomorrow. He's sure to be helpful."

"Tomorrow? Are you shittin' me? One damn day after my last final?"

"Read it, roomie. For all the fuckups, your government can be very efficient in some ways."

The following morning, puffs of white smoke trailing the defiant Plymouth, Al and I reached the designated downtown location, a square, fenced-in brick building with a banner nearly the size of the side of the building that read: Military Entrance Processing Station.

"Just in case we couldn't find it," I snarled. "And how convenient. Ample parking spaces."

Al opted to "first mull a few things" and headed for a coffee bar across the street. I reported.

Encouraged to enlist instead of being conscripted, I could then take the officer candidate school test, which I'd pass, it was hinted, if I could both read and write. I'd enter the U.S. Army as a commissioned officer.

Haunted by visions of my destiny as portrayed by Al, I declined, offering my assistantship as argument for an educational deferment. But as Al had informed me, the deferment was no longer in play.

I returned to my dorm room and sulked. Spoke to no one about it, as if silence could hide me.

* * *

"Once again I get to be the bearer of news, good or bad." Al held the letter with the familiar return address. He whistled "Over There."

"I've never known you to be such an asshole. Here I am about to read my death sentence and you're making fun."

"Just read it."

I was 1Y. He knew it. Had steamed the letter open then resealed it — a chemistry major, he knew all kinds of surreptitious shit like that.

"Congrats, little buddy."

But of course there is no such thing as unconditionally good news.

"Wait a minute," I said when I stopped jumping around the room and waving the letter in the air and hugging Al. "There must be something seriously wrong with me. They take everybody."

I uncrumpled the letter to look for the awful revelation. TB. Hepatitis. I'd heard polio was making a comeback. But there was no explanation. Just the 1Y, unfit for service.

I dropped on the bed to consider my impending death. "I'm going to have to go back down there and find out what's wrong with me."

"Roomie." Al hovered over me as I sat slumped, head in hands. "You're kicking the proverbial gift horse. You're out — at least for now. If you read the fine print, it says they can call you up in case of an emergency. I think this war qualifies. They can activate you any time, though you'd be toting a typewriter instead of a gun. I got two classmates from St. Louis, 1Ys, in uniform, stationed in some God-awful village in a desolate corner of Korea."

When time came to surrender my dormitory accommodations, I packed and left for Miami without leaving a forwarding address. Without me, the U.S. war effort would deteriorate.

But so would communism.

* * *

"Yes, operator. I'll accept the charges."

"Hi, Mom."

"My newest college graduate. And a scholarship to graduate school. We couldn't be prouder, Tom."

"It's an assistantship, Mom."

"You're gonna get a master's degree, just like your older brothers. And this time, your dad doesn't have to pay."

"How is Dad? Can I talk to him?"

"He's at the plant. Like every day. I wish he'd take some time off and enjoy life a bit."

"I guess he'd just as soon be there watching those lines run as lying on one of those beaches in Florida we used to drag him to every summer."

"All those years working so hard to build that business, and he's still got to be there to keep it all moving. Not one of you willing to help out. Not one of you to follow in his footsteps." It was a recurring theme, and not the last time I or any of my brothers would hear our mother's complaint.

"Maybe we learned from him to do our own thing? He's done his thing quite well, that's for sure."

"It's a good business, Tom. And you'd be a good one to run it. You're so much like him, you know. More than your brothers. All you'd have to do is say the word. Your father would be proud to add 'and Son' to the company name."

"Actually, Mom, I don't think…"

"It would be the right thing to do. After all these years him pushing himself for you boys, worrying he wouldn't make enough to pay for everything — schools, clothes, this house, and the cost to feed seven boys. It's worn him out."

"Well, you can tell him to relax. I'm off the dole. I'll make it on my own in Miami. I'll get paid for teaching, plus I've saved some money from my gigs."

"Your what?"

"Gigs. You know, playing music."

"You mean playing the guitar? You get money for that?"

"Yeah, Mom. Twenty-five dollars a night at the Village. Sometimes we played for more than a hundred people. And they all paid to get in, to hear us."

"That's nice. I'm happy for you, even happier that this guitar thing wasn't too distracting."

"It's not a distraction, Mom. It's what I do. It's who I…"

"Now listen to me, Thomas. It's all well and good that you had some fun during your college days. Heaven knows boys your age have had worse hobbies — including one of your brothers. But graduate school is going to be difficult, demanding. You're going to have to buckle down. No running around at night to some juke joint."

I'd been standing in one of the payphone cubicles in the dormitory lobby. I sat now, bent my head, and ran a hand through undisciplined strands of curly hair. I needed a haircut. Mom and Dad were never going to be okay with me as a musician. Explaining, arguing, wasn't ever going to change that.

"You better sell that guitar," she went on. "Or drop it off here on your way to Miami. We'll put it away for you and, when you get your master's degree you can come home and play it for us.

"And think about working with your father when you've finished with your studies. It's not the worst thing you could do, you know."

"Teach! Teach! Got a question, Teach."

I'd just mounted the platform serving as stage to the theater-style classroom. No guitar and microphone, instruments a textbook and class roster, audience a second semester make-up English 101 class.

"How encouraging, someone so eager to learn you can't wait for me to introduce myself."

"You ain't gonna make us diaphragm sentences are you?" Muffled laughter snaked through the class.

"Heavens, no. That would be anatomy class. Or perhaps sex ed. No diaphragms in English 101."

More laughter, less restrained. The questioning student standing, a hulking figure with a puzzled expression.

"Sir, I think he meant 'diagram sentences,'" interpreted a student seated next to him.

"Of course. And thanks for being so helpful." I tossed the textbook and laminated sheet on the desk. "That's one reason we're here. Why English 101 and English 102 are required subjects. Clarity. So that when you speak and write, others understand you and you understand others even when they have yet to learn to express themselves with clarity. What is your name, sir?"

"Ted Hendrickson, sir."

"And you, sir, whom I misunderstood? What is your name?"

"To-ny," the name spoken as if it were two.

"Well, Tony, I can state unequivocally that there will be no diagramming sentences in this class." Enthusiastic applause. "We're beyond that, hopefully, in college. Even you guys," I waved an arm spanning the entire class, "who've managed to land yourselves in make-up English."

Loud but affected booing. This was fun. I could do this for a year or so. A master's wouldn't hurt either. Especially if things didn't work out for me. Not that they wouldn't. But just in case. Not a bad gig, teaching.

I consulted the class roster. "Let's see. Do I have a Ms. Barrington?" A lanky brunette, large brown eyes peeking over tanned cheekbones looming like skyscrapers, stood at the back of the room, closest to the door.

A murmur of admiration from several male students and one unrestrained male voice, "Ooo, baby."

"Pardon me, Ms. Barrington. I'm inclined to join the others in their admiration of your...your stature. Ms. Barrington, why are you in this class?"

"Flunked it last semester." A sheepish smile revealed two rows of misdirected teeth held in place by thin wires.

"And you, Mr. Hendrickson?"

"Football, Mr. Cliffe. Not much time for classes in the fall."

"And Mr. Tony, you're a player too? What position?"

Tony, now seated, had draped a long right leg over the arm of the seat in front of him occupied by a student about my size. "Defensive tackle."

"Well, I hope you'll find tackling English 101 just as compelling." A few of Tony's classmates chuckled, several groaned.

I started the lesson by pointing out that English wasn't about diagramming sentences or even grammar. "It's about communicating. Sure, you want to use correct grammar in speaking as well as writing — we'll focus on writing in this class — and why is that important?" Again I consulted the roster. "Ms. Yardley?"

Another tanned, statuesque figure rose. Unquestionably, we were near a beach. "So we sound smart when we interview for a job."

"True. That's true. But sounding smart begins with explaining yourself and your ideas clearly and effectively. You see the cover of your textbook for this class?"

About half the class craned necks, looking left and right.

"How many have the textbook?"

About twenty of the eighty-three students sentenced to my class raised a hand or the book.

"For those of you who can't read it from a distance or upside down, the title is *Say What You Mean*. And that's exactly why you follow the rules, so that what you're saying is what you mean to say, and by extension, can be understood by whom you're saying it to."

The confused expressions on many of the faces made it clear that what I was saying was not understood.

My preparation for this first class had involved putting together ten sentences, each compromised by poor grammar,

[43]

a misspelled or misused word, or some other linguistic stumbling block. But the exercise generated no enthusiasm, and participation only when I called names from the sheet. It labored to the tenth and final sentence scrawled on the blackboard: "He was anxious to leave the classroom."

A bell rang. The class rose in unison and eagerly departed. Ted Hendrickson detoured to my desk.

"Mr. Cliffe. I think that was some pretty good stuff you started getting into, that stuff about communicating. But sir, nobody in this class is gonna be an English major. We just have to get English 101 and 102 out of the way."

He paused a few seconds, stroking a chin both prognathic and squared, like the jaw of a strong-man comic book character. "And sir, I'm not trying to tell you how to run your class or anything, but I wouldn't be too concerned with Tony. He's gonna get drafted into the NFL in a couple of years. He does his communicating with a forearm to the helmet. He's not worried about reading or writing, sir, just staying eligible for football. Anyway, his dad's the coach; he's already passed English 101."

"Mr. Hendrickson, they're paying me, or at least covering my tuition and giving me a place to sleep, to teach English. That means everybody here has to write essays and take tests. Tony will have to study and pass tests like the rest of you. Nobody gets a free pass because his dad's a coach."

"No, sir. I said *the* coach."

* * *

My musical performances at this point were limited to my graduate dormitory room; my audience — me, myself, and I. Despite an occasional "Shut the fuck up, I'm trying to study" from a neighboring room, I spent most hours of most evenings learning new songs, which I did by listening to records over and over again until I had transcribed the lyrics and could play most of their chords, though many of my progressions were not precisely those on the records.

As I'd transitioned to a new location and life, so too my music was transitioning. Rock was steamrolling the late '60s, but another music, more appealing to me, was also emerging, blending folk music's penchant for meaty lyrics and lush vocal harmonies with the rhythmic underpinnings of rock 'n roll.

It was even in some circles called folk rock. It came to pass in groups like The Byrds, who introduced it; Jefferson Airplane, who emerged from the San Francisco folk community to blaze the trail for its psychedelic expression; and eventually, in 1969, supergroup Crosby, Stills, Nash & Young. It defined itself in the songs of Paul Simon, then defied definition in the ultimate collision of folk and rock, The Beatles and their May 1967 release of the symphonic *Sgt. Peppers Lonely Hearts Club Band*. The singer-songwriter era would generate the most universally appreciated music, and the genre of greatest longevity, since the standards of the American Songbook.

Consistent with the folk-acoustic tradition, singer-songwriters were at their core solo artists accompanying themselves on guitar or piano, though with themes more personal than political. And like the singer-songwriters flowing from folk, I found my comfort zone in the new music. I built a playlist that included Gordon Lightfoot's "Early Morning Rain," a peppy folk carryover "San Francisco Bay Blues," and a new Neil Diamond tune, "Solitary Man." I added a few songs traditional in nature but not inextricably tied to folk, like Simon's "Scarborough Fair," and kept a few favorites from the Village days, most notably Buffy Sainte-Marie's "Until It's Time for You to Go."

Inspired by these solo artists to write my own songs, I'd spend hours hovered over my Goya fingering chords to accompany a melody I'd thought up. And lyrics, sometimes before a melody, sometimes to accommodate one. But I was rarely pleased with anything original, much better at interpretation than composition.

One night while practicing, I was interrupted, once again, by a knock on my door. But this time my callers were not there to complain. They came to listen. Other students coming or going stopped in, maybe twenty or thirty in all crammed into the confinement imposed by those bed-and-desk combos that described every dorm room in those days. I'd missed an audience terribly, and I played well past the ten o'clock noise curfew.

Some few nights later, I opened the door to see a couple of students who introduced themselves as the Dormitory Entertainment Committee. Talk of a fine singer and guitarist had spread, they said, and they could arrange for me to perform on a campus lawn on a Friday night. It would be billed "Tom Cliffe in Concert."

To be honest, I think I was more excited by the billing than the opportunity to perform, though both reminded me of how much I loved playing for an audience.

* * *

The committee arranged for a stool, microphones for my voice and guitar, and an underpowered PA. The students and their dates sat cross-legged on blankets scattered around the lawn. I opened with "San Francisco Bay Blues," about as spirited a tune as I could play, then "Unchained Melody," which I considered one of my most moving ballads. Maybe it was because on my own I was unable to replicate the Righteous Brothers' harmonies, but all the emotion I could pour into the song only left my crowd fidgety. I played "Mr. Tambourine Man" and "Ferry Cross the Mersey" amid a rising tide of conversation, giggling girls, and, despite administration's stern advance warning that no drinking would be tolerated on the campus lawn, clinking beer bottles. When I took a break about forty-five minutes in, a girl who had moved herself and blanket almost to my feet, whose eyes seemed to be following some cosmic body circling inside her skull, was the only one to applaud.

"Lesson learned," I thought, though I wasn't quite sure which lesson.

* * *

I was drawn to a more fitting environment: the nightlife of Miami Beach. The Collins Avenue hotels, each with at least one live-music club, would prove bastions of learning far more relevant than university literature classes. Several hotel clubs were piano bars where drinkers, whose lack of pitch and rhythm were matched only by their poor taste in songs, nevertheless were determined to get behind a microphone and prove the absence of the music gene from their DNAs.

I narrowed my attention to a couple of the clubs where I got to know the pianists, who were pleased to see me mount a stool, relieved to hand the microphone to someone who could sing. After a bad rendition of a clichéd song by an off-

[47]

key drunk, I'd collaborate with the pianist on a Cole Porter or Johnny Mercer tune, almost always to the amazement of the other "singers." I was often applauded and, occasionally, someone was sufficiently impressed to buy me a drink.

"Good evening, Mr. Reardon."

I climbed onto a stool immediately to the right of the pianist working through a tasty version of "Over the Rainbow." Artie Reardon, sixty-ish and always, at least every time I'd been by to sing with him, looking slightly disheveled, had held the nightly gig at the El Dorado going on two decades. He looked up and returned my greeting with his big, toothy smile.

"What are you singing for the beautiful people here tonight?" he mumbled into the mic. Artie, for all his unrestrained flair on the keyboard used the mic infrequently, and timidly when he did.

"'Rainbow' is good. In C?"

Artie reached up with his right hand, took the mic from its clip, circled it around the stand three or four times to unravel the cable, and handed it to me. I remember him doing all that with his right hand and the song never suffered in tone or tempo under his left. Nothing showy about it, but I couldn't do it if I practiced a lifetime. Then the transition to my key, the change imperceptible, as if we'd worked it out.

As we finished the tune, a man seated next to me nudged me, then slapped a ten-dollar bill on the bar in front of me. "Hell of a voice there, kid."

"Arlan," Reardon said, ignoring the tip that had come my way instead of his. "Damn near as prolific as Rodgers or any of them."

I sang two more, "My Funny Valentine" and a finger-snapping "Get Me to the Church on Time," before I surrendered the mic, stuffed a few more bills in my shirt pocket, and got up to leave. Reardon motioned me to sit.

"Gonna take a short break folks. Thanks for spending your time with us this evening. I'll be right back." Then to me, "Stay where you are for a minute."

I watched him go behind the bar and gesture a few times, waving his hands like flapping bird wings then bringing them together as if to say "please" to a dark little fat man in a black suit. I guess Artie Reardon was so glad for the break from the tone deaf singers he was determined to convince the bar manager to hire me. The fat guy shook his head defiantly a couple times, then at the praying gesture capitulated. The El Dorado would pay the small stipend to sing with Artie — one set, a half dozen or so songs, Friday and Saturday nights.

* * *

There is an expression that relates to coming to grips with one's beliefs and articulating them with confidence. It's called finding your voice. In Miami Beach's piano bars, I was finding my voice unaffected by inflections of some too-admired celebrity singer. Perhaps it was my baptismal folk career that had molded me in this fashion: unadulterated, honest. But I recognized it as an important distinction that separated me from the cover-band musician, a body in which so many players become trapped, where the aim is to copy a recording so well your version is indistinguishable from the original.

[49]

I was also refining my technique, like attacking notes more accurately and using head voice for resonance and a clearer, brighter tone than the guttural, throaty. No longer a mindless burst of notes, I was learning the craft. And the standards I sang with Artie, the Sinatra, Mathis, and Bennett tunes of my basement days, were again my teachers — more complex, more challenging ranges and reaches, requiring greater attention to things like pitch and breathing and tone than the folk songs of the Village days or the folk rock of my guitar-based repertoire.

The beach fueled my desire to perform. And with so many more places to sing than in the frigid and serious Midwest, it not only played to my passion but captured my concentration and time.

* * *

"Teach, Dean Mann wants to see you." Ted Hendrickson was arriving for the first of my summer English 102 classes, part of the University's program to accommodate students who had completed off-semester courses like spring English 101 and were eager to get required second-semester courses behind them before the start of a new school year. It was a very small class.

"Hmmmm...he say what he wants?"

"Like he'd tell me. Just caught me in the hallway and asked if I was going to your class today."

"Okay, thanks, Ted." Hendrickson headed toward the back of the room. "By the way, Ted, I know you worked hard on your 101 final essay." *You might have been the only one.* "Anyway, you did a good job organizing content and avoiding grammatical errors."

Hendrickson paused. He smiled at the compliment. "But that's just part of good writing, Ted. There's phrasing and rhythm, and most important, insight. You have to have something to say, then say it in a way that makes someone think about it. It's kind of like football, looks simple but there's a lot that goes into it, a lot of finesse required to make a good block or not miss a tackle."

"Much rather tackle than block, sir."

* * *

Dean Mann's office was well off the beaten student path, in a portable building assigned to the small staff that administered the school's modest graduate liberal arts curricula.

"Mr. Cliffe, please sit." He didn't offer to shake my hand, just motioned to a gray metal folding chair positioned squarely in front of and facing his mahogany desk, then stiffened upright into the black leather chair behind the desk. From where I sat, two framed diplomas on an otherwise unadorned ghost-white wall behind him appeared as extensions of his left and right ears.

"Mr. Cliffe, let me get right to the issue at hand. Complaints have been filed against you, from students, among others. I have a list that starts with your first day." He consulted a single sheet of paper centered on the surface of the desk, as if to state the charges exactly as they had been written. "Making fun of a student for mispronouncing a word and overtures to a female student." He looked up at me. If he was looking for an answer, I had none.

I just stared back.

"Oh, the list goes on, sir." Now he looked back at the paper. "For example, you've recommended questionable reading material. *Lolita*. Seriously?"

I thought to defend the novel — he was obviously more up to speed on other of the liberal arts than literature — but he appeared neither interested in nor waiting for any explanation.

"These are serious allegations. But before you try to excuse your actions, let me tell you that we're going to overlook your offenses. You seem to be a nice young man. Good upbringing. Very good references from that little college you attended out there in the Midwest. We're willing to overlook these transgressions and let you keep your assistantship…given some modifications."

It hadn't taken but a semester to rob me of any pride in my assistantship. Half the University's graduate students were on some kind of labor exchange, and all of us could have worked fewer hours serving hamburgers to earn the equal of the cost to occupy an otherwise empty graduate school desk. But I was unprepared for too quick a separation, especially from my dorm room, no matter how spartan.

"Yessir. If I've been a little loose with my students, I'll reel it in. And I'll be glad to submit my reading list to my supervisor for approval."

"Good, Tom. Good modifications. But there are others. You know, football pays for a lot of the education we offer here at the U. Sometimes we need to bend a little, accommodate some of those who work so hard to make a success of our football program, the support of which is vital to our academic initiatives. It seems you overlooked that with one of our players and, despite his best efforts, assigned him a failing grade."

"I don't think so, sir. I treat every student equally and I grade…"

"Hold on, Cliffe. Let's cut to the chase. You gave our head football coach's son an F. Do you realize how stupid that is? Tony Pate's dad is the most important man on this campus." Dean Mann's face was turning a reddish hue. "I want you to go back and change that to a passing grade."

"But sir, that bonehead showed up for class less than half the time, and a couple of times I'm pretty sure he was drunk. He didn't even take the final. What else could I give him but an F?"

"Change the grade, Cliffe. You don't have to make it an A, just a fucking C. You understand?" He was standing now and glaring, eyes so narrowed the slits made a straight line across the bridge of his nose, his face glowing now a brilliant red leaning in and down over me. "You fucking understand?"

A November Saturday night at the El Dorado. The season, northern migration, was beginning. Anticipating a full room of appreciative listeners, I arrived early for my twenty-dollar set. Artie Reardon was not at the piano.

The club manager, squatty, dusky, with matted black hair and sideburns that curled to a point at the middle of his pock-marked cheeks, rushed at me.

"Can you play that thing?" he waggled a finger in the direction of the piano, his marble-mouthed question more demand than inquiry.

"Where's Artie?"

Sweat dotted the pores and dripped from the ridges of his contorted countenance. Without Artie to entertain, he apparently had been using free booze to keep his customers on stools and at tables, enough that many who remained were hard-pressed to stand up much less walk out. Increasingly agitated, he glared at me, waiting.

"Gee, not like Artie. I don't really think…" But that I played at all was confession enough. He pointed at the piano again and ordered, "Play."

In preparation for the El Dorado gig, I'd been spending the better part of days on a piano in a practice room at the University music school. Years of piano lessons I'd suffered as a youngster were proving useful, opening doors to the music of the cabaret singers, the songs of Gershwin, Berlin, and Van Heusen, as well as newer tunes from people like Jackson Browne and The Young Rascals.

I slid in behind the piano. This was Artie's province. A little intimidated and a lot nervous, I began a very unobtrusive version of the initial verse of "It Could Happen To You."

One by one, patrons seated at the piano bar stopped talking and leaned my way, sliding their drinks with them. Slurred conversation quieted. I could feel their smiles and, with that attention, gained courage and enough confidence to launch into a brighter, happier, and louder "Pocketful of Miracles."

I survived the night behind the El Dorado piano, two sets in fact, even if the second half of the second set sounded familiar to anyone there for the first part of the first set. The early audience was joined by less inebriated couples over the two-hour span. They sat, listened, and stayed. And when I refused to relinquish the microphone, confessing that I was just filling in for Artie and only knew the songs I sang, no one got ugly.

* * *

Playing the piano is a lot like bridge, or golf; it takes a long time and a lot of work just to get where you can call it playing. Making music is yet another campaign. Different from saxophones, trumpets and other horns, and most string instruments most often, the piano requires of its player several notes at a time. Like the guitar, it fulfills all three musical jobs: melody, harmony, and rhythm.

But unlike the guitar, where one hand finds the notes and the other picks or strums them, the piano requires both hands to locate and strike. Furthermore, the left hand must do something, several things actually, different from the right hand — stroke the rhythm, play bass notes, form chords — while the right hand, in addition to completing chords, plays melody, and in more accomplished playing, interpretive, innovative flights recognized as improvisation.

My first night as a pianist, two sets of one-and-a-half sets worth of songs, was revealing. Those weekly lessons from the choleric Leon Sarnowski endured from age six throughout grammar school were imbedded in mind and muscle memory. I was better prepared for moving forward with the piano than the guitar where my knowledge was limited to the simplistic open chords common to folk music. I wouldn't totally abandon the guitar, but a better understanding of keyboard than fingerboard introduced me to a wider range of formats and songs. And that would undoubtedly broaden my appeal to my post-folk audiences.

But while learning the chords and melody of a song was easy enough, performing it required much greater familiarity and skill.

I had been scarred by the Sarnowski years, week after week of sour breath and attitude and simplified versions of classical pieces I'd never heard nor could appreciate. So, disinclined to seek out instruction, I tried to overcome the instrument by sheer practice-hour volume. But no matter how much time spent, I couldn't emulate the sounds of players like Artie Reardon.

One evening, talking between sets, I learned that Artie spent his days giving lessons "to recalcitrant children who despise practicing and weekly lessons, and who will abandon the instrument as soon as they wear down their mothers."

"You think you could help me?"

His eyes went wide. "You mean give lessons to someone who wants them?"

It proved a new beginning, a godsend. Artie showed me how to position my hands to allow them to move freely across the keyboard. He taught me chords of six and seven notes and how to form them, some as close as half steps. I learned more scales than I'd dreamed existed, and that would provide notes and patterns for solos.

But I still didn't sound like Artie. It would take years of practice, hours a day, to know well enough, to *hear* well enough to weave them fluidly, naturally, into playing.

"Your quest for skill and knowledge will always be at a beginning," Artie evangelized. "You're on a long and arduous journey that will not end. No matter how far you travel, something new and necessary lies ahead. You will never run out of things to learn and you can never allow yourself to stop learning."

* * *

Artie stopped me early in a lesson one afternoon as I began reciting an exercise in chord inversions.

"Let's just listen today."

He walked to the back of his teaching studio, a converted dining room in his small, spare Coconut Grove apartment, and opened a closet door to reveal no hanging clothes or even a clothes rack but a ceiling-high stack of LPs. He fingered a few, retrieved one, extracted the disc, walked it to a turntable near the piano, then handed me the album cover. "'*Waltz for Debby*, Bill Evans Trio,'" I read.

Artie's chords and scales came to life in the most musical hands I'd ever heard. Rich, lyrical, and so different than any pianist I'd ever listened to. What Bill Evans was doing was beyond my comprehension. And I knew it immediately, exactly what I wanted to learn. Those sounds, that technique, and to be that good, to play every note with that kind of agility and sensitivity and understanding.

I think I clutched the album to my chest. Then, a little embarrassed, tried to hand it back to Artie. But he just smiled, left me holding it, and let the cuts play. "My Foolish Heart," "My Romance," "Some Other Time" — all songs I'd heard before but had never really heard.

"You can't practice to be famous," Artie said as he lifted the LP off the turntable. "But if you work hard enough for long enough, you could become good, very good."

He stood over me and looked straight into my eyes.

"To get good, very good," he repeated. "That's all you can control and, in the end, the only thing that counts."

* * *

As the University of Miami's 1967 fall semester was about to begin, I was informed that my assistantship was not being renewed, and the related benefits — tuition, room, board — would expire at the conclusion of the first academic quarter. Then I missed four consecutive early morning Dylan Thomas classes and was dismissed by the professor — a failing grade for a course I failed to attend.

By substituting practice for classes, I'd built just enough of a repertoire to work in a Miami Beach piano lounge. Championed by Artie Reardon and begrudgingly approved by the El Dorado overlord, I was awarded the Fontainebleau daily cocktail gig, two hours of music for early drinkers.

A couple of weeks in, a bulky man with a gray ducktail and matching mustache approached during my break between sets. His hair was slicked front to back with an oily substance so noxious and acrid I could almost taste it. His suit — heavily padded shoulders allowed the jacket to hang loosely over his distended stomach — screamed cheap, a garish production from one of those downtown Miami discount clothing factories.

"Hey, Red, nice work," he rasped. His smile revealed an overbite of oversized yellow teeth.

"Thanks." I ducked to avoid the drift of smoker's breath and was about to move on when he draped a glossy suit-coat sleeve around my shoulders and breathed into my face: "How about a drink?"

"Little early for me. I've got another set." Hoping to escape his near-stranglehold I added, "and singing somewhere else later."

"Well, have a seat for a minute. You just might be interested in what I have to say."

I was unconvinced and considering my next excuse-me.

"Just give me a minute. Sit with me for one minute."

I sat — as far from him as a seat at the table allowed.

"My name's Dick Dollar." He held out a business card bearing an image of what appeared to be several conjoined musical instruments.

It read *The $ Agency*.

"Let me tell you straight, kid. I think you've got it. Star quality voice. I'd like to help you get started on your way."

Maybe I should have asked, "On my way to what?" But bad suit and breath aside, what he was saying was exactly what I wanted to hear. Maybe this was it. Maybe I was being discovered, just like it happens to everyone who becomes a star. I reconsidered the grease-riddled coiffure, and moved my chair a little closer to the table. He moved in, too.

"I'm going to put you on my club circuit, up and down the Florida coast, both sides, the best clubs. You'll play for good crowds and make good money."

When you grow up with a father who was the ultimate salesman, you should be able to recognize a sales pitch, and *good money* rang sales-pitchy.

Still, with an income limited to the cocktail hour gig and weekend sets with Artie, and further compromised by my impending eviction from the University dorm, I had but a few weeks to unearth an ongoing survival plan. There would be no money from home without going home, that was certain. And I couldn't see myself doing anything that would steal time from music. This could be my break, after all, or at least an adventure, even if these turned out to be less than ideal hands in which to place my future.

I took the card Dick Dollar held out. "Thank you. I'll think about it."

I didn't think long. As I'd been unwilling to do in Kansas City, I committed. Suitcase and guitar in hand, and pianos waiting, I took to the road.

[60]

* * *

Penny and I talked at least once a week. Some weeks when I was feeling lonely I'd call her three or four times. I'd reverse the charges — she insisted — but once I started making some money I called on my own nickel — or quarters. I'd come to the club early, get change from the bartender who'd taken enough of a liking to me to keep a bunch of quarters in the register, then step out of the El Dorado into the salty Miami Beach air and down the street to a payphone on the corner.

She was always cheerful. "Hey, Tommy," she'd say brightly.

"How'd'ya know it was me?"

"It was your ring."

It was our routine.

"So how're you doing — and Janice and your mom?" I was calling to tell her about my big break, but hadn't figured out how, exactly, to word it.

"Mom's fine as long as I keep her in Chardonnay, and Janice is a weed, growing right out of her knobby knees. You sound, well, light-hearted. Got some news for me? Maybe coming to see us like you've been promising?"

"Can't hide much from you, can I?" I loved that, her knowing me so well, better than anyone else ever, better than I knew myself.

"No. And of course you're not coming. So what is it?"

"I'm leaving school. I've got an agent, a booking agent, and I'm going to start touring." I stopped short of proclaiming I was on my way to stardom.

"Touring? Like with a band? Have you joined up with some big name band? Are you the newest Beatle?"

"Very funny. I'm going on the road…by myself. City to city. Playing nightclubs. A week or so at a time."

I thought she was sifting through my news, picturing what kind of touring this was, playing it out in her head — where I'd be, what kind of clubs I'd be playing, how I'd be moving from town to town.

I broke the silence. "It's a good start. Good clubs. Good money. He promises…him…my agent."

"Can he book you in Kansas City?"

I wanted Penny's approval and the hope I heard in her question made me think I just might have it.

"Maybe. Eventually. But he's got this circuit of clubs around Florida, up and down both coasts. That's what I'll be doing for now…for a while."

Another long silence made me less sure of her enthusiasm for my decision.

"I'm finally doing it, Penny, just like you've always said I should." I was pressing now. "No more teaching. No more anything but music."

More quiet, enough that the operator came on to ask for more coins. Long enough to make me anxious.

"Okay," she said after I'd deposited another dollar's worth of quarters. "Well, I'd better go. Stay in touch." The voice coming over the line was as chilly as a blast of Kansas City winter. Was she angry? Was she going to hang up? Even when we'd argued, mainly about when I was going to come for a visit, we never hung up before making up. Neither of us would risk that.

She finally spoke again, but I detected a note of resignation. "Tommy, I've been thinking a lot about us, wondering when I'd see you next, be with you, trying to be honest with myself. And now you tell me you're starting another new life, another life that doesn't include me. Oh, Tommy, I love you, and I'm happy for you. But I don't see me in your future…or you in mine."

"But Penny, you know I love you." I was sure of that. "Someday…"

"Tommy, I'm here, always will be. And you'll always be somewhere else. You can call if you want to talk. I hope you will."

I don't recall what else if anything was said, only the operator interrupting again to ask for more money. It was left at that, a simple, unemotional, crushing signoff. A clinical send-off — call me if you need me, but really, don't call. It would have been easier if she'd told me she didn't care, even had a new boyfriend. I stood, phone in my hand, looking out between hotels over the beach to the Atlantic and the waves resolutely backing away toward low tide.

My Penny. Standing bedside that first morning, her open silk robe, her unblemished beauty, her willingness. I loved her more than I'd realized. My chest ached, pained and heavy. I wanted to run back to the El Dorado for more quarters, call her back, tell her I was getting in the Plymouth — it might have had one last road trip in it — and driving to Kansas City that night. I wanted to say good-bye to the El Dorado, to Miami Beach, to my new agent and touring — to stardom — and head north.

But I didn't.

* * *

Given the call with Penny, I opted to tell my folks by letter.

> *I want you to hear the whole story and have a chance to think about it before we talk. I just arrived this week for my first job in a town called Punta Gorda on the west coast of Florida, right on the beach, the kind of place we used to go for our summer vacations.*
>
> *Of course, this means I'm leaving the University before I get my master's degree. I know that's not news you want to hear. But I can always go back and finish later. Frankly, I lost interest. I was teaching off-semester English classes, mainly for kids who'd failed English their first time around or missed it for some reason or other. Anyway, most of my students weren't the brainiest, and none of them were there because they wanted to be. What I learned from doing it was that teaching isn't for me.*
>
> *But I have learned what I want to do with my life. I know it's not what you'd choose for me as a career, but it's what I love. It's hard to explain, but there's nothing like playing music, no feeling quite like it. And I know I'm good because when I play and sing, people listen and applaud. My music makes them happy. I think that's more than just a good thing.*
>
> *It's important, really important.*
>
> *Now, I don't expect you to be okay with me quitting school, but I hope you understand why, or at least will some day. I've got work and I*

[64]

think I'll do well, maybe become well known and you'll hear me on the radio or be able to play one of my records for your friends.

I'll call soon. In the meantime, if you want to reach me, you can call the Dollar Agency in Miami.

Thanks for all you've done for me. I promise I'll make you proud.

Love,
Tom

As Dick Dollar promised, work on the road was steady, a week or two each in small cities up and down the Florida coast where life is on vacation: Ft. Lauderdale to Daytona, Ft. Myers to Sarasota, Pensacola to Ft. Walton Beach. The clubs drew good crowds, young people like me, who came for the music and to party. And the girls, well, were plenty enough and often willing. It was a series of short lives — work, friends, a romance, all stuffed into a handful of days. Then off to the next life.

One Saturday night in the Living Room, a cozy bar over a shop and restaurant at the entrance to Longboat Key, an upscale strip of sand bordered by the Gulf of Mexico and Sarasota Bay, I caught the stare of a twenty-something with round eyes and long dark hair. It was my final song of the evening, "Unchained Melody," and she seemed to be hanging on every note. I was developing a keen eye for that.

I finished the final, impassioned *to me,* then thanked "all of you for coming out tonight," advised them to "be sure to tip your waitress generously," and put my Goya on its stand. Count one, two, three, four. Then off the stage and nonchalantly to her table. Her two girl friends were standing, ready to leave; she was lingering.

"So where do people go to party this time of night?" It was terribly obvious, but I never was and never would be very good at this.

"Follow us," she grinned. She was even more stunning than I'd seen from the stage, commanding cheekbones and statuesque, taller than me by a substantial percentage. "The Viscous Cycle is playing Billy's Barn tonight." A deep-set green eye winked.

"You mean 'vicious'?"

"Hardly." She laughed, tossing back her head just enough that her breasts lifted and pointed at me.

Her two friends dutifully excused themselves.

The stop at Billy's Barn was pure protocol. An unremarkable band of unseasoned kids relying on volume played what sounded like the same song over and over. After a single drink, she offered "a decent bottle of wine at my place."

We were laughing at some untold joke as we left the bar, my arm around her waist. I valeted her into her red convertible, then boarded the delicately used, as the sign had said, Chevy van I'd bought with the last of my savings and a small advance from Dick Dollar before I left Miami.

I followed her deep into Sarasota, to a small, scruffy neighborhood, and pulled to a stop in front of a tiny stucco house unadorned except for a single, incongruous palm tree near the front door. She unlocked the door and quicker than a cork could be extracted from a wine bottle we were entangled and stumbling into a bedroom and onto the sheets of an unmade bed.

* * *

By seven a.m., I was headed back to the apartment at the Living Room. Ah, the rewards of life as a musician! My version of "Unchained Melody" played in my head and…blue lights flashed in the rearview mirror. I pulled to the side of the road, reached for my wallet, extracting my driver's license, and looked up to count five policemen around the front and sides of my van, each pointing very long, very large shotguns at me.

"Get out of the vehicle."

I did.

"Turn around, hands on the vehicle and spread 'em."

Before I could comply, he spun me around, pushed me up against the van and slammed the length of his gun across the small of my back. Another blunt object smacked the back of my knees, then, ever so meaningfully, was jammed up into my groin. I was breathless with pain. And thoroughly scared. Whoever they mistook me for must have done something terrible.

I was cuffed and head-pushed into the back seat of one of several police cars now on the scene. I hurt worse than I could remember ever hurting. In too much pain to speak. And when finally I could muster enough voice to ask why this was happening, the answer was, "Shut up or it's gonna get worse."

We rode in silence, interrupted only by an occasional undecipherable squawk of the police radio.

[68]

The police station was sparingly staffed on a Sunday morning. I was cuffed to a metal rail screwed to a wall where I stood for more than a half hour before the room's only other occupant, a uniformed policeman seated at what reminded me of an altar, looked up from his paperwork. He picked up a phone, dialed a single digit, and returned to his paperwork. I wasn't about to speak until spoken to.

Another ten minutes or so passed before another policeman entered and, taking me by an elbow, guided me to a room not much larger than a coat closet. He removed the cuffs and introduced me to the station's fingerprinting device.

My keys, taken by one of the arresting cops, were in a manila envelope to which I also surrendered my wallet and belt. All this activity was coalescing into something murky and unintelligible, preoccupied as I was with an increasingly dire need to pee. A trickle of urine was edging its way down my right leg.

"Sir?" I asked as politely as I could.

His thoughts must have been elsewhere because he didn't respond.

"Sir?" I asked again, a little louder, and with a little greater sense of urgency.

"What do you want?" His tone suggested he'd heard me the first time, just didn't want to be bothered.

"I need to go to the bathroom, sir."

"You'll get a chance soon enough." He escorted me from fingerprinting to another room, from the detective TV shows I'd seen, this would be the cellblock; opened a door and invited me to enter.

Call it stereotyping, but generally one does not meet nice people in jail. Whether it's running a stop sign or shooting your wife, you're all there together — and most of you have committed a crime more heinous than a traffic violation. By now the right leg of my tan khakis was dark with urine but I finished peeing in the open metal toilet, then cowered in a corner determined not to make eye contact with any of my five or six cellmates, a couple pacing and mumbling, others seated on the floor staring into their knees.

I knew I had a right to a phone call, but who? The only person in town I knew who might care that I was in trouble was the Living Room manager; I had no idea how to reach him. Dick Dollar was a first alternative, but when I gave the police the Miami phone number, I learned my right was restricted to a local call.

This wasn't going well. And did not go well for most of the day, through two inedible meals on tin plates. Sobriety left several fellow inmates grumpy. Few words were spoken, most interaction consisted of angry stares from men used to being in places where they were better off being aggressors than chance being aggressed.

Around seven o'clock that evening, nearly twelve hours after my arrest, the cell door opened and I was called out. Tired, ragged, and smelling evermore pungently of the previous night's sex, I was given my possessions and released. No charges. No explanation. No ride.

The long walk to my vehicle was therapeutic, a relief from the day's indignities. I wasn't angry, just relieved, and invigorated by my restored freedom. I got in and started the engine. As I looked up to pull out into traffic, I gasped and slammed the brake pedal to the floor. There, in the frame of my driver-side window, behind metallic sunglasses, loomed the face of the inflictor of pain.

"Roll down that window, boy."

I dared not disobey.

"Still wonderin' why you spent the day in jail? Smart young fellow like you certainly figured it out by now."

"N-no sir. Maybe you mistook me for someone else?"

"No mistake. I know damned well who you are. You're the guy who fucked my girl last night."

* * *

Sarasota police and jail aside, I enjoyed my first taste of the road. Being onstage made it easy to meet people and I enjoyed fitting into their evenings and fitting them into mine. In Florida's resort towns, where the world was on leave and holiday attitudes prevailed, there were always friends to be made, a coterie to join. They'd arrive at the club for the last set or two, genuinely enthusiastic, calling out their requests for my renditions of songs from *Sgt. Pepper*, Dylan, Simon & Garfunkel, and even, on the rare occasions clubs provided a piano, some of those standards that I'd learned working with Artie. Then they'd draw me along for their sorties on after-hours haunts. Happily drunk, I'd return to my club-provided hotel room or apartment at three or four in the morning, or on better nights, find my way to the bed of a more carefully vetted female admirer.

There were few nights when I'd finish the last set to retire to my room alone.

Except when Dick Dollar needed to fill a job in one of the many Florida towns that served as retirement communities for snowbirds, aged New Yorkers and Jerseyites who quit harsh winters of the Northeast to wither away more agreeably in the sunny South.

One morning in Ft. Pierce, at a seniors' sanctuary on the Atlantic coast paradoxically known as The Sunrise City, I was jolted from my sleep by a screech of microphone feedback.

"In lane two, Mrs. Ashton and Mr. Wisenstein versus Mrs. Winston and Mr. Bernhauer."

Lane two? What was going on between the Ashtons and Wisensteins at eight a.m.? I wrestled myself out of bed, shuffled to the window, and slid open the curtain to reveal a collection of bent figures, poles in hand, the spryest at least in their mid-eighties. Those not employing the poles to keep themselves upright used them to shove wooden discs from one end of a row of narrow strips of pavement to the other.

It was the opening round of what proved to be an entire morning of shuffleboard matches and screechy announcements of team partners and opponents, particularly annoying in that they were entirely superfluous, made with the competitors already in place and engaged. Several participants shook uncontrollably, some so severely it looked like even their shuffleboard pucks moved left and right erratically as they negotiated the concrete course.

Weeks in places like Ft. Pierce and other locales short on youthful partiers were tedious and plodding. Looking to pass the hours, I watched *Days of Our Lives* daily, knew almost line-by-line every exchange between Ralph and Alice in all thirty-nine episodes of *The Honeymooners* being rerun on TV stations everywhere in Florida, and vicariously competed with contestants on *Jeopardy*.

It was three successive retirement community gigs of two weeks each that prompted a call to Dick Dollar.

"Mr. Dollar, this is Tom Cliffe."

"Tom, how's Jupiter treating you?"

"I'm in Melbourne, sir."

"Jupiter bound though, eh?"

"Mr. Dollar, I appreciate that you're keeping me booked. And the folks here and in Fort Pierce and Vero Beach have all been very nice. Just a little old."

"But they love your music, Tom. Nothing but good reports."

"Honestly, sir, I don't think many of them can even hear me. I'd prefer to get back to clubs that cater to people more my own age, if you can arrange that."

Dollar paused, but only briefly. "As a matter of fact, I've been considering a new tour for you. We have an office in Chicago. I can book you for a swing through the Midwest. Some great folks up there, nice clubs, and good money."

As in Florida, nightclubs in the Midwest contracting the Dollar Agency were in small cities where otherwise anonymous acts could be heralded as near stardom. Following the final set of my final Florida gig, the Holiday Inn on Ft. Walton Beach, I drove forty-five hours, broken only by gas, bathroom, and fast food stops, battling sleep deprivation with open windows and Mountain Dew, to arrive just in time for my opening night at the Holiday Inn in Minot, North Dakota.

A week later, a 12-hour drive to Cedar Rapids, Iowa, to play the Buffalo Run. Then two weeks in Logansport, Indiana, followed by a week in Peoria, Illinois. Left to Lincoln, Nebraska. South to Salina, Kansas. North to North Dakota, the town of Fargo. Then around the horn from Duluth to Racine to Kalamazoo. And on and on.

An unspectacular circuit to be sure, but while many bar owners considered musicians an annoying necessity, an amenity required to draw and keep drinkers, these clubs booking Dollar Agency acts showered their touring entertainers with respect: staging, lights, and sound that presented us as artists, something worthy, something from out of town superior to what was in town.

My unvarnished style played well here. All about the music. I might deliver a low-key introduction to a song or a short story about its composer to an audience I sensed would find the detail of interest. But I'd learned early in my stage life not to tell jokes. "Just sing," Artie Reardon had suggested not so subtly. A voice strong and tuneful, guitar and piano work tasteful if not dazzling, recognizable material, I won over most audiences. By a third or fourth night at a club, I'd see familiar faces, and more as the week or two unfolded.

Stepping down from the third of four sets one evening in a Duluth, Minnesota, bar perplexingly named Mike's Canadian Pub, I stopped to say hello to two couples there for a third straight night.

"Thanks for coming in again. I hope it's the music that's bringing you back." They were younger than they looked from the stage, considerably younger than most of Mike's customers, middle-aged couples and after-work drinkers.

"Th-thanks for c-coming to D-Duluth," said a boy with a shock of brown hair that drooped over his eyes.

"We don't get much good entertainment in the winter," said the girl who sat next to him, probably his date, equally young with a crooked nose, bad case of acne, and coarse brown hair that had been bleached, though not recently, and stretched into a pony tail.

"The better acts don't start coming till it thaws," explained the other boy, another late teen, also with severe acne and asymmetrical features, likely the girl's brother. He wore black-rimmed glasses too big for his face, reminding me of a math major I'd been in class with as a freshman at Immaculata.

"I'm kind of used to it, growing up in Missouri." Their remarks had put me a bit on the defensive, though that didn't seem to be their intention. More, it stirred my resentment for Dick Dollar for taking advantage of me, and disappointment in myself that I'd not been suspicious enough to realize it. "As long as the snow doesn't get so deep I can't make it out of here when I need to get to my next gig."

"Sit down and have a drink with us," ventured a girl with a face more pleasant than plain framed by a halo of tight black curls, likely the math major's date. She cocked her head and smiled, the kind of inviting glance a girl might learn watching too many sappy romance movies.

By this time, several years on the road in nightclubs, I'd learned it wasn't a good idea to respond in kind to a come-on from the date of someone in my audience. I wasn't likely to fare well in any kind of physical confrontation; there were my hands to protect, after all. It was better to hold off. She might come back alone another night—and there was little else in Duluth to make me look forward to another night.

I sat between the two boys and the waitress brought me a bourbon. As she left the table, the shock of brown hair leaned into me and asked, "If you c-can handle the c-c-cold, I've g-got a j-joint of some k-killer shit in my tr-tr-truck."

"Marijuana?" I guess in my surprise my reply was louder than he expected, and he jerked his head around to see if anyone might have overheard. But the evening's crowd had filtered out of Mike's, the only remaining guests on stools at the bar across the room, a couple of guys in rolled-up sleeves and loosened ties too long at a bar after office hours.

"What'd you th-think? S-Smack? Just w-w-w-weed. You g-got something s-stronger?"

"Not at all. In fact, I've never even tried pot."

"You're k-kidding. A m-m-musician, and you never s-smoked a j-joint?"

"I've seen it around, but never cared much for smoking anything. The voice, you know."

"Tonight's the night," the math major's date teased.

There was no reason to hurry back to the stage.

"Just g-give me a c-c-couple of m-minutes." Shock of brown hair rose from the table. "I'll b-be in the white p-p-p-pickup." Math major's date whispered something in math major's ear and followed shock of brown hair. I watched them go, a bit nervous about what I had evidently agreed to.

"Fire on, brother," math major coached my exit after a couple of minutes of the two of us sitting and smiling at each other, and I headed for the door.

I was greeted by a blustery Lake Superior wind and sub-zero temperature. Headlights halfway across the near-vacant parking lot flashed twice. I alternately stepped and slid across the icy blacktop to the truck and, shivering uncontrollably, stepped up through the open passenger side door into the front seat. Math major's date, now nestled between me and shock of brown hair, was touching the truck's cigarette lighter to the end of a long, thin, and apparently freshly rolled joint. She took a prolonged draw and exhaled slowly, then reversed the joint, putting the lit end into her mouth, and turned to me. Holding my face in both hands, her lips tight around the joint, she blew a stream of smoke at my nostrils, some of which I managed to inhale before convulsing into a violent choking cough.

"Sorry, sorry," I wheezed as smoke belched from my nose and mouth. She giggled, then offered me the joint. "Just inhale it like a cigarette, only hold it in as long as you can."

I held it in as long as I could, maybe a couple of seconds before another fit of coughing cost me most of the smoke.

The three of us passed the joint until it was smoked so short I couldn't hold it without burning my fingers.

"That ought to do it, mister music man," shock of brown hair slapped me on the back as we huddled in our parkas and pushed through the wind.

"I really don't feel anything," I whispered to the girl and tripped over the threshold at the club entrance. I gathered myself, and we both found it all hilarious.

"Better go back for my last set," I whispered again, not sure why I was whispering. As I walked toward the stage, I stopped at the table for my bourbon. A pizza and a pile of nachos had been ordered in our absence and much of shock of brown hair's face was already smeared with cheese, tomato sauce, and sour cream.

My finger picking of Gordon Lightfoot's "If You Could Read My Mind" had never been so precise, my voice so much in control. I heard every note, sung or played, with absolute distinction. And the rhythms, steady and solid, pulsing, pulsing, up from my feet to my hands, straight into my veins.

In "Vincent" by Don McLean, I heard my voice as pitch perfect, the high notes effortless, guitar work subtle and

[78]

smooth. It was as if the songs were playing themselves; I merely had to let them go.

> You're not a dream
> You're not an angel
> You're a woman

I'd never sung it with more feeling or focus; never realized how perfectly the melody and lyrics suited each other. I thought the set the best music, maybe the first real music, I'd played.

"Phenomenal!" math major's date applauded as I stepped off the stage and approached their table.

"Smooth," shock of brown hair flashed a peace sign. "Best set of the week."

"A little slow and uneven to a straight ear," math major countered. His date nodded.

"Really? It didn't seem like that."

"Eddie doesn't know why it stops his stuttering either." And we all laughed a hearty laugh.

* * *

Though warmly received and treated well by these Midwesterners, I was left wanting. There was a certain lack of *joie de vivre* here, somber men and their weary wives, out of office buildings and off the farm, drinking to put cold days and gray lives behind them. It was hardly the devil-may-care vacation spirit that imbued the sun-drenched Florida coastlines. *Hey pal, you know that song about raindrops? You know, dot dot dadee dadee dadee?*

And so my drinking became less partying and more anesthetizing: a glass of wine after the first set to help me through a second, a bourbon to accompany a third set, at least one more bourbon to numb me for a fourth.

Days as well were mostly steeped in apathy and lethargy, my only relief reading, a habit acquired as a youngster looking to books as well as music to escape the homespun chaos. In the mornings, before picking up my guitar or heading to a closed club to spend time alone with the house piano, I'd find a mall with a B. Dalton or Waldenbooks. A satisfying morning might include breakfast at a nearby grill, or more frugally, a McDonald's, then meandering through the mall, buying a new shirt or upgrading my underwear collection, then spending an hour or so checking titles and pulling hardcovers from the bookstore's shelves.

One night, middle of the night, I awoke abruptly to find myself upright, drenched in perspiration, throat parched and acrid. In my dream, I'd been in a van parked in front of a club where I was to perform. But the van door was locked and though I was trying frantically, I couldn't lift the handle to unlock it. Passing people talking casually walked toward the club. They didn't see me struggling and when I tried to call to them, I had no voice.

I rose and paced. I could perish having only wandered from dismal town to dismal town, dragging on, emptiness to nothingness, an aperitif to sustenance of no consequence. I could fade away, leaving nothing of value to remember me by, and no one to remember. I was locked in, just like these trudging, stolid Midwesterners. Or my college mates who'd graduated to a bank building or an accounting office or to sell insurance and come home every night to get drunk in front of a television. I'd been determined not to live a life of quiet desperation. Yet, here I was, quieter and more desperate than those who followed the conventional paths prescribed by our fathers and insisted on by our mothers, paths I'd so adamantly proscribed for myself.

What is more ordinary than confrontation with one's own meaninglessness? But in my restive state, I couldn't rid myself of it. The intensity of it would subside for a time, but it remained entrenched, gnawing, migrating to a melancholy underscored one night after performing as I sat alone in a hotel room, hovering over a glass of cheap white wine, passing my thirtieth birthday, and miserable enough to pick up the phone.

"Hi, Penny."

"Tommy." Not a hint of surprise in her voice. But that was Penny, I remembered, never bewitched, bothered, or bewildered.

"You still know my voice?"

"Your ring."

I had forgotten. She hadn't.

"How are you, Tommy?"

"I'm fine. A big hit, you know, out here in the hinterlands."

"Where's that?"

"Somewhere in between the Midwest and the Northwest. Yeah, somewhere in between."

"Not enjoying life on the road?"

"It's just that I'm not getting anywhere. But hey, never mind that. I just called to let you wish me a happy birthday, The big Three-O, you know."

"Oh my gosh, Tommy. I used to remember your birthday, think about what you might be doing, where you were. I even tried to get in touch not long ago. Called your booking agency. But they weren't much help. Probably thought I was a crazed groupie stalker."

"I'm not exactly famous enough to be stalked...even here...though it would be a welcome break from the boredom. So what's up with you? And Janice? She's almost a teenager now, right?"

"Twelve going on forty. She's quite the grown up. Thinks it's her job to watch out for me."

"So there's no one else on that job? No husband?"

"Not with Janice around. She puts anybody I bring home through the wringer. Nobody's good enough as far as she's concerned. Most of the time she's right, but she *has* run off a decent prospect or two. So, happy thirtieth. Is that really why you called?"

"Truth is I just wanted to talk. I haven't really talked to anyone since you. I guess I'm just feeling sorry for myself out here in Bumfuck, Nowhere. Thirty years old and nothing to show for it."

"You knew it wasn't going to be easy, Tommy." Her counselor's tone reminded me of that last call I'd made from Miami Beach. "How many people back in the '60s wanted to be singers and guitar players? And how many had the talent and the determination to actually do it? It might be small crowds and small towns, but you're entertaining every night and being paid for it. You should be proud of that. The crowds will get bigger and the places better. Besides, what else are you going to do? Give up? Go back to teaching?"

If I'd called looking for sympathy, I should have known better. And damn, she was right. What the hell else *was* I going to do with my life?

THE MUSICIAN

Still, I felt stale. My progress toward getting to very good had stalled. As many hours as I'd practice in a day, day after day, my learning was limited to expanding my repertoire on guitar, songs from James Taylor, Carole King, and Cat Stevens; and on piano, material from a new era of singer-pianists including Elton John and most recently Billy Joel; plus more standards from Cole Porter, Billy Strayhorn, and the Gershwin brothers. But playing alone I was restricted by what I could teach myself; never in one place long enough to seek out instruction, even if I could find someone like Artie Reardon.

My discontent compounded one week in Des Moines.

Arriving opening night, I was surprised by a glistening white baby grand, the centerpiece of an elevated stage. A row of variously colored stage lights pointed at the piano from three sides. At the wall behind the piano on a waist-high stand sat a multi-channel soundboard, sixteen channels and more knobs than I'd seen anywhere other than in the music magazine photos of recording studio control rooms. Cables were strung neatly along the back wall to double-stacked speakers just off either side of the stage in a setup worthy of an orchestra or at least a big band.

I mounted the stage, stood behind the grand and ran a scale the length of the keyboard: bright yet warm, and perfectly tuned. I positioned my guitar and amplifier — I'd long surrendered the Goya and followed Dylan into the world of electrics, a Gibson ES-150 — and cradled the Shure mic that cost me a month's wages into its boom stand.

I began to unravel the microphone cable and noticed a weathered, white-haired man standing in front of the stage wearing a faded blue suit, pants of which the legs ended a couple of inches short of glossy black wingtips.

[83]

"Tom Cliffe, right?" He offered a right hand. "I'm William Knoll from AFM Local 75."

"Nice to meet you." I bent to shake the hand. At the insistence of Dick Dollar, I'd joined the musician's union in Miami. It would be required, he'd said, in some cities where unions held sway. "Want to see my union card?"

"Yes, thank you, Tom."

I fished the card from my wallet and handed it to him.

"Tom, I'm pleased to welcome a member of the Miami local to Des Moines. You know Ed Greenberg down there? Or Paul Stazinkowski?"

"Can't say I do, Mr. Knoll." I'd acquired the habit of using the name of someone I'd just met as soon as I could work it into the conversation, though it rarely helped me remember the name for more than a few minutes. "I left Miami soon after I joined the union."

"When you get back, you tell them I said hello."

"Will do." I returned to my cabling.

"Our rules here are a little different than Miami's. We require you to be a member of our local to perform in our nightclubs."

So he's here for a piece of the action. "Yessir. So what's the fee?"

"Well, there's a little more to it than that." Knoll's tone lacked the pretense of friendliness in his earlier remarks. "You can join, of course. We're pleased to have you. But there's a waiting period of a month before you can work as a leader in the jurisdiction."

I was bemused. "I'm not a leader. It's just me."

"That makes you a leader, son."

I stopped working with the cable and gaped at the man. Here I was in the biggest city on this tired circuit, on the most musician-friendly stage with this magnificent piano and sound system, and I was being told I wasn't going to be allowed to play.

"Now don't panic, Tom. We're not inhospitable here in Des Moines." He stuck the little finger of his right hand in his right ear, twisted it a few times, then examined it. "Wouldn't want the boys in Miami to think poorly of us. I've got a local member for you, a bass player. He'll serve as leader and the two of you can work the week."

"But I'm hired here, contracted, as a single. And besides, there's no time. I'm supposed to start in twenty minutes."

"If you're worried about the money, the money here is enough to cover scale for both of you. Your leader will make sure you get your dough."

Scale. It couldn't be much. At best, maybe half of what was in the contract.

I sat at a table and signed the membership form. Knoll folded the paperwork, stuffed it in the breast pocket of his suit jacket and motioned toward the club entrance where a man who had to be well into his eighties stood, hoary and bent. Knoll waved again, a little more animatedly this time, and the octogenarian began making his way to the stage dragging a full-size bass fiddle with his right hand and carrying a small metal staircase in his left. Without acknowledgement he passed me, hoisted the instrument onto the stage, then gingerly, one foot at a time to each step, ascended his staircase.

"Guess you don't got no charts, eh boy?" He didn't wait for an answer. "None of you hippies do. Most of you can't read a note." He stood the instrument, then unzipped the cover, let it fall to the stage floor and kicked it off to the side.

"No worries though. Old Ed here's played about every song ever written. I'll follow you."

He did follow, in a truer sense of the word than musically acceptable. He stood where he could see my hands on the guitar and then the piano, and played bass notes that agreed with most of my chords, just slightly later than me.

"Don't let it get you down," a waitress caught me as I stepped down from the stage after a disastrous first set. "Happens everybody's first night. What most of our acts do is have him stand off to the side, as far from them as he can get without falling off the stage. He won't argue with you. He's used to it. Then, about halfway through the week, he'll stop showing up, just come Saturday, late, for the money."

It played out just as the waitress forecasted. When I returned for my second set, I directed Old Ed to the back corner of the stage. He grumbled, but relocated, then played only sparingly, and mercifully, too quietly to be heard.

He did not come the following night or any night until Saturday, arriving just as I was finishing an uninspired final set to a few remaining couples drunk and talking louder than my singing.

Emerging from the office behind the bar, Old Ed dragged himself to the stage and handed me my pay: seventy-five dollars, all that was left after the leader's take, a hundred dollars for a union initiation fee, and twenty percent workweek dues as the newest member of the Des Moines chapter of the American Federation of Musicians.

* * *

THE MUSICIAN

While Des Moines might have been the proverbial straw, Waterloo was, well, my Waterloo. A second two-week stint in John Deere country called for my surrender and an end to my sojourn in the wilderness. I was hardly on my way to bigger stages and better shows.

A better alternative, I decided, would be to pick a city with a vibrant music scene, move there and find work. New York was an exciting idea, but the competition was famously formidable and intimidating. Denver, San Francisco, Austin — each had appeal, havens for live music as they were. Maybe New Orleans. A chilly fall wind warning of another Midwest winter reminded me of warmer, more cordial days. I'd been comfortable in the South. And I knew someone in New Orleans, a lawyer named Evan Fontenot I'd met during one of my weeks on a Florida coast, as friendly and fun a person as anyone I'd met in what was now more than eight years on the road.

"Mr. Dollar, this is Tom Cliffe."

"Tom, how's Indiana treating you?"

"I'm in Iowa, sir."

"Indiana bound, though, eh?"

"Mr. Dollar, you know I appreciate your keeping me working all this time. But I'm kind of burnt out, being on the road by myself."

"Uh-*huh*." I pictured Dollar running his nicotine-stained fingers through his greasy ducktail. "How about if I hook you up with another player, and you could travel as a duo, say, another guitarist or a good-looking chick singer? How'd you like that?"

The idea had its allure: a sinuous blonde contorting on the closed lid of a glossy grand piano while I chorded an accompaniment to "Makin' Whoopee." But in the ennui of a Waterloo Ramada Inn room even that quickly lost luster.

"I think I'd like to go somewhere and settle in, get established someplace where there's a lot of music. I was thinking maybe New Orleans. Could you book me there?"

Dollar laughed, then tried to cover with an obviously bogus cough.

"Clubs in New Orleans do their own booking. They don't use agents. There are so many good musicians, hell, great musicians available to them. Same for all the big cities. If you want to keep working, Tom, I suggest you stay on the road. You're building a good reputation, doing what you need to do to get to the next level."

He sounded like he was chewing on a cigar as he laid out a plan I couldn't refuse. "Tell you what. I'll get you back to Florida and those young folks' clubs you liked working."

Dollar's offer rang faintly desperate. He'd book me anywhere he could to keep me in his stable. I'd played well enough, sure, and was, as one club owner reported to Dollar, "a nice kid who shows up on time." I was not prone to trashing hotel rooms or starting fights with barroom patrons which translated into calls for return engagements — and hassle-free management for Dollar.

But, since agreeing to life on the road, there were too many awakenings as a piece in Dollar's chess game, ambling a square at a time in all directions around the board, no captures, always stalemate.

"Evan, it's Tom Cliffe, the musician. Remember? From The Den in Naples?"

"Uh, Tom…sure. You in New Awlins?"

"No, but I'm thinking of coming, seeing if I can land a gig there."

"*Mon ami*, of course. There's plenty of places to play. Where are you now?"

"In the Midwest, a little north of that, actually. I've been on a circuit up here for several years, moving around, playing a week or two in each town. Kind of like Florida only it's Minnesota, Iowa, the Dakotas, Illinois."

"Sounds cold."

"Way too much snow. It wears on you. But more than that, being bounced around like a pinball isn't doing me any good. I mean, I'm working steady, but that's about it. I need to be where there's more music, you know, good musicians and better audiences."

"Well you're thinking right if you're thinking New Awlins. We love our music and our musicians. No better place in America to be a musician than here. And it's warm, a little humid sometime, but always warm. So, when you coming?"

"I've got two weeks in Bloomington — that's Indiana, I think. Then I'm done. But Evan, I haven't exactly gotten rich out here. I was wondering, do you have a couch I could crash on for a few days while I look for a gig?"

"*Bien sur*. Come stay with us as long as you want. Or as long as you can stand us all — me, Mama, and my sister and her poodle."

"Gosh, Evan, that sounds like I'd be intruding. I don't want to intrude."

"*Pas de problème*. It's a big house. A little rickety, but roomy. Built before God created crawfish. You're welcome like family."

* * *

The Fontenot residence was an Uptown shotgun, so named because a bullet fired through a front door could exit a back door without colliding with anything along the way.

The architectural style dated back to the nineteenth century, as did the buildings, originally cheap housing for Haitian refugees, then expanded up and out over the decades, and by the mid-twentieth century bought and renovated by the young: lawyers, doctors, and accountants who found cachet in quaintness and living in Uptown.

As to Evan, a photograph or passing glimpse might not have qualified him as handsome. His looks, in particular his deep, dark eyes, benefitted from his Cajun ancestry, as did, he would later make a point of it, his *savoir faire*.

"Cajuns came to Louisiana from Canada later than the Creoles; they were more sophisticated and better educated."

But somewhere, his pedigree was compromised by what must have been a jolly Irishman, evidenced in a reddish round face, and, I was to learn, an inbred disrespect for authority revealing itself in a slightly curled upper left lip.

Evan's shotgun belied his description. From the street it looked considerably bigger than neighboring houses — two stories and as wide as his Uptown property lines seemed to permit. Evan met me at the door before I could knock or ring and ushered me into an expansive sitting room, bright with white pine floors and floor-to-ceiling windows.

"Drop your bag and let's get you a beer," he said. I followed him toward the back of the house, through a dining room narrower than the sitting room but spacious enough for a large black buffet — I couldn't help take note of the ornately carved drawer panels and cabinet doors — and a boarding-house-size mahogany dinner table (I would soon learn of the Fontenot's need for a twelve-foot-long table). Next along the ballistic path, bedrooms left and right, then a kitchen with rows of high-hanging pots on hooks and stainless steel appliances gleaming in the afternoon sunlight that streamed through glass doors at the back of the house.

"Evan, this isn't exactly what I'd call rickety."

"You should've seen it when we bought her, *un véritable désordre*, a real fixer-upper."

He pulled a couple of Dixie beers from the refrigerator, popped the caps, and pointed to a chair at the kitchen table. He wanted a full rundown on my years in the Midwest, which I managed to condense into a summary description of the considerably less than noteworthy venues where I'd been the "featured" act and thus why I was looking for somewhere, something, more opportune.

We returned to the front room to find Evan's mother, Eunice, and sister, Elaine, lounging with tall brown drinks. They were billowy women, nearly round as high, the daughter a replication of the mother in facial features as well as stature, the two distinguishable only by marks of time. The first minutes of conversation proved them unhesitatingly welcoming, neither pretentious nor judgmental. And they were having cocktails at three o'clock on a Tuesday afternoon.

Promising our return for a get-acquainted bourbon, Evan showed me to a small bedroom on the second floor. A twin mattress under a patchwork quilt on a metal four-poster frame was fenced by three walls of overstuffed floor-to-ceiling bookshelves. The legal collections were identifiable by the uniform severity of their spines, but what must have been hundreds of other hardbound and paperback volumes and an occasional magazine had been haphazardly crammed wherever shelf space allowed.

"If you have trouble sleeping, you won't run out of things to read."

"I really appreciate this, Evan. I'll be out of your hair as soon as I get a gig."

"You won't bother anybody here. Hell, there's all kinds of people here virtually every day for drinks, dinner, whatever. You'll hardly be noticed."

In fact, the Fontenot home was a virtual halfway house frequented by neighbors and friends, from well-wishers to ne'er-do-wells, at all times of day and night. Even Dropsy the poodle received visitors.

[92]

The guests, as many uninvited as invited, came to sit in the parlor and talk about what a lousy job Mayor Landrieu was doing ("Hell, Moon can't be counted on to keep the vermin out of the gutters on Bourbon Street.") and how fruitless the efforts of their beloved Saints were ("How do you keep a coach who gets you two lousy wins in one entire season?")

They came for a drink and stayed for dinner at the big table, gorging on Eunice's cooking: mounds of rice and sausage, duck breast gumbo and shrimp jambalaya. And on weekends they gathered in the backyard around the fifty-quart King Kooker, from which Evan poured piles of Zatarain's-flavored boiled crawfish onto pages of *The Times-Picayune* spread across a long wooden picnic table. The one thing all the callers had in common was drinking. Beer, wine, and liquor flowed around the clock in parlor, dining room, kitchen, and backyard.

* * *

I was rarely alone in Evan's house, waking to coffee in the kitchen with a cheerful Eunice, who spent most of her day at the stove or pulling something from the refrigerator or scrounging through cupboards for just the right serving dish. Something was always over a flame or being dragged from the oven. For *Mère* Fontenot, a guest was a happy obligation, and hostessing required by definition an onslaught of food and drink. The only way I could offend was by turning down a second helping of some savory mixture of meat, vegetables, and rice submerged in one or another of her gravies or brown roux sauces. Life in the Fontenot home was unflaggingly engaging.

Early mornings over coffee netted all I needed to know about Evan. Not that I had to pry it out of Eunice. She was an open book, and so proud of him.

Eunice, born a Bertrand, was the daughter of an army lieutenant from Thibodaux who moved to New Orleans following World War II. According to Eunice, he "drank himself to his early grave." Evan's father attended Tulane University, met Eunice at a St. Patrick's Church social, and was long employed at the Whitney Bank, where he worked late, a habit that cost him his life: a heart attack at his desk one night, alone and undiscovered until the morning.

Evan also attended Tulane then law school there, where he absorbed enough of the diverse set of French, Spanish, and English codes that complicate Louisiana laws to earn his J.D. and pass the Louisiana bar.

"You know those made-for-TV movies," Eunice complained. "They make Cajun men out like swamp people who care for nothing more than a Saturday night fight and another beer. That sure isn't Evan, and it wasn't Evan's father, no sir."

One morning as I dallied over coffee and a biscuit submerged in Eunice's red gravy, I listened to her describe a performance she'd watched on television the night before.

"You should've heard him, Tom. He was up and down, all over that piano, hands like lightning, but the sound so sweet and mellow as you ever heard."

The passion with which she described the pianist's competence and sensibility and the pleasure she got from his music filled me with guilt. I hadn't touched a piano in weeks, and removed my guitar from its case only when Evan pressed me into playing something for one of those

[94]

nightly soirées. I had to start looking for work; I needed to find my place in the city's music.

It was, after all, why I came.

But my anxiety abated like a late afternoon New Orleans rain shower. For weeks I slept late then passed the remaining morning hours in the kitchen with Eunice, Elaine, and Dropsy, only leaving the house to meet Evan for lunch in the French Quarter at Brennan's, a Royal Street bistro just around the corner from Evan's law office.

Evan himself didn't leave the house until nine-thirty or ten, and I wondered just how much lawyering on behalf of his clients, mostly injured maritime workers, could be done in the hour or two before our lunches, which habitually began with a bottle of wine and a Bloody Mary with three olives and a spiced green bean — "Our vegetables for the day," he'd toast — the subsequent piece of fish or plate of pasta a mere formality.

Evan rarely returned to his office after lunch, preferring to extend mid-day merriment to one of his many favorite Quarter haunts where we were invariably greeted warmly.

"Hey, now, Evan, so good to see you. Saved you your table in case you come in today."

I excused the little time I dedicated to my music as a well-deserved break from my diligence on the road, substituting lessons about New Orleans' *laissez les bon temps rouler* lifestyle under the tutelage of one who lived it to its fullest. And Evan clearly enjoyed his role as guide, introducing me alternately to Uptown, Midtown, the Garden District, the Central Business District, as well as the French Quarter, at least to the bars and bistros. "Our city's lifeblood," he explained.

On the rare mornings I was out of the house before ten o'clock, I noticed traffic was light. And when Evan and I were still roaming the Quarter late at night, I learned that New Orleanians rarely ceased partying before a morning hour, and that many bars still bustled with revelers as the sun sneaked over the sluggish Mississippi onto debris-laden French Quarter streets.

How apt New Orleans' motto "the city that care forgot." Not just a tourist come-on, it was how New Orleans lived. From the Metairie real estate salesman to the Uptown banker, from the Canal Street antique dealer to the Bourbon Street bartender to the Jackson Square portrait artist, New Orleanians were committed to the good life.

While I was captivated by New Orleans' distinctive charm of trolley cars, po-boy sandwiches, fried oysters, and French Quarter boy strippers prettier than most girls, Evan cautioned against being too wide-eyed.

"So much mystery in people's minds about New Awlins." Evan stood at the wet bar in the Fontenot sitting room fresh from late afternoon court, still crisp in a three-piece suit and white shirt. He dropped a couple of square ice cubes into a crystal water glass then reached for the Scotch.

"But we're no different than other cities. Yes, we've got good restaurants, but all big cities have good restaurants. Some neighborhoods are dirty and dangerous, but not any nastier than parts of Birmingham or Atlanta." He turned from the bar, a forefinger stirring his drink as he sank into one of the taupe suede chairs facing an ivory-colored leather sofa where I lounged in worn jeans and frayed tee shirt.

"We're a hodgepodge of cultures and origins, like any city. And the unhurried, carefree style we're famous for is bullshit. We're as paranoid and scattered as any other citified folk, day working and night crawling.

"Just because we're further south and we live under a blanket of humidity and the inescapable French Quarter odor of stale beer and rotting fish doesn't make us anything more than nothing in particular."

I didn't say it, but I believed living his whole life in New Orleans had robbed Evan of an ability to distinguish the unusual. And the more I saw of New Orleans, the more I believed it exceptional, if only in the collective attitude of its residents.

* * *

In New Orleans in the 1970s and '80s, superstar bands like The Meters and The Radiators filled rooms with locals who followed their musicians like nowhere else.

They crowded into the most unlikely halls for the most informal collaborations, as much to hear a particular player as a popular band. Straight-ahead jazz or Dixieland, rock, zydeco, bluegrass: if a player did it well, they drew a crowd wherever, whenever, and with whomever he or she played.

Much of the gigging in New Orleans was spontaneous, late afternoon calls from a horn man for piano, bass, and drums for a gig that night at The Warehouse or Maple Leaf Bar. The loosely connected assemblage would be capable players, know the same tunes, and sound like they'd played together for decades.

The portrait Dick Dollar painted of New Orleans as overflowing with accomplished musicians was accurate. What Dollar hadn't shared was that work was plentiful for a singer-pianist, in the French Quarter and outside it, from legacy Bourbon Street piano bars like Lucky Pierre's to ornate hotel lounges like the Fairmont in the Central Business District. Restaurateurs knew music was as essential to their fare as hot sauce and filé powder, and a piano as essential a piece of furniture as a four-top. Few neighborhood bars would sell many drinks without someone in there attacking a keyboard.

One afternoon late, after a particularly long and wine-infused lunch at Mr. B's, Evan and I crossed the street to Hotel Monteleone. One of the Quarter's and New Orleans' many fabled hotels, the Monteleone was best known for its Carousel Bar which circumnavigated at a speed of one revolution every fifteen minutes — enough to evoke comment, not enough to induce nausea.

The Monteleone also boasted one of the Quarter's busiest piano lounges. In a room two steps down from the rotating bar, stools bellied up to a padded rail built around a grand piano. Tables and a row of banquettes against the back wall also faced the pianist featured by a bank of white and blue spotlights.

"Cyril," Evan snagged the bartender as we rotated on the Carousel, "Tom here is a singer and pianist. He's new to the city, looking for work. I heard him in Florida. He's great. Know any place we can get him in?"

It wasn't the first time Evan had introduced me to a bartender or club manager in this way. But it was the first introduction to elicit interest.

"In fact, they been talking 'bout gettin' a body down there afore Sylvia. That room's dark till she come in at ten, and they think someone around seven might put some butts in them seats a little earlier." He wiped the bar in front of me and looked me over. "You as good as Evan says it?"

"Well, yes, I guess. I mean, it's what I do for a living."

"Follow me, you."

Cyril ducked underneath the rotating waitress station, stepped down into the lounge and reached behind the grand. A brief squeal announced a live microphone. Two blue lights aimed at the piano stool.

"Lemme hear what you got."

I sat behind the piano and cleared my throat. I hadn't auditioned for a job since…well, Immaculata's Talent Night '63. Maybe something dramatic, big, I thought, and started the intro to "MacArthur Park," then stopped. Maybe a little too dramatic, and my voice a little too rusty. Better stick with something more comfortable.

> *I'm not a dream*
> *I'm not an angel*
> *I'm a man*

It was the first time I'd sung it with piano. It came easy, felt natural. When I finished, Cyril and a manager he called into the bar halfway through the song were standing at the steps to the lounge. They applauded. As did three or four revolving customers. And so it came to pass: five nights a week, three hours a night, at the rate of fifty dollars a night paid by check at the conclusion of the week's sets — in the storied Hotel Monteleone in the storied New Orleans French Quarter, no less.

As pleased as I was about my first New Orleans gig, Evan appeared even more delighted.

"We are going to cel-e-brate," he proposed. "Let's have one at the Nap House, and make a perfectly good plan," *perfectly good* being the superlative Evan applied broadly to persons or activities that could be identified as appropriately as good.

We left the Monteleone through the garage exit and turned right past Exchange Alley without a nod of recognition on Evan's part to his office there or the slightest indication that he might want to check in. We walked to Chartres, then two blocks to St. Louis and the corner door of the Napoleon House.

Many bars in the French Quarter, especially along Bourbon and Royal Streets, were well known by tourists. Many more, like the Chart Room on Chartres, Cosimo's on Burgundy, and the Napoleon House catered more to locals, those like Evan who would stop for "one more" at hour one or more in the morning.

THE MUSICIAN

The Napoleon House had been so-named because then-mayor Nicholas Girod was presumptuous enough to believe that Napoleon, in exile in 1821, would accept his invitation to sail to the Vieux Carré for refuge.

It was quintessential New Orleans, a clash of idiosyncrasies, from aloof waiters and bartenders who locked deprecatory stares on patrons, to an interior that hadn't been painted since Napoleon turned down Girod's offer, to an overdose of classical music, most famously Beethoven's *Eroica*, which he initially titled *Bonaparte* then withdrew the dedication when Napoleon declared himself Emperor, clamoring that "Now, too, he will tread underfoot all the rights of Man, indulge only his ambition."

We found an empty table at a window facing St. Louis Street. "I need to get to a piano. My chops are in need of tuning. Serious fine tuning." I was starting to talk in bursts like Evan.

"We'll work on that tomorrow. I'll get you into a practice room at Tulane. Tonight, we party. Two Pimm's Cups," he shouted at a waiter.

It was to be another New Orleans lesson, though neither of us could stomach much gin. Without acknowledgement, the waiter — his and fellow servers' crisp white shirts, black bowties, and creased black slacks amid the crumbling architecture, another "Nap House" paradox — turned to a bartender and raised two fingers, the cocktail such a Nap House staple it only needed identification by quantity.

The drinks were delivered, and thanked by Evan by name, the waiter dropped his customary smugness.

"How you do, Ev?"

"Perfectly good, thank you, Camille. How's Arthur?"

"Oh, Ev, dat boy just can't stay out his own blame way. Got into it with some lesbians at Johnny White's the other morning, and got hurt real bad. Four or five of them took to beatin' on him. Then threw him right out onto Bourbon. Thank the Deity nobody run over him, but he's broke and swol' up something terrible."

"*Pauvre.* Need my help?"

"No. No trouble with the cops. Don't need to get him from jail this time. Just wish I could convince him not to get to fighting every time he gets a few drinks in him."

I was struck by the waiter's reasoning that it wasn't the drinking that needed elimination, only the kid's urge to fight when he drank.

"Camille and his wife are good people, as nice a folks as you'll meet," Evan confided as the waiter headed back to the bar. "Just not so bright. Did a shitty job raising that boy. Grew up angry. He'll get killed here one day and they'll be miserable as hell the rest of their lives."

Evan finished his gin. I was still thinking about how or where I could get to a piano.

"Hey, here's an idea. I'll invite some people to the house and we'll announce your gig. We'll cel-e-brate, and you'll have a built-in audience when you start next week."

A second drink, in plastic for the road — for Evan, a Johnnie Walker Black on the rocks; for me, the house bourbon — and we retrieved Evan's Mercedes from an Iberville Street garage and headed toward Uptown.

"Don't you ever worry about getting pulled over for drinking and driving?"

"In New Awlins it's illegal not to have a drink in the car." Evan was on autopilot, more concerned about finding a holding place for his drink, since I was using the sole available slot in the console between us, than the Royal Street pedestrians he was barely missing.

"It's no big deal in the parish. Booze is our industry, the P on our P&L. Besides, I've been in front of every judge in this district. Nothing's going to happen to us for driving with an afternoon cocktail."

Upon arrival at the house, Eunice and Elaine greeted me with vigorous applause. Evan had used the Carousel Bar phone to share the news and the evening's plan, and they had gotten a head start. Eunice was rattling pots and pans and Elaine was on the phone with invitations, both with drink in hand.

Overall, the evening unfolded not unlike many others. The afternoon gave way to visitors and cocktails. Neighbors and friends milled inside and out while Eunice served up a huge pot of shrimp étouffée, many on their second bowl and third drink before dark erased the shadows of the live oaks that marked the boundaries of Evan's backyard. Conversation ranged from the skullduggery of city council members to how miserable the Saints were, vehement pros and cons on topics, all New Orleans related, that would go unresolved and about which there would be little concern in the morning.

And as usual, no matter how long the evening and arguments persisted, guests were loath to take their leave.

It was past midnight when Evan closed the iron-gated front door behind the last guest.

"One more little celebration." He steered me to the countertop in the middle of the kitchen, waving a tiny clear plastic bag in my face. I knew about cocaine — in the '70s everyone from acrobats to zoologists was snorting — but had never tried it.

Evan emptied a portion of the baggie's contents on the kitchen counter, used a kitchen knife to draw out two white lines and produced a manicured straw. He inhaled one line, half into each nostril, his head jerking backwards with each sniff, then handed me the straw.

I might have turned it down as I had several times before when someone where I was playing had offered me cocaine. But I was emboldened by multiple bourbons over the course of the evening.

And it was Evan offering.

The unanticipated sting of a first snort and almost simultaneously a sense of exhilaration. How fond I was of Evan. What a great guy. What a friend.

"Evan…man…like…I don't know. Just thanks for everything."

"Hey, let's take this into the parlor and get comfortable."

Another couple of lines on the coffee table and a game of backgammon. Evan was occupied with the checkers and dice while I blathered on about my time on the road, the good and the bad, the dreary club owners, and the women I'd met along the way, "most of whom were fucked up, except for a girl back in Kansas City, who I really miss."

Suddenly guilty about dominating the conversation, I looked across the backgammon board at Evan. "So tell me about Vietnam."

Evan closed the baggie and folded the board. "Better hit the hay. I'll call in the morning and get you a practice room at Tulane."

* * *

THE MUSICIAN

Given an 1886 opening, Hotel Monteleone had been housing tourists long enough to become legendary, a celebrity that included status as the most haunted hotel in the voodoo city. But mostly, it was just old. The piano lounge was draped in sorry, wistful blacks and browns and the aroma of decades of excessively employed sanitizers.

Thanks to my Miami Beach experience, I was comfortable with people who liked to camp at the piano bar and able to manage them as a listening, as opposed to singing, audience. They did, however, dictate my repertoire. I could mix in a song from a well-known singer-songwriter, say Carole King's "You've Got a Friend," or something recognizable from Billy Joel or Elton John. But requests for contemporary songs were more likely to be for the simple earworm melodies of pop performers like The Carpenters or Barry Manilow.

The room also called for Broadway show tunes. And I wore several standards to the bone, the Cole Porter, Gershwin, and Rodgers and Hart tunes Monteleone patrons were most familiar with and wanted to hear.

But some requests went unfulfilled no matter the denomination of the bill dropped into my tip jar: "Rollin' on the river" as it was more often requested by lyric than title ("'Proud Mary' is not a tune for piano and voice, especially my voice."); "Rhapsody in Blue" ("Sorry, wish I could."); "Help Me Make It Through the Night" ("Please, no."); and of course, "Feelings," the most melancholic of woebegone lounge material. Still, I wasn't completely unyielding and played "The Impossible Dream" and "My Way" sometimes twice, even three times, in an evening.

Initially, Evan and his friends were there to listen and applaud, but their loyalty waned. My typical audience proved a mix of hotel guests and locals who liked rotating in the Carousel Bar. Generally, they were indifferent to my music, even the tourists who came to see the room where Liberace had played.

There is such a thing as a piano bar musician. They range in talent and skill, but are defined by their voluminous repertoires, including every over-played song that piano bar devotees over-request. Like a jukebox, their buttons are pushed by deposits in their tip jars. But I wasn't one of them.

The bloom was off the Monteleone rose. I needed something better.

* * *

"You work a single?" a balding saxophonist who referred to himself as Hacksaw asked rhetorically. "You'll always eat."

We leaned on a corner railing in the Old Absinthe Bar, another venerable French Quarter establishment. A row of linked French doors along one side of the long, narrow space opened to Bourbon Street traffic. Opposite, the bar stretched nearly the full length of the club, the wall behind papered with more than a century's worth of autographed currency, foreign as well as U.S.

Hacksaw was on break from a set by a band named Metropole: two horns, guitar, bass, drums, and a vibraphonist. They played a mix of straight-ahead jazz and jazz fusion. An uncoordinated-looking bunch — the bassist and trumpeter tall and athletic; the guitarist and saxophonist shorter and wider, a Twiggy-thin girl playing vibes — their disparity in appearance was refuted by how together they played. They worked instinctively, supporting solos,

[106]

creating moods, and often sounding more than their number, nearly orchestral.

"Good stuff, man," I offered.

"We kinda sucked most of that set. At least I did. These new reeds just don't cut it."

"I thought you played great stuff. I mean, some really interesting lines. Sounded like Coltrane on *Giant Steps*."

"Don't give me that shit, man."

I'd run into Hacksaw's kind of cynicism before. I'd seen it in some older players, club players soured by unremarkable careers and decades of scant earnings. Most were horn or bass players, or drummers, dependent on bands for work and only rarely fortunate enough to play a job or with a group that endured long enough to sustain the ability to eat.

"I guess you're right about playing a single. It's regular. But that's about the only thing that's good about my Monteleone gig. I mean, I got off the road because I'm tired of playing alone. The only playing I hear is me. Nobody pushing. Nobody playing something I want to learn."

"You're in the right place. Lots of good players in New Orleans. Lots of good things going down every night."

"Yeah. Like here. One of my buddy's friends told me you guys were kickin' ass." I paused to watch Hacksaw wrestle with the compliment. "And that you were doing it without a keyboard."

He was quick to respond. "The vibes fill well enough."

The bartender slid a brown drink toward him and he caught it deftly just as it was about to topple off the edge of the bar. They exchanged nods. Hacksaw turned back to me.

"But your buddy's maybe a little clairvoyant. She's movin' on. Wants to play hip-hop. A Roy Ayers protégé, but rather be with her criminal bros. Maybe knock off a 7-Eleven after a gig." He ran a hand over the top of his head as if he had hair. "Actually, Doreen's cool. Just young and tired of the tunes she had to play in school."

I swallowed hard. "Listen, if I can get my hands on an electric, can I sit in with you guys one night?"

Hacksaw stepped back. He looked at me like he was sizing me up for a fight. "I'll be straight. You don't want to come in here if you can't keep up."

Through all the transitions, transformations, and crossovers in American music, jazz remains relatively constant. Born in the back streets and Black clubs in New Orleans, jazz spread to Chicago and beyond, most famously through the influence of Louis Armstrong but simultaneously by a flurry of New Orleans jazzmen. Players came and went, styles varied, but the concept, the intention, was the same: take a melody and make it swing.

It had been another of those lessons with Artie Reardon with little or no hands on keys, me at the piano and Artie deep into his closet of LPs extracting record after record like he knew exactly where in the stack each waited.

"Swing was the *sine qua non* of the big bands — Dorsey, Goodman, Miller," he waved albums in the air, "and Sinatra, Bennett, and their crooning cronies. Before teenagers swooned to the Beatles, Sinatra was swinging a generation of screaming Bobby Soxers, the first young pop music audiences."

Given my affinity for Sinatra and his contemporaries, I could've countered with a long list of swingers and an anecdote on each. But Artie was on a roll.

"Aside from the teen idols, there were pure jazz singers, like Ella and Nat and Billie." Two and three albums in each hand spread so I could see at least parts of each cover.

"Swing translates as syncopation."

More and more albums pulled from the closet. Once displayed they lay in chairs and on tables around the room, an audience of the greatest jazz artists of all time staring in tacit approval of Artie's every claim.

"In four-four; it's also called 'common time,' though that's hardly used anymore. Take a four-four measure transcribed as eight eighth notes. But you play them as alternating sixteenths and dotted eighths, with the sixteenth as a pick-up and the emphasis on the dotted eighth."

He replaced me on the piano stool.

"Consider the title line of 'Do Nothin' Till You Hear from Me.'" He played the melody line, the first two measures. "It's like poetry in iambic pentameter."

I remembered a reference to swing jazz from a college English professor, and completed the thought for Reardon: "Only Shakespeare doesn't swing."

"The roots of our so-called modern jazz were in the nineteen-forties," Artie continued without recognizing my contribution, as if he had completed the thought himself. "Dixieland revivalists like Eddie Condon and Bud Freeman established the structure: a jointly played melody, an exchange of solos over accompanying horns, and a closing four-bar drum tag answered by the entire band.

"We might name it Modern, but the tunes, all our repertoires, are from the '20s, '30s, '40s, and '50s, the Great

American Songbook, the songs we've
like Hoagy Carmichael's 'Stardust' a
With the exception of an occasional
''Round Midnight,' the standards a
chestnuts we call them. Serious players kn.
five hundred chestnuts and can play them all in virtually
any key. But what really makes it jazz is improvisation.

"The composition is secondary to how it is played."

He returned to his straight back chair and tilted back
precariously on its hind legs. His hands folded behind his
head, he studied the popcorn ceiling.

"In classical music, musicians play the notes on the
page." He snapped forward, the chair's front legs thwacking
the wooden floor. "The difference from player to player is
how they interpret the notes. Don't add notes or alter
Beethoven's chords, even if, in fact, Beethoven himself
rephrased a line or added a trill or two as he performed.

"Improvisation applies to the melody line, not only how
it is interpreted but how it is altered."

He was now leaning forward from the edge of his chair,
again exuberant and animated. "As well, altered applies to
scales and chords; they add depth and complexion and, by
the way, are the most annoying to those who find jazz
troubling. It's called playing outside, not within scales
traditionally associated with a key or chord."

Artie paused as if to let it all sink in, or perhaps to see if
it was sinking in. He must've liked what he saw.

"The overriding rule is stay true to the form. No matter
how far outside the melody you play, you never really stray
from the architecture of the song. It's mortally sinful to
abandon the tune."

tie's teaching had been nudging its way into my
ing in the years since. And now, as noncommittal as
acksaw had been, the mere prospect of sitting in with these
accomplished players was inspiring. I would take measure
of everything I'd been taught and exploit all I had learned.

Preparation would include zealous pursuit of the best
jazz the city had to offer, to glean what I could from the best
players. Which was how I came across Ellis Marsalis.

* * *

Ellis Marsalis was better known outside New Orleans by
his progeny: saxophonist Branford, trombonist Delfeayo,
drummer Jason, and the revered trumpeter and composer
Wynton, the only artist ever to win Grammys for both jazz
and classical recordings. But the pianist-father was genius in
his own right — to wit, his LPs with Blue Note, Columbia,
CBS, ELM, and a host of other labels. He was also highly
regarded as a teacher if a bit intimidating. But I was in need
of education.

"Let's start with a common two-bar melodic tactic," he
said. The master played the first four bars of "Don't Get
Around Much Anymore."

"See how the notes and timing of the melody are
repeated? And see how different they sound when you play
the same notes over the different chords in the second half of
the line?

"It's also a way to think about improvisation: repeat the
line but change it up a bit." He played a few notes, then
altered their order and timing in a second pass.

"Of course, improvisation demands that you find new
lines and new ways to work a line every time you play it."

He played a simple, straightforward melody, then played it again changing the notes and chords, the altered lines sounding more interesting and colorful.

"The best players are distinguished by the quality and complexity of their innovation, which demonstrates their mastery of both technique and taste, of melody, harmony, and rhythm.

"Not that everything comes off the top of your head. You don't have to come up with something original every time you play a line or a song. Players have their patterns: Oscar Peterson's a good example. They learn to play them in all keys and are familiar enough to modify them on the fly to accommodate different tunes and applications. There's a lot more of that than you would think, or hear."

He gave me an assignment. "Take 'You Make Me Feel So Young,' and make up a phrase of as few as three or four notes played over a couple of measures. Repeat the same two-bar pattern over the chord changes as you play through the tune. Then go back and do it again, embellishing your pattern with complementary notes: first, simple half-tone steps leading up or down to a targeted note; then a series of arpeggios based on the key of the song, then on the landing chord, then your major, minor, and altered scales.

"It's those connectors that allow you to build tension and interest."

Marsalis had been playing throughout the lesson, it appeared absentmindedly sometimes, never taking his eyes from the keyboard, never pausing to see if I understood.

"Like a diminished scale to connect one chord to another, or passing notes to resolve a dominant chord to a minor chord. There are endless varieties and therefore endless ways to interpret and play songs."

He turned from the piano to catch my empty gaze. "It sounds more complicated than it actually is." Then waved a hand in dismissal.

* * *

Knowledge and performance can be distant relatives. Turning theory into music takes time as well as talent and technique. My greatest asset was persistence. That virtue had been challenged, subjected to the malaise and indifference that followed long nights with Evan spirited by bourbon and cocaine at Cosmo's or the Chart Room, or on the most careless of peregrinations past sunrise at The Dungeon or Johnny White's.

Evan appeared impervious to it all, rising and out of the house well before I surfaced. "If you're going to soar with the eagles, you got to be able to sing with the birdies," he'd waggle a stubby finger. I wondered how he could be so excessive so regularly without the consequential morning-after payback. Could there be a New Orleans gene, a twenty-fourth chromosome pair that imbued New Orleanians with herculean resistance to the after-effects of alcohol and drugs?

Under any circumstances, a workday that began after dark allowed me plenty of daytime for practice. To make the most of those hours, I bought a generously discounted, almost-new electric piano, paid for with the majority of my savings from the road, money I hadn't needed to draw on, due partly to my weekly Monteleone paycheck but more to free room and board, the benevolence of Evan and Eunice.

Crammed between bed and bookshelves, my own keyboard made practicing much more convenient. No more negotiating the Tulane campus. No more outmaneuvering a student to a practice room. No more distractions from exuberant clarinet scales leaking through penetrable practice room walls.

The appeal of the Yamaha electric, a pioneer product of its day, was its weighted keyboard and near-acoustic sound, the closest to the real thing. Unconnected to an amplifier, it could be heard only through headphones, so I could practice any time of day or night without fear of testing the limits of Fontenot hospitality.

Its drawback, which I learned as the Werlein's House of Music clerk and I wrestled it from the store's second floor to an elevator, out onto Canal Street and into Blue, as I'd named the van, and Evan learned as we dragged it from Blue across the Fontenot front lawn into the house and up the narrow staircase, was its weight, egregiously heavy due to the feature that provided for the piano-like sound: its detachable harp.

Even disjointed, getting this package anywhere was a two-man job, and not a comfortable haul for the pair.

The Saturday night following my talk with Hacksaw, I hurried from the Monteleone the few blocks up Royal and over to Bourbon. The Old Absinthe Bar was packed, the crowd raptly attentive to an arrangement of the theme from the TV series *M*A*S*H*, particularly clever in how trumpet and sax harmonized their way through the melody. The rhythm section was its solid self — effortless, synchronized. The vibraphonist struck chords only occasionally; she was bored, clearly.

A subsequent arrangement of "Birdland," the just-released Weather Report tribute to the iconic New York jazz venue: synthesized opening replicated by bass then solidified by snare drum rim shots and open hi-hat, savage roll of descending quarter notes by both horns, frenzy of wildly dissonant thirty-second notes from Hacksaw's tenor sax. Clearly comfortable in this fusion groove, Metropole at least doubled the six-minute Weather Report recording, concluding with violent four-beat bursts from each player and the melody repeated in unison to one, final, exquisitely extended note.

Thunderous applause.

Bows and a break.

I waited at the bar for Hacksaw to work his way through the admirers. Better prepared now for his aversion to praise, I remarked, "Not bad for a little Bourbon Street funk band," and was rewarded with something close to a half-smile.

"Some nights we're not too bad. How are the pretty people at the Hotel Monteleone? Big tips tonight?"

"I'm eating well, thanks. So how about if I come by and sit in one night next week?"

"What keyboard did you get?"

"A CP70. It's the closest thing to…"

"Oh, man, no. Those fuckers should come with a warning from the surgeon general."

"No problem. I've got a buddy who'll help get it in and up on stage."

"We'll have to rearrange the whole fucking setup to get that behemoth on stage."

"Come on, man, you've got those vibes up there." If space were the issue, I would have returned the Yamaha for a Wurlitzer.

"You can put it on the floor next to the stage."

"Cool. What night?"

"Suit yourself. We're here all week." Hacksaw turned to work his way to the stage, then turned back and stepped to where his nose was but a few inches from mine.

"Look, man, don't get too high on this. These guys have all worked with killer keyboard players. Hell, Walter played with Stevie Wonder. Lee and Mark have gigged with Dr. John. A few weeks ago we opened for Herbie Hancock in Lafayette, and he got our rhythm section up to jam on 'Watermelon Man.'"

I was duly intimidated. But not enough to pass on the opportunity, my chance to step up the ladder, to climb into the world I so desperately wanted to live in.

* * *

The following days were spent alternating between anticipation and anxiety. I practiced constantly, breaking a rigorous daily routine only once, on Monday, a night I didn't play the Monteleone, for "one" with Evan at the Nap House then dinner at Café Sbisa. Over and over I ran through two tunes I believed the band would be willing to do with me: a Billie Holiday ballad, "God Bless the Child," that I'd sing, and an instrumental, a Brazilian chestnut I'd heard Metropole play, "Blue Bossa."

On Wednesday afternoon, Evan helped me bounce the CP70 harp back down the hallway stairs and slide it into Blue. Then came the keyboard section and the guitar amplifier that would now broadcast piano notes.

At the Old Absinthe Bar we hoisted the harp from Blue, shuffled it into the bar, and leaned it against the side of the elevated stage. We unloaded keyboard, amplifier, and finally, boom stand and a bag of microphones and cables.

There were a few day-drinkers at the bar, and a bartender and waitress juggled serving and setting up for the evening. No one spoke to us or even seemed to notice as we assembled the piano, positioned amp and microphone, unraveled and connected cables.

"I guess your parents never considered violin lessons." Evan fell into a chair near the stage, and ordered a drink.

The setup completed and leaving for the Monteleone, I wasn't surprised by Evan's parting comment, "Think I'll just hang here till you get back." He and the waitress, an Ann-Margret clone, seemed to have found some common ground.

As usual, I did little talking during my three sets below the Carousel Bar, moving from song to song with only brief pauses, often connecting tunes with two- or four-bar turnarounds. Twice I sang "God Bless the Child"; twice I played "Blue Bossa."

As I entered the Old Absinthe Bar, Metropole was still in its first set — the better the music the later the start was the New Orleans way. They were playing the ballad "Little Sunflower," a Freddy Hubbard composition, with a Latin rhythm. Following a harmonized sax and trumpet head, Hacksaw and the trumpeter switched to flutes and exchanged solos. The tune has but a few changes, which were being chorded apathetically on the vibes.

As they finished, Hacksaw motioned to me to approach, and as a way of introducing me to the other band members, said, "This is the guy who belongs to that monstrosity." Then to me, "Whatcha got?"

An innocuous enough overture, but I was stalled, struck dumb. I could only summon his warning. Something crawled in my belly.

THE MUSICIAN

I was usually nervous before I played. It is an occupational condition that affects many, maybe most, musicians, actors, speakers, anyone preparing to face an audience. To the audience, the stage appears a place for the bold, the poised, the self-assured. But to the performer, the audience can loom a critical lot ready to call you out — or worse, dismiss you — for the slightest flaw or unimaginative passage. Anticipation bubbles. Adrenaline flows. Hands cripple. The throat dries. Stage fright is a meddling neurosis with a debilitating physical manifestation.

"How about 'Blue Bossa'? C minor?" I finally croaked.

"'Blue Bossa,' Real Book," Hacksaw patronizingly referenced the standard fake book key for the song. The vibraphonist rolled her eyes, put down her mallets, and, addressing no one in particular, announced she would sit this one out.

"Two, three, four," and sax and trumpet started the head. I missed the pickup and was already two measures late when I joined in. But I caught the correct F-minor seventh chord when I did, and followed the rhythm through the head with the right changes at the right intervals.

A few times during the Midwestern swing I'd dropped in on local players at their after-hours sanctuaries. But this was the first time I'd played with musicians this competent, not to mention players I wanted so badly to impress, and jangling nerves were making it hard for my fingers to find the targeted keys. I sourly misplayed the E-flat minor seventh at the beginning of the bridge, but recovered — and rather cleverly, I recall — with a Marsalis passing chord to the A-flat seventh, then another to the D-flat major seventh.

"That was almost jazz," I thought and completed the form's final four bars, then the turnaround with a series of substitution chords I'd discovered during my practice sessions. With a compassion I hadn't expected, Hacksaw took the first solo. Settling in, I began to take advantage of the freedom supplied by a full rhythm section, playing chords complementary to the guitarist's and some fills where Hacksaw's soloing allowed. My playing was still stiffer than I would have liked — but the band, what a thrill to be part of this, each player executing his own idea but all in agreement, the drummer driving, the bass player holding everything in place.

A guitar solo, then me. The guitar so brash and dissonant, I thought contrast a workable idea. A simple four-bar phrase, repeated over the second four bars (more Marsalis emerging), countered in the next four measures. Then to the bridge where I modified only slightly the line I'd used for the first eight bars and back to the original line for the final four bars.

A second time through I expanded on my theme, adding passing notes, flavoring with arpeggios, and supporting it all with alternate chords and syncopated rhythms. It was as far as I could comfortably go, and I played the composer's melody through the final four bars, signaling Hacksaw and the trumpeter to return with the head.

The applause was genuine and generous. Though I'd done nothing spectacular, I'd played capably, survived early mistakes, and blended well with the other players. I was swelling with self-satisfaction.

"Folks, this is Tom Clifton over here on the piano," Hacksaw announced, bending into his microphone, which, except for his occasional flights on flute, he kept at the level of the bell of his tenor saxophone.

I couldn't have cared less what he called me; that he felt compelled to recognize me was exhilarating.

"He's agreed to sing something for you tonight as well." A smattering of applause and I nodded in appreciation, then began the introduction to "God Bless the Child" that I'd spent hours working out: the final four bars of the song rubato, the two two-bar phrases separated by an arpeggio based on a diminished scale. Maybe not original, but interesting enough. Hacksaw joined in on clarinet at the turnaround, and I leaned into my microphone.

With three hours of singing behind me that night, I was in control, strong and steady. My voice was supple and dynamic, delicate and pitch perfect through the song's tender denouement, its complaint and confirmation that God's blessings are truly reserved for the wealthy.

Robust applause spread through the crowd. Some, led by Evan, stood.

* * *

"No one will confuse you with Billie Holiday," Hacksaw smiled, this time without reservation. We were leaning on that railing at the corner of the bar. "Doreen's got one more week, probably would like to get out of here tonight if she could. If you can comp the tunes, you're welcome to come in and play."

I couldn't keep from giving a huge, grateful smile. I wanted to hug Hacksaw, though that might have been a deal killer. "That's great. I mean, how cool to get to play with you guys."

I'd join the band nightly as soon as I completed my Monteleone sets. I was not so daring as to surrender my early gig yet, at least until my place with Metropole was secured. It was, in Hacksaw's manner of speaking, keeping me fed.

But there was no mistaking it. This was where I wanted to be, what I came to New Orleans for. This was the world of jazz…and I was in it.

"Not tonight, Ev."

Palms up and begging for mercy, I countered Evan's familiar, foreboding, "We are going to cel-e-brate to-night, *mon ami.*"

Avoiding the Bourbon Street procession, we stood in one of the open entrances to the Old Absinthe Bar, Evan proud as a father how his Tom had "blended in like you'd been playing with them all along."

I'd have preferred to get the piano back to the house and immerse myself in the Metropole repertoire. But Evan was to lead and I to follow, and we were off to the Nap House.

"Two bourbons," Evan shouted to Camille and headed for the bathroom; I scouted for an unoccupied table amid the congregation of Nap House faithful. A few minutes later Evan was inconspicuously passing a miniature baggie and halved soda straw, and I was pocketing the pair.

In the bathroom I entered a stall and slid the lock shut. The words "Napolean was NOT here" were scrawled in black marker above the toilet on a brick wall that many years previously had been painted white. Straw to bag, straw to nostril. The familiar jolt.

"Balance," I chuckled, remembering one of Evan's rules of cocaine: straw to bag, straw to other nostril.

Back at the table, Evan was engaged in conversation with a thin-faced, brown-skinned, black-eyed beauty.

"Tom, this is Olathe, but she swears she's not from Kansas." She sat cross-legged, facing Evan, her left elbow on the table, a forefinger to lips full, pouty, and painted blue, her brown braids draped behind and over the back of her chair. She stared into Evan's eyes, head tilted, face expressionless, as if she hadn't heard the introduction.

"Nice to meet you, too," I countered with not one note of sarcasm. The cocaine had me way too giddy.

A lanky young man in a stained apron delivered a tray of glasses to the bar, and I hummed the notes they gave off as the bartender clinked them onto shelves. "B-flat I think, and that one a C-sharp — or of course, D-flat," and grinned, quite pleased with myself.

Another round of bourbons and to the stall to reinforce my energy and ebullience. Then back at the table, laughing at Evan's story of a client, a rig worker who had to remove his pants in court and hold out his penis so the jury could examine his injury, "the *root* cause of his suit against his employer," Evan quipped, prodding the girl, still expressionless.

A third trip to bathroom to shore up the second. But only momentarily. Vigor, spirit, and goodwill were giving way to a very different feeling, a sort of anxiety. Another session in a Nap House stall, a brief revisit of competence, then deeper into angst. I worried about my piano, left at the club. And microphone, that Shure, in its clip on the stand, so easy to steal. Would everything be there tomorrow?

Now Evan was working the crowd, amicable and animated, talking to anyone and everyone, locals and tourists alike, the braided pouting beauty on his arm, silent and several inches taller.

"Tom, come on over and meet Jimmy Valentine. He's with one of the big, successful New Awlins law firms." I was barely able to speak, trying to say things that wouldn't be said, convinced people were picking up on my paranoia.

Again to the bathroom, this time intending to flush the remainder of the baggie and straw. I could get caught, even arrested. Maybe just a little more in each nostril.

The more cocaine I inhaled, the more ephemeral the relief. I needed out. The only way was to leave without notice or being noticed. I waited at the table for Evan to captivate another Nap House customer, then walked quickly to the door and out onto Chartres, hailed a cab, and announced Evan's Uptown address. Teeth grinding and nose draining, I rode wordlessly home.

It was hours before I slept, motionless through the wait, huddled in a ball under the sheets.

* * *

My practice routine was now dedicated to the Metropole song list. I'd agreed to leave the piano at the A-Bar. "Better to go to the mountain than move the mountain," Evan reasoned. Most days, by midmorning, headphones on, I was at it, impervious to the rumblings of staff and grumblings of the bar's morning regulars.

My diligence was rewarded. I comped tastefully to tunes like The Crusaders' "My Mama Told Me" and "Carnival in the Night," and Jeff Lorber's "Tune 88," arrangements

[125]

driven by bassist Lee Carter and guitarist Mark Brown, and even to the more intricate straight-ahead jazz, Miles Davis and John Coltrane tunes that featured Hacksaw and trumpeter Walter Hess.

And my solos were well executed if guarded.

The Metropole players were from Minneapolis, Los Angeles, Boston, and two, Hacksaw and Lee, from Alabama. So we avoided traditional New Orleans music, anything that smacked of Dixieland, leaving that to the cats at Preservation Hall. We steered clear, too, of Louisiana rock, avoiding the turf of the Neville Brothers and The Radiators.

Unlike most music where the emphasis in a four-beat measure is on beats one and three, jazz leans to two and four – the four makes it swing; the upbeat of four, even more. Drummer Ricky Stallings found no satisfaction in this simple formula. Stallings, rarely where expected, committed to variation and improvised rhythms that sometimes lost me.

As Stallings left me guessing, Hacksaw snickered, "Find the one."

Nor was I used to the speed. The more complicated the tune, take Coltrane's "Giant Steps," the more pedal to my mettle. Would I ever be able to match the comfort of these players with such breakneck abandonment, especially Carter, Brown, and Stallings who handled the frenetic pace so effortlessly? "It ain't easy being white," Hacksaw quipped after one searing conclusion to a set that had me lost and left him and Hess spent.

As the band's unofficial leader, and perhaps because he had invited me in, Hacksaw took responsibility for my integration. Between sets he corrected chords that didn't fit the funk format or accompaniment that intruded on solos, or chastised me for a faulty rhythm. "Keep it simple, steady. Block and tackle. Ride the bass."

The others said little, but were tacitly welcoming. Except Lee Carter, who was openly cordial.

"As African Americans go, I'm more brown than black." A huge smile spread Lee's cheeks, reflecting enough time in New Orleans to understand the significance of the distinction. One of the first American cities with a ruling African American political class, the incoming mayor and associates were universally light-skinned.

As the band's bassist, Lee's job was to hold the beat, particularly in light of Stallings' flights of fancy.

Contrary to a broadly held misconception that the drummer controls pace, it's the bassist who lays the foundation. The bass player is also likely to be the nicest guy in the band; drummers, feral and most likely to be late for the gig; guitarists, self-centered and most likely to get girls, then get them pregnant; piano players, pensive and most likely to wear glasses; horn players, comfortable standing around not playing at least half the time and most likely to be happy to have work.

Lee, who stood more than a full foot above my five feet six, leaned over and whispered the question as if the answer would be a secret only the two of us would share. "Where you from, Tom?"

"Midwest." I considered my upbringing so commonplace as to be uninteresting, yet Lee persisted, each remark or question muttered as if in confidence.

"What's winter like there?"

"Wow, seven boys! Your poor mother!"

"What made you want to be a musician?"

I was finally able to redirect the conversation. "How about you?"

Encouraged by Lee's childhood growth spurt, his parents committed his youth to athletics, eventually parlaying his height and minimal athleticism into a basketball scholarship at a small college in rural Georgia.

Lee lost his place on the team and the scholarship in his sophomore year when a pregnant cheerleader accused him of rape. She later recanted, admitting fear of her parents' wrath had they learned of the actual impregnator, a teammate of Lee's whose off-campus exploits included two arrests for breaking and entering.

Thanks to the intervention of the head of the music department, whose only hope for the college jazz ensemble was Lee's ability to cement the rhythm section, Lee had remained in school. Until a touring funk band convinced him playing for money was preferable to unpaid college performances, marking the beginning of his music career and the end of his and his parents' aspirations for a degree.

* * *

As nights and weeks played on, I grew more enthralled with Metropole — the groove, the funk, the fusion, the Latin rhythms — and less enthusiastic about the Monteleone. I never arrived late to the piano bar but left earlier each night to get to the A-Bar. When a Monteleone waitress dropped in one evening and saw me with the band, I was outed.

"No wonder you're out of there so fast," she teased. "Don't blame you. This has got to be a lot more fun than singing 'Tie a Yellow Ribbon' to those fat fucks from Buffalo."

"I would never stoop to 'Tie a Yellow Ribbon.'"

The following evening at dinner — it was one of the rare dinners in the house attended only by the Fontenots and myself — I decided, as Eunice and Elaine hauled huge bowls of fricassées and étoufees to the table, enough for any number of others who might drop by conveniently at dinnertime, to share my dilemma. Eunice was always in my corner, encouraging and cheering my successes. Elaine too, had been friendly, though I kept my distance, wary of a romantic interpretation that wouldn't be fulfilled and that might result in my eviction from the Fontenot premises and Evan's company.

"Don't think I can keep up with both the Monteleone and Metropole. They're kind of clashing, and last night a Monteleone waitress came in and called me out for leaving the Hotel early to get to the A-Bar. She was right. So I'm thinking of giving up the Monteleone."

One by one, they convulsed into wet, choking laughs that evolved into bona fide howling.

"Damn, Tom, we've been listening at your door to hear if you were practicing 'Feelings,'" Evan sputtered, and they roared anew with laughter. Until kind, caring Eunice came to my place at the table, hugged my neck and announced, "Let's eat." It was her approval, all of theirs, and I attacked dinner with the zeal of a man unburdened.

The following weeks were utopia, my only concern that the band rarely rehearsed. We learned new tunes on the job, sometimes from charts Hess worked out, more frequently playing through a chestnut called by Hacksaw.

Playing their core tunes nightly, I was getting more comfortable with the band's repertoire. Daily, like an apprentice at the forge, I spent most waking hours hovered over the same tunes again and again, looking for fresh ideas. I was less successful with charts and chestnuts, though I managed to keep up with most of the chord changes, enough so that the other band members didn't complain.

But euphoria was short-lived. Hardly two weeks after I'd relinquished my Montelone income, Metropole, after nearly three months as the A-Bar house band, was dismissed. We were being replaced the very next night "by a Blues band with a lead singer named 'Blind' something," Hacksaw groused as we rolled cables and packed our instruments. "Typical asshole club owner figuring we'd no-show or fuck the place up if he gave us any notice."

I was crushed. And so much more than the others.

Truth was that while the Metropole musicians were fine players, they lacked the slightest bit of business savvy. They had no contract with the A-Bar. Comfortable with their house band status, they sought no other work, had no manager, no agent, just Hacksaw whose business model was to play the gig until it ended, then wait for something else to come along. In the meantime, they'd scatter to pickup gigs, with whomever, whenever a call came.

Which, to their collective thinking, worked well enough. They had been in New Orleans long enough and had reputations good enough to get calls: Hacksaw, a night with a trio at an Uptown wine bar; Lee and Ricky to fill out the backup band for a visiting celeb at an upscale hotel lounge in the Central Business District; Walter for a Canal Street hotel's Sunday jazz brunch.

Except me. I got no calls.

There was work — a New Orleans piano bar could support as many as three full-time players — and I was not one to be okay with not working. But in taking a job as a single I risked being unavailable for Metropole bookings. I didn't think I'd engendered enough loyalty to render myself irreplaceable, so I was not willing to risk not being available. I would use my time to study and practice.

* * *

In the month following our release from the A-Bar, Metropole got only two calls. We played a late afternoon mixer for the Loyola University student union on the school's St. Charles Avenue campus and opened for a touring blues band at Tipitina's. Given the band's aversion to rehearsing, we saw little else of each other. I feared what was happening to us was what happens to all bands: We were disintegrating.

Then again, maybe I could help Hacksaw find us work. It would be another way to secure my seat in the Metropole rhythm section. So I invited Hacksaw to join me for burgers one afternoon at the Camellia Grill.

"Don't see much out there for us right now." Hacksaw dragged a fistful of fries through a body of catsup the size of Lake Pontchartrain. "But if you want to spend time buttin' your head up against club owners' doors, be my guest."

"Eighteen-fifty." The waitress bent over the counter and scowled, impatient as I fingered through a short stack of insufficient funds.

"Hack, sorry man, but do you have, like, three dollars?"

"I thought you were buying…"

"I am and I was." I returned the waitress's glare. "But who'd ever guess two hamburgers cost eighteen bucks?"

"I don't price the stuff, honey, I just serve it. You applying for a dishwashing job?"

"Don't know what you're waitressing for." Hacksaw pulled a ball of wadded bills from his pocket and straightened out three singles. "You're obviously a talented comedienne. Great timing. Great look. The whole package."

"Can't wait to see the tip," was her retort.

* * *

I was likely the best suited of Metropole to negotiate with club owners. Maybe all that private schooling would show up in a presence that would seem legitimate, worthy of respect. Still, I didn't have much experience finding work, even for myself. That and my limited knowledge of New Orleans made it challenging. It was time again to consult with the sagacious one.

"Evan says to meet him in a half hour at the Nap House," his secretary informed me.

Well aware now that being on time was not one of Evan's virtues, I wove my way through the quarter, Conti to Bourbon to St. Peter and toward Jackson Square, then back up Chartres, stepping into a few bars along my route, none of which seemed big enough to support a band. At the Nap House I took a seat at a table by a window looking out on St. Louis Street and, not wanting to offend, ordered a bourbon, even though it was still early afternoon.

I'd just been served a third when Evan arrived, about an hour late. "*Je m'excuse, mon homme. Les clients!*"

Evan's specialization in maritime law was determined by his first job out of law school, assistant to the general counsel of an oil refinery in West Louisiana near the Texas border. Victimized by principles, he soon changed sides of the courtroom to represent workers injured on refinery-owned Gulf of Mexico rigs. It proved not only a righteous but a profitable move, moral indignation playing little part in his arguments with oil company lawyers that led to handsome settlements for clients, from which he netted a morally gratifying thirty percent, fifty percent when a case went to trial, though that was rare.

"There's a guy at Aucoin & Babineaux whose clients are mainly chophouses and saloons. I'll see if he'll introduce you to some people."

That being, to Evan's thinking, sufficient progress for one day, I received the well-rehearsed tap against my knee, accepted the baggie and headed to the men's room.

"Just one line tonight," I professed to Evan upon my return, passing the baggie and straw back under the table. "I don't need the paranoia."

But soon I was the one doing the tapping, countering each cocaine jolt with bourbon, attempting the fine dance between high and low in search of even.

For Evan, it was pure invincibility. He did not hesitate to burst into others' conversations at the bar, to drag me down the street to another of his Quarter haunts, to get his Mercedes from Solari's Garage and drive us to Uptown, to fuel himself through an entire evening. And there was me, huddling below all that noise, commotion, a near-silent partner, sinking, sinking.

Well past midnight. We'd made our way to the third floor, two-room French Quarter flat of a Café Sbisa waiter. It was the kind of residence peculiar to New Orleans: an unkempt box in a crumbling building in the heart of what in any city that care hadn't forgot would be a premium-priced luxury rental market. The front room contained all but the bed: a tiny kitchen just big enough for sink, gas stove, and a small, rusting refrigerator, and a smattering of furniture — a salvaged square wooden table, scarred writing desk, and recycled Naugahyde couch.

The waiter and Evan sat at the table where the host capitalized on Evan's beneficence, inhaling his cocaine and negotiating the sale of one of his drawings, the stuff of a vocation that had earned him a long career as a waiter. I slid deeper into the Naugahyde.

Evan looked toward me and rose to leave. "Be right back. Gotta check in at Cosimo's." Cosimo's was only a few blocks from the waiter's apartment, but while I was hesitant to let Evan out of my sight, I was grateful not to be going anywhere in my state of anxiety.

About an hour later, Evan had not returned. The waiter, buzz expired, excused himself to the bedroom, offering me the night's accommodation on the couch, tossing me a pillow and blanket to protect me from a chilling night air that breathed heavily into the room through gaps between door and frame and windows and sills.

I was uninterested in spending the night in the chill on a slippery couch with bedding that reeked of cigarettes and other less identifiable malodors. And gradually, thankfully, the cocaine buzz and paranoia waned. Still, it was nearly eight in the morning when I finally summoned the confidence to leave the apartment, to find a way back to Evan's house and somehow evade Eunice and Elaine en route to my room and refuge between clean, crisp sheets.

[135]

I descended six flights of stairs, leaning gingerly on uncertain wood railings, and slinked through the gated entrance onto the morning street.

I was bedraggled, ragged, aware of blending too well with the morning-after French Quarter sour and spoil. My wrinkled black pants and shirt were further compromised by splotches of white lint, courtesy of the waiter's blanket. Mouth arid and teeth wooly, my head throbbed with the remnants of the night's bourbon. My nose wept an acrid mix of snot and blood, and when I moved to wipe away the unseemly soup with the back of my hand, I saw my hand tremble. I reached Royal Street where I might find a cab, and turning the corner came face-to-face with a crisp young woman in business attire. She averted her eyes and hurried to cross the street.

* * *

"*Mon ami*, so sorry. I came back to get you but the gate was locked to the street." Evan, with support from Dropsy, was at the door to get me in and up the stairs before Eunice could emerge from the kitchen to witness my unsightly homecoming.

"But hey, I've got good news," he whispered. "The lawyer I told you about knows a guy who books New Awlins bands. Has connections with clubs all around the Southeast. That's who I was meeting at Cosimo's last night. Given the shape you were in, I thought it best to wait another day to make the introduction. I'm in court this morning. Get some sleep and we'll talk about it later."

I was a step from the top of the stairs before I could distill his words. "Court? Haven't you been up all night?"

"*Pas de problème.* We'll settle before I put a foot in the courtroom. I'll be home before noon."

Compelled to shower and brush my teeth before crawling into bed, I slept uninterrupted through midday, waking late afternoon. I rose and dressed and, awkward and humbled, descended to join the family. Eunice was, of course, in the kitchen.

"You boys and your late night sporting." She was sifting flour into melted butter in a large black skillet. "Don't know how you all do it. And Evan. He's still in court or at the office or out again somewhere." She paused briefly then began again with the sifter crank.

"He worries me something terrible, Tom." She remained focused on the contents in the skillet. "We all like our drinks, but he just goes on and on. Once he starts there isn't no stop in him."

She turned from the stove. "You think he might be alcoholic, Tom?"

"No, Eunice, no." How else could I answer? "He enjoys being out and with other people. And wherever we go, they love to see Evan. And they look up to him. He's respected."

She was back at her skillet, whisking now, gingerly, never too vigorously, adding ingredients from shakers and jars. "That's a real sickness here in New Awlins. Most folks, they drink so much. How do you call 'em? *Couyon.* But Evan, he's even worse than most. And I know he uses that dope. Ever since he's back from Vietnam. Something horrible happened to him there, Tom. Or things he saw. But he won't talk about it, no, not even to his Mama. But something happened that has him act like he does, something keeps him going so hard.

"Were you in the service, Tom?"

[137]

I hadn't thought much about it since I'd left Kansas City, but now, suddenly, I was ashamed. Eunice's talk of Evan and Vietnam and what must have happened there compounded my embarrassment over my previous night's self-indulgence, made me feel like somehow my escape from the Army was an affront to Eunice and Evan.

Still it was easier not to complicate matters. "No. I got a notice from the draft board after college, but I told them about graduate school. They let me go."

"Huh. Evan just went. Wanted to see what it was like, he said. I tried to tell him don't go, what with him accepted at the law school and me knowing what war did to Papa. I just pray to the Lord that's not how Evan's headed."

* * *

It was past even a workingman's cocktail hour when Evan entered the house looking, I was amazed, little worse for wear. He went directly to the wet bar. I was not drinking.

"Those puppy lawyers from the oil company." He was shaking his head. "Refused to negotiate and announced to the judge they were ready to go to trial." He dropped two cubes into a glass and reached for the Scotch. "So there we went. Selected the jury before lunch and argued the case in the afternoon." He turned to me and raised his glass in a toast. "Dumbasses. Jury came back with twice what I was going to settle for."

"How in the hell did you last?"

"Bathroom breaks, every hour or so." He raised a celebratory glass. "*Voici á ma victoire.*"

Claude Avery of law firm Aucoin & Babineaux considered himself a music business insider. In courting owners of New Orleans' celebrated restaurants and bars, Avery befriended many of its prominent musicians, which led to negotiating their bookings and recording contracts and anything else that required legal wrangling.

He was familiar with Metropole. "Been to hear the band several times. Don't recall a piano."

"Just started playing with them a few weeks ago. I replaced the vibes."

"Oh, *that* girl — something special about her. Star quality. Mesmerizing. Can't take your eyes off her."

The voluble Avery sat in an oversized chair at an oversized desk gesturing with each point, punctuating every half sentence with specks of spittle. Although barely forty, a gray ponytail, cavernous forehead wrinkles, and in the middle of his right cheek an unseemly brown growth with a single protruding unclipped hair, suggested at least an additional decade.

[139]

"She prefers to play hip hop, from what I understand," I conceded.

Avery reached for a fresh pack of Marlboros, upended it, rapped it on the surface of his desk, swiveled it upright, and pulled the thin gold tab.

"You know, there are entertainers who have that…what would you call it? A magic about them." His voice crackled like a scratched record, his words cast like darts. "She isn't good looking by any measure, but there's something there that gets your attention. She plays magnificently, then just stands there absolutely detached. Mysterious, I guess."

"Yeah, well, like I said, she's gone to hip hop."

"Too bad. I guess that's the next thing after disco." An unlit Marlboro danced in the corner of his mouth. "Now that's been a real killer, the disco craze. Put a lot of guys like you out of work. It's worse in other towns where people don't care so much about live music. Club owners have adversarial relationships with musicians anyway, so a few grand for a sound system and strobe lights is a no-brainer. But the bump and grind set don't drink as much, or drink the pricey stuff. They'll get the message soon enough."

"Evan said you might have some ideas for me, as far as getting work for the band. Said you might know somebody. Losing the A-Bar gig so suddenly left us without much work. I was hoping you could maybe help us get something regular."

Avery flipped open a Zippo and lit the Marlboro. "There's really not much of that going on, unless you want to buy your own club, like Al Hirt, or hey, Chris Owens."

This wasn't going as I'd hoped.

Or as Evan had suggested.

"But seriously, you guys have a good enough rep to gig at all the best places — Tips, Maple Leaf. You just need to knock on some doors."

I thought to restate my case for *regular*, but reconsidered, given his apparent dismissal.

Avery pawed his mole with a knuckle. "Would you guys be interested in gigs outside New Awlins?" He flicked an ash into an oversized ashtray.

The road was still an unpleasant recollection. But it *was* work. Maybe being on the road would make us more productive. With all that time together, we'd be more inclined to rehearse, learn new tunes, maybe write things that could get us into a recording studio and get the kind of work, like touring and concerts, reserved for bands whose music is broadcast even to the limited audiences of jazz radio stations.

Hacksaw was my first call. "I'll go if the rest of the guys want to."

"Sure. I kinda miss tourin'," Lee agreed.

And the others fell in line, including Walter, who had taken the lamentable day job and was the most pleased with the news: "Beats painting houses."

I called Avery who, after several irrelevant asides about recordings and bands, read me the phone number of an artist representative named Johnny Star, "an okay drummer in his day who played clubs all over the Southeast and made lots of contacts." And because the phrase *a New Orleans band* was alone sufficient — no recordings or touring history or promotional materials necessary — there were plenty of those contacts where Star could place groups like Metropole.

* * *

Hacksaw was taking inventory of the kitchen in a much-abused condo reserved for musicians working the Pensacola Beach club where we were beginning a two-week stint, and speaking with the conviction of twenty-five years on a saxophone. "Not to diminish the importance of innate talent, but no one would write a book called *The Natural* about a musician."

He was searching in vain for a coffee pot, trying not to make too much noise as the other Metropolians were still nestled all snug in their beds.

"The greats work hard at their craft. Coltrane practiced during breaks between sets. The first time I heard 'Giant Steps' I thought, 'Listen to those changes.' How brilliant that he worked out this thing of playing a minor third tune that moves in major thirds. To understand that much, that deep, he had to be working at it all the time."

"I think there are naturals," I said, sitting on a stool, resting my chin in cupped hands with my elbows anchored to the streaked and cracked yellow Formica-topped breakfast bar. "You have to be born with certain capabilities, like timing and a sense of pitch."

"Sure. There are people like Michael Brecker. Even as a young player, he had that chromaticism and was hip to the Coltrane substitutions and putting them into funk tunes. But he worked hard. You can hear it, how polished he got."

He opened a cabinet under the sink, moved a few pots and pans around in his as yet unsuccessful quest.

"The better jazz players, you don't usually see music in front of them — except maybe a big band where you're playing charts. They've got those tunes memorized. A bass player I know here in Pensacola, Artis Wellmore, recorded with Harold Land. He knows all the standards, can play them in any key. That takes a lot of work."

He slapped the counter as if to drive home his point. "Ain't nothing *natural* about it. Even Miles. Up every morning working: writing tunes, listening to tunes. That's the profession. People think you just play at night and mess around the rest of the time — sleep late, go to the beach. It might be true for some musicians. But even the most talented jazz artists have to work constantly. The music drives them."

He was preaching to the choir. Back in the Midwest and before that in Florida, there was little to keep me from practicing most of my day before I went to work at night. As a single, learning and arranging songs occupied my practice time. Now as a member of Metropole, it was working on the band's tunes, hunting for more interesting changes, unearthing more compelling lines to play on my rare solo excursions and, thanks to Hacksaw, listening to recordings — Monk, Brubeck, Corea, more and more Evans — as essential as museum tours for a painter or reading to a writer.

For horn players like Hacksaw, practice habits were developed from a different perspective, persistently at the mercy of a bandleader, careers spent on call. Better show up and know the tunes.

"I'm with you, Cliffe. There's no substitute for talent." Hacksaw had given up on a coffee pot and was boiling water to pour over the Hill Bros. he'd dumped into a strainer. "Several times I thought I should get out of this because I don't have the gift to be a great player. "

He generated two cups of dark, grainy liquid, then flavored his with Belgian Toffee, a cloying creamer he'd found at half price on his early morning expedition to a neighborhood grocery.

"Want some?"

I deferred.

"I played this job once with Wellmore. We got to the gig and it was embarrassing. I had to play the heads of some tunes, so we were down to what I could play from memory and get by, like 'All the Things You Are' and 'Green Dolphin Street' and 'Have You Met Miss Jones?' But then they'd call a tune like 'Along Came Betty' and I couldn't remember it. I used to know more, especially when I was playing those years out of Mobile with the big bands at the Grand Hotel. You have to memorize the literature."

Hacksaw had picked up a dozen eggs on my promise to scramble them. I took his place at the stove; he moved to a barstool.

"Listening to Brecker, I wish I could play lines like that, but I never will. Can't hear them. I probably play better than I did years ago but still within my limitations. I'm a working musician and that's the best I can say."

* * *

It's the jazzman's cliché: *If you want to play jazz, do nothing but play jazz*...with the emphasis on nothing. By extension, because jazz is complicated and hard to understand, it plays to a small audience, like physics classes at a liberal arts college, which translates to fewer opportunities and meager earnings.

"Who'd want a part of this life?" Walter considered the recent breakup of his marriage and separation from his son. He emerged from a bedroom, the next to rise as Hacksaw and I were finishing our eggs and savoring the last vestiges of the parboiled coffee. He dropped into a threadbare wingback chair.

A capable studio as well as stage musician, Walter had attended Berklee College of Music. He'd immersed himself in the school's heralded jazz studies program, graduated, and went on to work with several notable artists and bands, including a couple of years with the Stan Kenton Orchestra. He was lanky with a mop of blond hair cut evenly all around that sometimes looked to me more like a hat than hair.

But most conspicuous were his glistening white teeth reflecting an obsession with brushing, evidence of which was the head of a toothbrush invariably peeking out over his shirt pocket, which I at first thought an oversight but came to understand as more of an accessory.

"What attracts women to musicians is exactly what drives them away," was Walter's position. "She loved being the girl of the guy on stage. When all the fawning was over, the other girls sent on, she'd be the one leaving with me, the chosen one."

But the reality of life without routine — working nights, touring weeks at a time, never enough money — wore her thin eventually.

"They're excited by it at first," Walter theorized, "something so different from what most people do, but then it's drudgery."

Hacksaw sipped, nodded.

Walter was in most ways reserved. He spoke little, and succinctly when he did. "A man who does his talking with his horn," Hacksaw would introduce him from the stage. But this morning thoughts of his ex-wife had Walter chatty. Perhaps he'd stumbled across her that night in a dream.

[145]

"I thought maybe with the kid, she'd have something to keep her occupied, you know, feel settled," the word *kid* less painful to say than his son's name.

"Which she was," Hacksaw snickered. "Enough to forget your ass and settle in with somebody else."

The remark struck me as particularly callous, even for Hacksaw, but Walter took no offense. The two had worked together for years, whenever they could arrange it, and Walter appreciated Hacksaw's carping, considered it an admirable trait. "Can't say as I blame her. He's not a bad guy. Probably good for her…and the kid."

Most who find a career in music are led to it early on. As children they have a knack for it; fundamentals come easy. They or their parents have been told by teachers that they are *gifted*. And their gift has proven itself in some way: a soloist in the school orchestra, or the best player in their garage band.

While the parents might boast of their children's genius, virtually none encourage their virtuosos to pursue music as a career. On the contrary, they warn, threaten, then command them to abandon a course they believe certain to leave them destitute. Few of the young and talented are able to escape the well-meaning parental ties that bind, to withstand the pressure, to deflect what most often proves good advice.

Those who persisted in the '60s and '70s would have found little support outside the home. Had I chosen to study jazz instead of English literature, my options would have been few. As of the early '70s, only a handful of institutions of higher learning offered a degree in jazz studies. Even fewer turned out real players. Performance degrees were reserved for classical musicians.

Music departments of most colleges and universities prepared students for teaching careers, the squeaking clarinets and awful oboes of high school band rooms and discordant football Friday nights.

Working musicians, nightclub players, guys in touring bands, jazz musicians, they all learned from each other, sometimes in formal lessons but more often on the job, that and listening incessantly to the recordings of the greats and practicing ad nauseam. Few jazz musicians I met would've even considered attending college, no matter which kind.

"We weren't groomed for it." Hacksaw paused his warm-up routine, running scales and playing long notes, as we got ready to leave for our night's work. "Most of the better players I know weren't born into families with two parents, two-and-a-half kids and a pedigreed beagle. Music was our hiding place, our protection from the noise."

For Hacksaw, the noise had been an angry father, angry that he worked ten and twelve-hour days for a paycheck that was never enough; angrier that his wife, who had burdened him with three children from two earlier marriages, was drunk most nights when he got home; even angrier that his only natural child, James Howard Reynolds, would rather spend time alone in his room with a battered saxophone he had found in a trash pile than with his father; and angriest that he couldn't do anything about any of it.

"Mama was a happy drunk," Hacksaw smiled. "At least until the old man got home. Then it was mostly just staying away from him. Not that he ever hit her. Just so fucking negative. Can't blame her for checking out. She's a lot better since he moved on."

Little wonder musicians lived so haphazardly. And why I, enthralled with jazz and eager to establish my place in it, still felt like an outsider. I gravitated to organization: a made bed, clothes on hangers, underwear in a drawer. I had a sense of direction, was concerned about my future, while my fellow players seemed unbothered by their indetermination. Always someplace to play and musicians to play with; play well and everything else will take care of itself.

* * *

Given our fusion rhythms, Metropole's appeal was broad enough to play more than straight-ahead jazz rooms. Where there was a dance floor, Metropole funk could keep it crowded. We were well received in most of the clubs where Johnny Star booked us, in nearby Baton Rouge and Hammond, and along the Mississippi Gulf Coast — Gulfport, Biloxi, even a jazz club in Pascagoula. But Star was not always conscientious about matching bands to clubs, thus we occasionally found ourselves in a venue and locale that did not cotton to our style.

In a pine-paneled basement hovel in Houma, an oil town in the South Louisiana marshes still frothing over its desecration at the hands of Union soldiers in 1862, a burly man in an oil-stained blue work shirt with rolled up sleeves approached the bandstand halfway into our first night's first set and stuck a napkin with something scrawled on it in my face. It took a few seconds to work through the penmanship, and when I did, I found it amusing, which must have shown, because even before I could begin to explain how inconsistent his request was with the music we were playing, the man slammed his fist on the deck of my CP70.

"If you don't know no Johnny Cash," his face inches from mine, bloody filigrees branching through bulging eyes glaring menacingly, "you better git outta town."

The room was small and subdued. The angry ultimatum could not have gone unheard. Yet no one seemed to notice or care. Except us. So sudden and brash the outrage, everyone in the band was stunned into silence, though I thought I heard Hacksaw mumble "asshole." The man leaned even closer, a meaner and more belligerent posture than I ever encountered.

"Sir, we're a jazz band," I began to apologize. I was scared and unable to hide it, shaking. "I'm sorry but we don't know any country songs."

"Listen to this, Willa." An enormous woman, platinum hair piled at least a foot above a narrow forehead and flabby jowls, wheeled around on her barstool. "He says," his hands on his hips and waggling his butt in mock effeminacy, "'we don't play no fuckin' country music.'" And at that, the entire row of barstools twisted to attention.

It was like the prelude to a barroom melee in an old Western movie: town meanies gather for afternoon whiskies, achin' for a brawl. Settlers just off the train from back East, naïve and vulnerable, walk in. And…

"Birdland!" I barked, hoping our most energetic song could counter the developing enmity or at least overcome it with volume. And as we started in, one by one they turned back to their drinks. Except Willa, who slid off her barstool, waddled to the bandstand, grabbed the man under his armpit and jerked him away from the piano.

"C'mon, Deaton," she yelled above *Birdland*, "leave them boys alone and get back to your drink."

Deaton was dragged to the bar, all the way his glare remaining fixed on me. Playing through mechanically, I watched every conversation at the bar and the few occupied tables. They might all have been related. I was convinced they were planning vengeance.

We completed "Birdland" to nothing but the mumbling of the drinkers. We gingerly set aside our instruments. We were on break, but none of us was moving from the bandstand. Then a bartender motioned to me to follow him. We skirted the bar to a door that opened to a small, rectangular pine-paneled office.

"Maybe this ain't the right joint for you boys." A displeasing figure — meaty hands and arms sprouting thick black hairs, flab spilling out in all directions from an unbuttoned shirt, no neck, shaved head, face the color of corned beef — rocked in an incongruously rich leather chair behind a metal desk littered with papers and clumps of cigar ash. A nameplate at the front of the desk read "Gilley." He rolled an unlit cigar from one side of his mouth to the other as he spoke.

"I think you and your niggers might want to git back to New Orleans." He shifted the cigar to the opposing corner of his mouth. "Like, now."

It had been but a few years since the Alabama freedom marches, and civil rights laws fresh on the books had done more in some quarters to harden attitudes than pave the way to mutuality. I retreated from the office timidly and decided not to share Gilley's phraseology with the band, not so much to spare Lee's and Mark's feelings but to avoid what might ensue. I'd heard enough about how Evan's clients in Houma entertained themselves after several drinks on a weekend night to know that a quiet departure, even unpaid, was the sensible decision.

* * *

"Mr. Star, it's Tom Cliffe. We were fired in Houma and we're back in New Orleans."

"Yes, Tom, I'm aware of that."

"Do you know what happened? They wanted country music. We were threatened and then the owner used a nasty racial slur."

"Perhaps you should learn a few country songs, Tom. There are some good ones out there you could sing just fine. Take Willie Nelson, for example, your voice is meant for some of those songs. Like 'Crazy.' That'd be perfect…"

Now off the Star circuit, my fellow players again dispersed to rented one-room flats and girlfriends' apartments and playing one-nighters when calls came. I felt more and more invasive returning to the Fontenots, though there was never anything less than a prodigal welcome awaiting me — Evan, Eunice, and Elaine gathering in the parlor to mix Sazeracs and gimlets, a Scotch for Evan and bourbon for me, all quizzing me incessantly: Where had I played? How were the crowds? And from Eunice, did I meet any nice girls?

On the occasional evenings at home when no guests were on hand for one of Eunice's prodigious feedings, Evan and I would retire to the parlor as the women repaired to the kitchen to hand-wash plates and silverware and the multiple glasses that had been arranged so meticulously at each table setting, and to scour the myriad pots and pans Eunice would engage in her nightly culinary campaign.

"I thought being on the road all day together with nothing else to do and no one else around would be just what was needed to get serious about new material." I'd assumed the white couch as my natural place in the parlor and sprawled as Evan worked the bar, using bronze tongs to pluck two perfectly square ice cubes from a refrigerated drawer, dropping them into two snifters. He added a splash of water to a jigger of Maker's Mark for me and poured his Johnnie Walker Black uncensored to the brim of his glass.

"No one is interested in writing anything, or for that matter, even rehearsing. Walter arranges something from time to time, and charts it out for us. But a half hour over a chart is about as long as anyone can stay focused."

"Is that all it takes, a half hour to learn a new song?"

"Mostly we just read our way through an arrangement on the job."

"And it comes out okay?"

"Yeah. That's the problem. These guys are good enough to read a chart for the first time and it sounds like music. Every night's a jam session. But if they were really committed, we could work over a Walter arrangement, kick around some ideas, you know, come up with something much cooler."

I'd barely touched my drink when Evan rose for another. "Some of the stuff you guys play is really strong," he said, fishing more ice from the bin. "I think it's as good as anything going on in New Awlins. And not just me. I could see it in their faces at the A-Bar. And if you didn't notice, some of those faces were back night after night."

"I'm not sure that was because of us or they were just A-Bar freaks." I sipped on the bourbon. "Hell, same derelicts hang out at the Carousel every night."

Evan sat back in his chair and folded his hands behind his head, sympathetic, I could tell from his expression, if not thoroughly convinced.

My concern was legitimate. The band was inherently averse to rehearsing. We were good enough to hold a crowd, to play good rooms, but not much beyond that, not a sound or style that would be recognized as original or distinct.

I knew we could do better.

* * *

I was now getting an occasional call from bass and guitar players for pickup gigs at bars or private parties, though rarely with much enthusiasm. Wasn't I the guy who got the gigs for Metropole? Shouldn't I be calling them with work opportunities?

But the only work I could land was solo. Most evenings found me in a New Orleans neighborhood bar, singing my Paul Simon, Billy Joel, and Elton John tunes, and the standards that were the stuff of my Monteleone days. The good news, there were so many places for me to work; the bad news, there were so many places to keep me occupied with that kind of work.

Still, my playing was maturing, aged since the Monteleone, influenced by Metropole-brand funk, infested with the seamy, liquid New Orleans nights. Jazz was burrowing bone deep. There were hints of dirt in my music, an emerging rasp in my voice, intonation cured by time, seasoned by experience. My singing more communicative if less silvery; my playing more daring and interesting. So the rooms I played, if less fashionable than posh hotel lounges with their overstuffed chairs, catered to better crowds, more locals than tourists, more listeners than socializers.

Well, maybe not all the rooms I found myself in.

* * *

Mid-summer in New Orleans. So oppressively humid the French Quarter streets were sweating. I was on an hour-long break following a set at Bourbon Street's Lucky Pierre's, by legend the infamous "House of the Rising Sun." I stood outside the club with a bartender also on break watching one of the kid tap dancers con yet another tourist with the "betcha ten bucks I can tell you where you got them shoes" scam.

Described by a journalist as "the kind of place that made New Orleans seem like an endless Fellini movie," Lucky Pierre's no longer invited its guests to the bedchambers that encircled the second floor of its back room. Instead, it upheld its reputation for being "the ruin of many a poor boy" by hosting a select cache of young hookers who sat demurely on barstools in the front room waiting a negotiation, then to whisk their customers to one of several nearby sponsored apartments. The back room long ago had been converted to a restaurant serving late-night breakfasts, the ostensible reason for most visits to Lucky Pierre's, including those by its most faithful visitor, the parish's chief vice cop. "We call him 'our vice cop,'" one of the prostitutes whispered in my ear one night as he arrived.

The musical showcase of the evening, most evenings, was Frankie Ford, a one-hit wonder from the '50s crumpled beyond his years by the rigors of amphetamine-fueled one-night road shows.

THE MUSICIAN

Frankie's trademark was the glissando, which he used repeatedly to embellish show tunes that monopolized his Lucky Pierre's repertoire. I found little in Ford to admire in terms of skill, but I was dazzled by the energy he brought to his work. No matter how sparse the Lucky Pierre's crowd, Frankie was *on* every night, every set, every song — including every one of the multiple nightly executions of his career achievement, the bombastic "Sea Cruise," launching that honking vessel three sometimes four and five times a night as patrons of pussy paused to put a twenty into the huge glass bowl set conspicuously atop the spinet.

Lucky Pierre's stayed open until four in the morning, every morning, requiring two players to cover eight hours of music. I exchanged sets with Frankie five nights a week at seventy-five dollars a night plus tips — and the girls made sure their clients were generous at the tip jar. That is, when they came, for most nights the room stayed nearly empty.

"How can they stay open?" I questioned the bartender, both of us on break and out on Bourbon taking in the nightly parade of Quarter dwellers. An elderly woman in a faded and soiled wedding gown, a duck cradled in her arms, whizzed by on roller skates, tattered veil held aloft by a trailing teenage boy, hairless, wearing only a diaper and riding a tricycle.

"Don't ask." The bartender crushed a half-smoked cigarette on the sidewalk. "Don't ever ask."

Frankie's ten o'clock set concluded, I squeezed in behind the piano. Halfway through a half-hearted version of "Summertime" I was distracted by contentious voices at the bar. I played on. The conversation grew more strident. I played on. One of the girls yelled something angry and profane, and a barstool went spiraling into a table. I played on, then looked up to see a couple of guests bolting for the back room. I was about to take cover beneath the spinet's keyboard when an authoritative voice bellowed.

"Everyone out. Now!"

As the hookers and their johns scattered down Bourbon and around corners, I stood on the sidewalk with Frankie, the bartender, and a couple of waiters, and watched as the officer who'd cleared the club padlocked the front door.

"I knew they were coming, just not when," Frankie enlightened us. A bust by the Orleans Parish Sheriff's Office had been anticipated for some time. A trust had been violated.

"They'll kiss and make up," the bartender offered.

"Won't happen here," Frankie said.

Lucky Pierre's liquor license was pulled, and the rising sun gave way to an unaccustomed afternoon glare welcoming ladies' social clubs to vegetarian lunches. Lucky Pierre's former owner would need other French Quarter registers to account for the nightly takes generated by his cash enterprises. Of less consequence, it was the end of my best-paying New Orleans gig, not to mention Frankie Ford's sweetest deal since his recording of Huey "Piano" Smith's "Sea Cruise" climbed into the Top 20 in 1959.

I was developing a reputation as a solid singer-pianist, and it was opening doors at more rooms around the city. I could laze through a cocktail hour set or two in a hotel lounge, then move to a grittier location for a more committed effort. I was even building something of a following, mostly thirty- and forty-something couples already nostalgic for the '60s and '70s. A following allowed me to charge something of a premium, which, combined with a knack for drawing attention to my tip jar, a skill I'd picked up from Frankie Ford, could generate two hundred dollars and more on some two-venue nights. Not only could I feed myself regularly, I could afford my own place.

"It's time for me to stop sponging off you and Eunice," I raised the subject one afternoon halfway through a bowl of seafood gumbo at Brennan's. "I looked at a little house up by the Lake this morning that I can rent. Couple of bedrooms. Enclosed porch in the back where the band can rehearse."

No response or reaction by Evan, as if he hadn't been listening. That lawyer thing, I thought, and added, "And have a girl spend the night when the mood strikes."

"Strikes who?"

"Hey, I could hook up with somebody soon. There's a group of five or six girls that have been showing up at my gigs. Maybe one of them."

"I'd say you're due." Evan smiled his agreeable smile, laughed his affable laugh. Then, as he did so often at such moments, affected the Bronx-like accent of New Orleans' Lower Ninth Ward. "Sure, *mon ami*. It's time you done blow the Fontenot coop. Only 'ting you got to do is tell Mama. She done got partial to her little curly-headed Tommy."

I caught his glimpse for a few seconds, then grabbed a corner of French bread and slowly mopped up the last vestiges of my gumbo.

"I know, Evan. She's treated me like her own." I drained the last of my Chardonnay and stared into the empty glass. "Like a son."

I swallowed hard and reached for my water glass. Evan leaned in and threw his arm around my shoulder. "Let's get out of here before you get weepy on me."

* * *

I rose the next morning intending to make the announcement at breakfast. I'd watch Eunice and wait for an appropriate moment. But any plotting was scuttled upon my arrival in the kitchen. Eunice was spilling over with excitement, flush with pride at the revelation that Elaine was pregnant, and even more blessedly, of a related marriage proposal. Before I could pour myself a cup of coffee, Eunice thrust a photo of the smiling couple into my hands.

"Oh, Tom, are they not just perfect for each other?"

Except for beard and bald spot, the intended was a mirror image of the portly Elaine. Eunice was certain to be feeding yet another round person, and another after that, an expanded family of snowmen and snowwomen.

Elaine's prospects made my announcement less momentous. And certainly I would come by often, for drinks, and dinner of course, every night I could.

* * *

Consistent with their laissez-faire attitude, most New Orleanians lived in modest homes in neighborhoods defined more by location than wealth. Lakeview was one of the city's more upscale areas, home to its professional class. Still with rare exception the houses were unassuming.

The terra infirma of a locale three feet below sea level marked the exteriors of houses with wavy clapboard siding front to back, and inside, ceiling cracks and roller-coaster floors. The attraction of Lakeview was, like other parts of the city, its quaint bars and small grocery stores, and its long-standing eateries, specifically the fresh-catch crab restaurants along the docks around Lake Pontchartrain.

Dwarfed by music equipment, my otherwordly possessions consisted of a second pair of jeans, four pairs of dress pants (two were red bell bottoms) which, with Dingo boots and floral print shirts, screamed *stage clothes*; and a large paper bag stuffed with underwear, socks, Dopp kit, a couple of sweaters, and a leather jacket. I needed but one trip in Blue to move.

[161]

While I was ready with the four hundred dollars for my first month's rent and a deposit of the same amount, furnishings were an afterthought: a bed and mattress, guaranteed flea-free, from a homeless mission thrift shop, and a chest of drawers from a yard sale near Evan's house. The living and dining rooms would be furnished with table, chairs, and a sofa Eunice had been keeping in a Tremé storage unit.

For me this was palatial. So much room all to myself. For the first time since my Immaculata dorm room, I felt rooted — and in a city vibrant with music, where kids grew up wanting to be jazz musicians as opposed to rock stars, where there were so many good players with whom I could mingle and from whom I could learn.

Once again I was on track, just as I'd hoped when I first traded the road for New Orleans.

The subsequent weeks and months provided time, convenience, and focus. Despite a late-hour solo gig or the occasional Metropole appearance, I was up and working by midmorning. My growth was fueled, as always, by practice, relentless and determined, working my existing repertoire as well as adding to it, more chestnuts mainly, but always tunes with enough structural depth to challenge my skills and expand my knowledge.

If not yet brimming with confidence, I'd become somewhat self-assured. Enough to audition for and win a seat at the piano in the prestigious Fairmont Hotel's Sazerac Bar for the lounge's Sunday Night Feature Performances. I'd play a solo set, then accompany a guest vocalist, usually a touring singer with some name recognition.

I'd pursued the job, for one, to see if I could win it. But Hacksaw had advised it as another educational opportunity.

"You'll have to play from charts for singers with different ranges. The material won't be in fake-book keys."

The Sazerac Bar was among the most elegant in the city: comfortable, spacious, and bright. Sofas and stuffed chairs covered in floral patterns of pinks and mauves and baby blues were placed around the room with purpose, to allow for quiet conversation among small groups — more the feel of a large living room than a bar.

Singers contracted for these special performances were always women, most often from the cast of a touring musical theater production. Occasionally the Fairmont engagement was a stop on a multi-city tour of an up-and-coming starlet — or one fading sufficiently to take one-night, late-night hotel bookings.

The first couple of Saturday nights went smoothly: a hopeful ingénue and an aging diva. I met with their managers beforehand who handed over clean, printer-rendered charts. As I was used to accompanying myself, I was sensitive to playing in a complementary way, neither interrupting nor disruptive, and the singers waved appreciative hands as they stepped off the Sazerac Bar stage.

But misfortune befell my third Sunday Night Feature Performance when a drunk Debbie Reynolds tripped over the microphone stand and fell into my lap as she was mangling the bridge of "Bridge Over Troubled Waters." En route, her face collided with the top register of the piano, bloodying her lip, several of the ivory keys, and, in due course, my crotch.

Two weeks later would prove to be my final Sunday at the Fairmont. As I completed a rendering of "I Can't Get Started," a waitress came to the piano waving a drink napkin. The night's guest singer was ready to go on.

The waitress read from the napkin: "You are to announce Ms. Williams to the introductory bars of 'Stella by Starlight.' I'm not sure what this next part means." She squinted at the writing. "There's just the letter F and the number sign." She then affected a haughty pose, resting her right hand on an extended right hip and fanning herself with the napkin. "Ms. Williams insisted I make sure you understood. You understand?"

"Where's her chart?"

The waitress straightened and gaped. "What's a chart?"

I was about to explain, then noticed a chalk-white face encased by stringy black hair above a silvery silk sleeveless floor-length gown moving toward the piano. Dressed as she, the stride was decisively he. I was still hunched over the side of the stage — the waitress had fled — as if some final part of the message was lingering there to be heard. The singer mounted the stage, adjusted the microphone stand to her, or his, substantial height, looked out at the crowd…and waited.

"Uh, ladies and gentlemen, Jackie Bryson," I announced. Then leaning away from my microphone and behind the singer's back, "Excuse me, uh, Ms. Bryson, do you have a chart for this?"

The singer turned a cold stare on me and wrapped blood-red lips around the live microphone, then growled, "What piano player doesn't know 'Stella By Starlight'?"

Stunned then embarrassed, I ducked back behind the piano. Of course I knew the song, but in such an impossible key? Without a chart? I began playing the introductory changes in G, mumbling "What singer can't sing this a half-step higher, in a reasonable fucking key?"

A single bar into the introduction, the singer turned from the audience to face me full on. "I believe instructions called for the key of F sharp," directly into the microphone.

Damn, perfect pitch, but I can get through this, I figured. Just think a half-step lower. And I began again, working hesitantly through the diminished chords in the introductory bars. Jackie started the song then began snapping the fingers of her free hand, a signal to me to hurry the tempo. But I was barely keeping up at the slower pace. Faster, I missed an early change, badly, and then again. Halfway through the first verse, the singer, with no change in commitment to tone or lyric, sang: *Through years of B over Bb...The murmur of a Eb minor...at even F sharp diminished.*

Through my scrambled thoughts I heard chuckling in the audience. Even a chart, would one miraculously appear, couldn't save me now.

The small stage was bordered by a curved brass railing with an opening in the front, the only way to enter or leave the stage. The piano was tucked into the back of the curve, the space around it barely enough to stand in.

At the beginning of the second verse, Jackie stepped toward the piano. "That great symphonic theme," the singer crooned, then dropped down next to me on the stool, and in a singular swift athletic motion, butted me to the floor, simultaneously striking the B minor seventh chord and continuing the verse in tempo. There Jackie stayed and played, through two forms including a two-verse solo, to a resounding finish...and a final arpeggio.

Jackie stood, bowed to acknowledge the mix of resounding applause and hearty laughter — her accompanist standing fast, hemmed in and humiliated, sharing the spotlight that had moved with the singer to the piano. Great comedy. Wonderful routine. I rolled my microphone cable, placed the Shure in its protective sleeve, and walked out the front door of the Fairmont. I didn't play the final set of the night. I wouldn't return to ask for my night's pay.

"A great lesson," Hacksaw commented as he worked over a reed. "You have to know the literature and be able to play in any key."

* * *

On nights I didn't perform, I was out gleaning ideas from other pianists, Ellis Marsalis at Snug Harbor and others nearly as accomplished. More and more my singing was taking on the grit and gravel that flavored the voices of Fats Domino and even the tender Aaron Neville. At home, I practiced evermore earnestly. When not practicing, I listened: Evans and Peterson, Corea and the percussive Bud Powell, even the esoteric Keith Jarrett, moaning and all.

As I was building my reputation independent of Metropole, so too Metropole, despite sporadic work, was establishing itself in certain corners as an assembly of fine players. A few weeks following a return engagement on the Loyola campus, students voted us ahead of the famed Radiators as their Band of the Year. Word got around. We were contracted by the student union at Mississippi State and for a commemorative program at Jackson State. An off-campus frat party in Tuscaloosa led to a week in a Birmingham jazz club. Then came calls to open for name acts: at Tipitina's for the Neville Brothers, and for Houston-born, New Orleans-influenced Joe Sample in a sold-out appearance in Lafayette.

Our stock was surely on the rise. These bookings were high-caliber, so much better than the sort being doled out by the Dick Dollars and Johnny Stars. More than gigs, these were events; and just as gratifying, calls were coming not through an agent but directly to me. It was Metropole they wanted, not just a jazz or funk band. And the money, well, I probably wasn't asking enough, probably not getting the going rate for a name band, but it was better than the clubs had paid. And the work was definitely of a higher calling.

Then, for the first time, concert status: the marquee act in a four-band lineup to reopen a renovated Saenger Theater in Pensacola. I was as excited as the others were unmoved, jaded perhaps by their earlier work in impressive venues with name players.

"If we're our best in Pensacola, it could lead to more concerts and maybe even a chance to record." I talked excitedly as Evan and I negotiated Chartres Street, passing a line of expectant diners waiting at the door of K-Paul's, then maneuvering around a tour group blocking the sidewalk leading to the Chart Room.

"This could be a real launching pad for us. So I'm going to propose two things, a set program and daily rehearsals. We'll take our four or five best tunes and shake 'em up, add dynamics, like new harmonies and rhythm changes. Get it all down so tight it'll sound like it's right out of a studio."

"Ah, commitment." Evan had been following tourists' gazes upward toward some historic window and inadvertently bumped an elderly woman. She fell backwards to the sidewalk. Flushing with embarrassment, Evan quickly helped her up. Brushing the French Quarter from the seat of her pants as Evan apologized, she returned an adoring smile, then toddled on.

As did we. "It's how you turn an idea into an accomplishment," I pleaded. "It's what makes the good great, the ordinary extraordinary."

"Of course you know better than I," Evan suggested as we slid onto a couple of Chart Room barstools. "But isn't spontaneity the essence of jazz? I mean, aren't you supposed to play the song different every time? Make stuff up as you go along?"

"I'd just like there to be a plan, when to get loud and when to play soft, a few places where we all break together and some lines of harmony that have been worked out. Not just play the head, take turns soloing, then play the head out."

"Fortissimo and pianissimo! Tom, if you nail that bunch to that kind of discipline, I'll call Guinness," then in the same breath, "Good evening, Evie, you luscious thing you."

At four feet eleven and sloop-shouldered, with a nose that seemed to spread from ear to ear and caked-on makeup that couldn't entirely hide a deep scar running diagonally across the width of her forehead, Evie was hardly luscious. But there was only kindness in Evan's greeting and she took the comment gratefully, like she believed it.

"A Johnnie and Bud chaser, s'il vous plaît, and a Kentucky oil change for the piano man here."

We were quiet for a time, Evan sipping Scotch, me pensive over my bourbon. But I was bristling. I wanted Evan to understand my dilemma, that I wasn't just whining.

"In your business," I began, "in any real business I can think of, there are things you can do to improve your lot — advertise, come up with a new service or product, do something as simple as stay open later. If you work for somebody else, you can work harder, get an MBA, suck up to your boss. Tried and true ways to get ahead. But musicians, you just have to put yourselves out there and hope opportunity finds you."

Ordinarily Evan would deflect my complaints with humor or counterpoint, but he must have sensed how truly distressed I was.

"Tom, I understand. Your business is, well, no business at all. I see how hard you work just to make the tiniest bit of progress. And no matter how good you get, it doesn't seem to get you any closer to what most people would call success."

"Exactly. It's frustrating." I chugged the bourbon, and raised my glass to signal for another. "Fucking frustrating. The guys I work with, they've been rats on this treadmill for a long time, even if they don't think of it that way. About the best they can hope for is to get enough work to keep playing. It's damned unfortunate."

"La vie telle qu'elle est. They take life as it is, my friend. You might also say they've learned to take things as they come. I don't think you can convince them that practicing more or writing new arrangements will make one bit of difference for them."

I studied the scarred wood of the Chart Room bar, the carefully carved initials, the angry wounds. It was as if it was saying, "No matter what you do to change me, I remain what I am."

* * *

"You had good intentions."

Hacksaw apologized for Mark and Ricky who, on the first day of the two-week rehearsal schedule, were yet to arrive an hour after the eleven o'clock scheduled start. "Structure kinda goes against the grain."

He was spread-eagled on my sofa while Walter paced in front of us running scales and Lee sat at my piano rolling a joint. I sat at the edge of one of Eunice's dining room chairs, head in hands. "Afraid they'll get stale."

"Or just lazy motherfuckers."

"Careful now." Lee handed me the once-toked joint and gave me a toothy smile. "No racial epithets."

I took a hit and slid back from the edge of the chair.

Hacksaw broke the silence. "Look. I'll get with Mark and Ricky and we'll get straight for rehearsing the day before the gig. Nobody's going to lose their edge running through these tunes one more time."

We gathered on my back porch the afternoon before the gig, but not a note was played. Ricky didn't bother to bring even his practice drum set. The best I could do was to get everyone to agree on the songs we'd play and the order we'd play them in. We'd been playing those tunes on every gig; most had been on the Metropole playlist well before I joined the band. They were the arrangements —had morphed into arrangements as we played them again and again — that generated the most enthusiastic response from our most attuned crowds. And given the pre-concert radio and newspaper promotion, a receptive Saenger audience was assured.

* * *

What was not assured was the ability of the venerable theater's renovated staff to manage four bands eager to prove themselves in a concert venue. Each of the first three, more local to Pensacola than the New Orleans headliners, played well beyond their allotted time.

We sat and waited.

Lee and Hacksaw knew some of the other musicians, and there was a considerable exchange of stories and joints as the hours dragged on. I paced, grimacing with each additional tune, and incredulous at the time it took each band, more interfered with than helped by an inexperienced stage crew, to tear down and set up.

Even before the last of the "warm-up" bands had exhausted its repertoire, the refurbished venue was half empty. It was near midnight before amp and mic checks, and fifteen more excruciating minutes before we began. Anorexic strains of an uninspired effort on "Birdland" ricocheted off freshly gilded walls, empty seats, and vacant concrete aisles, bringing the event to a muted dissolution.

Paragraph four of the four-paragraph November 8, 1984, *Pensacola Journal* article covering the Grand Reopening read:

```
By the time Metropole made it to the
stage, the audience had depleted its
cannabis supply and was drifting off
with the smoky cloud. So, too, the New
Orleans headliners must have been lulled
comatose by the combination of second-
hand smoke and the previous three dreary
efforts. While those of us still awake
at the midnight hour could recognize
some talent among these musicians, we
also shared their disinterest in their
caliginous role, for which, as it turned
out, they should have been issued scrub
buckets in place of saxophones and
guitars. As opposed to featured act,
theirs was more akin to ablution,
```

mopping up the musical excrement of
their predecessors, their most
appreciated effort being an appearance
mercifully short for the few of us
either required to stay or too stoned to
leave the not-so-grandly reopened
Saenger.

New Orleans admits all, admonishes many, admires few. On the strength of our opening for the Neville Brothers, and a Tipitina's waitress whose admiration for Walter had been rewarded that same night, we were invited to return as headliners, the featured Saturday night band at the city's most revered music venue.

Tipitina's was more music hall than bar: open space, high ceilings, row upon row of concert seating. In 1977, new owners had named the building for a composition by Henry Roeland Byrd, the beloved Professor Longhair, the "Picasso of keyboard funk." Fess was credited with birthing the "New Orleans piano style," a freewheeling, driving jambalaya of rhythms. He played Tipitina's so regularly the last years of his life — he died in 1980 — that his and the bar's history are one, the song "Tipitina" as much his legacy as "Big Chief" and "Go to the Mardi Gras."

There was always worthy music at Tipitina's, always a line at the door with a cover charge of whatever amount in hand.

"Atlanta?" I asked.

The man had stopped me on my way to the bar after our first set and introduced himself as Mr. King. I suspected another disingenuous booking agent. He talked of Cousin Ned's, a nightclub in an Atlanta neighborhood called

Virginia-Highland. "It's emerging as the hip area of the city, and our customers are the city's new breed of hipsters."

I was feeling a little full of myself. It was what a venue like that and the crowd that came there did to you. We'd played exceptionally well, especially Hacksaw and Walter, but all of us at our best. I was hardly interested in hearing about some club in some other town. But I'd also learned to listen when someone talked about work.

"We started as an acoustic house, singer-songwriters," said King, identifying himself as Cousin Ned's owner. "They were a little too serious about themselves, and once the new wore off so did the crowds. We switched to blues bands. That's been better, but we don't have the vibe just right yet. I'm here getting a feel for some of the places in New Orleans that figured it out."

"You got it right about Tip's. Good as it gets in New Orleans, maybe anywhere."

"You guys seem comfortable here, I mean, in a club atmosphere."

"We are. We do a concert gig from time to time" — okay, I exaggerated — "but clubs are what we do most," then recalling the Saenger debacle, "and do the best."

"Do you travel or just play New Orleans clubs?"

Most visiting music junkies thought of New Orleans as a closed society, a clique of inbred musicians who'd never leave. With so much music here and people coming from all over the world to hear it, why would you want to play anywhere else?

"Unless you have a regular house gig, you need to travel some. Hard to stay busy picking up one-nighters. Which reminds me, we better get back."

He raised his right hand with an extended finger. It reminded me of something I'd seen in an Agatha Christie TV movie, a Poirot gesture. "Well, you might consider Atlanta."

Consider Atlanta?

"Try us out for a couple of weeks. Your funk groove could play well with our crowd."

I didn't think so. Doubted there were places like Tipitina's in Atlanta. Doubted if any of us would want to settle in anywhere again outside New Orleans. I shook King's hand and started toward the stage.

"How does two grand a week sound? Two weeks, three nights each."

I hesitated a beat, maybe a whole measure, and in perfect time he landed on the tonic.

"Starting Thursday."

For most of several years now, I'd held the band together crisscrossing Louisiana and contiguous and near-contiguous states. The others had gone along willingly, despite mismatches like the unfortunate Houma booking, as long as we returned home with enough cash to last until a next gig.

But we rarely ventured farther than a few hours' drive home. Atlanta was a leap of miles as well as faith.

But a two-week engagement at almost seven hundred bucks each with nothing else on any of our calendars?

It was enough to send everyone packing, and the following Wednesday we were headed to Atlanta.

* * *

I steered Ol' Blue, Lee with me, through a cloudy drizzle, the band equipment jostling over ribbed floors and against the metal walls of its unfinished interior. Ricky, the rest of the band stretched out comfortably in his '74 Cadillac Fleetwood land yacht, followed perilously close along Gulf Coast Highway 98 through Mississippi and into Alabama, then from Mobile north along a recently completed stretch of I-65 to Montgomery and east on I-85 into Georgia.

A couple of hours later we were in Atlanta, a city, it was immediately apparent, that shared little with New Orleans. Lee and I were alternately stunned, amazed, humbled, and frightened by the traffic. Three interstate highways, two major arteries north and south and one east and west, poured into each other in the middle of the city, spawning a nightmarish traffic jam despite multiple lanes in all directions.

Off the interstates and into the city, another distinction from New Orleans: the pace of traffic and associated roar. We were passed, honked at, cut off, and verbally and visually cursed. A young male face encircled by a heavy beard leaned out of the driver's window of a glossy red Camaro and shouted something angry but unintelligible at Lee to the accompaniment of a booming, thumping disco base line.

It took several stops to find a convenience store clerk who knew enough about the city and could speak enough English to guide us to the apartment building where Mr. King rented space for his visiting bands.

The club-provided lodging test is ritual. The sequence of test events might differ from place to place or band to band, but the collective list is much the same: refrigerator for anything of use left behind by previous tenants, like a jar of mustard or a stick of margarine; beds for adequate support and, for Walter and Lee, long enough that nothing more than feet hang over the bottom of a mattress; chairs and couches for cleanliness and structural integrity; and the television set, probably the most telling indication of how the gig will unfold. If the TV is of recent vintage, and stations are received clearly, maybe even by cable, chances are the club and its owner will prove accommodating.

For Hacksaw, whose priority was the television, especially during football season, the indication was of a happy engagement, despite the troubling broadcast that greeted us: a news report about a group of felons who'd escaped from the state penitentiary and were very much and for very long at large.

"Welcome to Atlanta." Hacksaw turned from the TV, arms spread like a preacher welcoming his flock. "Impenetrable traffic, ubiquitous disco, and a prison break — and we've only been here a couple of hours."

* * *

Cousin Ned's was new enough to look, even smell, fresh. An elevated, wide, and well-lit stage suggested respect for the music. The club's centerpiece was its bar, and around a glittering rectangle of suspended glassware three bartenders were already hustling to keep up with unwavering demand, even at such an early hour.

A polished concrete floor separating bandstand from bar was crowded with twenty- and thirty-something clean-shaven men in starched and sharply creased blue jeans and dry-cleaned collared shirts and a bevy of storybook blondes and dazzling brunettes dressed just as crisply — all with cocktails, conversing.

As we set up for this our opening night, I was enjoying the view from the stage, pleased that I'd booked us into a good room, a haven for live music, a crowd hungry for Metropole fusion, so different from the numbing, flashing discos I'd associated with Atlanta.

Even Hacksaw's habitual discontent was muted: "See anybody without a haircut or a beauty appointment in more'n a week?"

We launched our first Atlanta set with enthusiasm, a nonstop sweep through three recognizable selections: from the Crusaders and Bob James, then "Birdland" to its stentorian conclusion. Heads nodded, then returned to their conversations. Three more of our strongest arrangements and the set concluded to a smattering of applause.

I made my way through closed circles of couples to the bar. "Can I get a bourbon?"

"Pick your poison." A bartender motioned to a long row of bottles, only a few brands I recognized.

"Your house is good."

He pulled a bottle of Maker's Mark, measured a shot, poured it over ice, and marked a sheet with the band's name in bold at the top.

"Better keep individual tabs," I told him when he delivered the drink.

The bartender's uniform was standard issue: black pants, white shirt, and a black bowtie. A bronze-colored badge that read "Jeff" was pinned perfectly horizontal to and less than an inch below the ridge of his shirt pocket. He was maybe twenty years older than the rest of the wait staff, likely entrusted with overseeing the young waiters and waitresses, just as likely college kids keeping themselves afloat on Cousin Ned tips. He returned to the sheet, drew a line through Metropole and wrote "piano."

"You guys sound pretty good. I think the crowd digs it."

"Really? Couldn't tell by the reception we're getting. Or not getting."

As the night progressed, the crowd grew, clustering on the dance floor and around tables, talking, laughing. Some broke from conversations to watch us, particularly through a well-played horn or guitar solo; several women appeared interested when I sang a ballad.

No one danced.

During breaks, a few customers approached, congratulating Hacksaw or Walter on a well-played solo, making a comment to Lee or Mark about an artist whose composition or recording we'd played, offering to buy one of us a drink. Yet the mood was distinctly low key, nearly cerebral, as if they were analyzing the music.

"Ain't like New Orleans," Lee remarked as we stepped down from a third set.

"I don't think anybody here is even drunk," Hacksaw observed.

By midnight, Cousin Ned's was a mob. I announced to a crowd too preoccupied with each other to listen that, "Metropole will return for our final set of the night after a short break." A few seconds of polite applause let me know at least some in the crowd realized we'd stopped playing.

Stepping from the stage, I worked my way through the throng toward the bar when my path was blocked by a girl so stunningly beautiful I froze. I stared wordlessly into limpid blue eyes. Somewhere played the conflicting themes of "Hallelujah Chorus" and "Jungle Boogie."

"Buy you a drink?" she asked, then raised a hand to her mouth to stifle a giggle. She had the flawless alabaster complexion of a porcelain doll bracketed by honey blonde curls that bounced at her shoulders. And her eyes...so blue, so deep, so remarkably round.

"Sorry, didn't mean to holdya up," the words slow and languorous, a hint of an extra syllable in several of them. "We sure are enjoyin' y'all's music."

She stepped back to let me pass. But I was stuck in place. Those eyes. Say something, I told myself.

"I'm s-sorry," I finally stammered. "A drink? Sure. But you'll have to let me do the buying."

It was hardly brilliant repartee. How unsophisticated I must have appeared among all those starched young Atlantans.

"I'm not usually so forthcomin'," she drawled as we climbed onto a couple stools at the corner of the bar. "That song about stayin' with someone till you have to go?"

"'Until It's Time for You to Go.' I've been singing that for years. It kind of suits my voice."

Jeff set two drinks in front of us, a chardonnay for her, Maker's over ice for me. He made two marks on my tab, then straightened his bowtie in the mirror behind the hanging wineglasses.

"It sounded like you really meant it. Not like it's just somethin' you sing every night."

"That's something I learned a long time ago, when I was a kid actually. It's like reading to someone. Think of the words as you sing, no matter how many times you've told the story."

"Well, isn't that smart." That made me flush. She continued, "And it works 'cause the message got through to me — I mean, us." She tilted her head in the direction of three girls sitting at the table closest to the bar, who weren't talking, just watching the two of us.

We chatted on, mostly about nothing, laughing at everything. Her name was Muriel, and when she said it, how she said it, it was poetry: *And all that's best of dark and bright / Meet in her aspect and her eyes…*

The band was on stage, waiting. It seemed the shortest break ever taken. "Is there any chance, Muriel, you'll be here when we finish?"

"It's pretty late. I think my friends are ready to go. But I'll try and come back to hear y'all tomorrow night."

"Great. Maybe we could go out after, I mean for something to eat."

"That's a very nice offer, Thomas."

She pulled a set of keys from her purse, eased off the barstool, and glided from the bar. I watched her leave Cousin Ned's on the loveliest pair of legs I'd ever seen.

* * *

"Tom, you guys enjoying the club?" Cousin Ned's night manager asked following our first set on our second night. He was a lengthy, serious man about my age with a narrow, pock-marked face and a long, thin nose slightly bent so it appeared as if he were leaning marginally to his left. In a blue blazer over a bright yellow Izod golf shirt and tan khaki pants, he looked more accountant than bar manager.

"Yessir."

The night before, back at the apartment, we'd been giddy over our opening night at Cousin Ned's. The acoustics were good: "You can hear every note," Mark said.

Management seemed happy with our performance: "Saw that guy King standing at the bar watching and smiling," Lee observed. The crowd was interested if not ebullient: "An intelligent group," Walter assessed. "A little self-absorbed," Hacksaw felt compelled to add.

"Our crowd likes you guys, too. Lots of good comments. If you're not committed somewhere else, Mr. King would like to extend you for an additional two weeks."

A couple of weeks on top of our first two weeks translated into our longest engagement since the A-Bar. Only Ricky, his wife in mind, was hesitant, but coaxed by the rest of us, consented. This was a comfortable gig, we agreed, and four weeks of two grand a week was not to be scoffed at.

I was again optimistic. Away from New Orleans, living in the same apartment, with four nights off between our three-night weekends and the club available during the days, everyone would certainly be more inclined to rehearse new arrangements, perhaps collaborate on an original.

But onstage the following night, the Cousin Ned's job and Metropole's future were hardly top of my mind. I was having difficulty concentrating, even missed a few pickups, and was unusually lax in calling out tunes, another responsibility Hacksaw, with the exception of an occasional late-night unrehearsed chestnut, had abdicated. I was taking my time and using it to survey the crowd.

It wasn't until the final set of the night that she appeared. And in the timing of her arrival, her purpose was clear. Not about the club, not for society, not even for music.

Opening a nightclub or restaurant is a crapshoot. Paying customers are capricious, their choices arbitrary. Experience, reputation, skill — all are less consequential than one would suppose; a next opening is just as risky as a first.

Late twentieth century Atlanta was particularly subject to fad. When a nightclub or restaurant became the *in* place, often for reasons unknown or at least unapparent, the employed and unencumbered young flocked to it. No matter how long the wait at the door, or how uncomfortably crowded — crowded, in fact, was magnetic — you had to be *there* to be *in*. But the fortunate restaurateur or bar owner suddenly in the favor of the in-crowd could not afford to enjoy the success, only work harder and smarter to delay the inevitable evolution of fad to fizzle.

Whether Atlanta was primed for Cousin Ned's brand of nightlife, and whether Metropole was contributing to the attraction, the place was packed nightly. And we rode the wave: from four weeks of three-night weekends to five nights weekly as Cousin Ned's house band.

I was gratified by our success, but also troubled. It was life on the road without being on the road. I missed the privacy and freedom of my Lakeview house. I missed everything about New Orleans. I phoned Evan regularly to stay current on the bars and restaurants and the movements of favorite bartenders and waiters; on Elaine and the baby and how Eunice delighted in caring for the extended family despite the husband's perpetual lack of employment and ugly, booze-fueled episodes; on the city's unfathomable love affair with its disheartening football team.

But there was that rare pleasure, a weekly paycheck. And Muriel, she alone enough to make it better here than anywhere else. Not since Penny — and Penny seemed so long ago now — had I felt, well, in love.

Muriel had signaled the beginning of the relationship with her return to Cousin Ned's that second night. We sat at the bar and talked until closing, then continued our conversation for another couple of hours at one of Atlanta's ubiquitous Waffle House all-night restaurants before I finally, reluctantly, drove her back to her car in Cousin Ned's parking lot.

The course of that night became our routine. Night after night, every night Metropole played, Muriel arrived during our final set. And no matter what was happening on stage, in the middle of a tune or between tunes, I never missed her entrance. I'd nod to her as she came through Cousin Ned's door, and she'd respond with a smile and understated wave, more fingers than arm or hand. I'd follow her every move as she drifted through the crowd to dangle those legs from a stool at the corner of the bar nearest the stage.

Many a young man called at her barstool. Some she knew and talked with; others trying to know her were dismissed. As we concluded an evening's final tune, she and I would hurry from Cousin Ned's to our Waffle House, where I'd ignore my coffee, watching Muriel's delicate hands and long pink fingernails bounce a tea bag in a cup of boiled water that rarely touched her lips.

We talked some of music but more about each other, likes and dislikes, what we were good and not so good at, about families and friends. I found myself digging into my past, even dredging up old anxieties: Mother, "so stern and unyielding about how a Cliffe should behave"; Father, "not one who'd take you to a ball game or fishing; there was a factory to run, and most nights, clients to entertain"; and brothers, "our relentless competition."

"Do you miss them, I mean, not seeing them anymore?"

"I really don't think about it that much. Guess because I could always go home and see them. Mom still wants me to come back and work with Dad, learn to run the business. But he'll never let go. He'd die without that factory to go to. Besides, being trapped in that steamy building all day watching them twist metal into fence posts and railings and the like — that's the last thing I'd want to do with my life."

"Is anyone else a musician?" She steered me down an easier path.

"Dad played banjo in a band of eight he called an orchestra, which I guess was what they called a bunch of guys playing together back in the '20s. But you wouldn't confuse them with the London Philharmonic. About the closest they got to orchestral music was Dad's solo on 'Has Anybody Seen My Gal,' on which I must admit he could shine. But the only thing I ever learned about music from him was how to finish a piece unresolved. It drove him nuts."

Being with Muriel made me feel warmer toward everything, including my father. "I'd be playing something like 'Clair de Lune,' and stop before the final chord and get up from the piano. He'd lower the newspaper and order me to 'get back here and finish that.' It was all in fun, but you

[186]

could tell it annoyed him. My brothers loved it…which was cool."

"So you got along well with all those brothers? I can only imagine how chaotic life would be in a house with nine people in each other's way all the time."

"I liked my three younger brothers best. Used to stop at Larry's Corner Confectionary on the way home from high school and buy them a whole bag of penny candies. In good weather, I'd take them to a lot at the end of our street we called a park, and hit grounders and fly balls to them, teach 'em to catch and throw. Two stayed in Missouri. One's a CPA, the youngest, a divorce attorney. Both married. Kids."

"And the other?"

I peered into my coffee, picking up a spoon as if there were something in the cup I needed to remove.

"Dead."

I raised my eyes to hers. His suicide in my senior year of college, even that long ago, still hurt. But with Muriel, it was a sadness I didn't care to hide. "Couldn't brook living. Couldn't make any sense of it."

For a few poignant seconds, she held my stare, then looked into her cup and started again with the tea bag. "And Thomas? How did he survive all that brotherly love?"

"Spent most of my time listening to music and reading. Pretty much tried to stay out of the way."

Muriel shared little of herself other than that her family was considered Old Atlanta. She was still living at home in the house she grew up in. Like me, she'd graduated from a single-gender liberal arts college.

"Agnes Scott." She was almost apologetic, a reticence, she confessed, that had become habit in light of the usual response as the school was known for educating the daughters of Atlanta's wealthiest families. She'd graduated with a degree in marketing and worked at her father's ad agency "doin' whatever, for now."

She appeared much more interested in me: my life as a musician, what I liked about performing, favorite places when touring, expectations for Metropole. She seemed particularly interested in my thoughts on New Orleans, so interested that it had me wondering if — more like hoping — she was thinking about what it would be like to live there with me.

It was hardly ever before three in the morning when I'd return with Muriel to Cousin Ned's parking lot. We'd say our goodnights — for the longest stretch, weeks — without even a parting kiss.

Then one night, a long, tender kiss. Soft, barely parted lips caressing, gentle, innocent. She shivered, an almost imperciptible tremble.

"Muriel, I think you're wonderful, the most wonderful woman I've ever known." I pulled her closer to me to kiss her more fervently. But she leaned back and just looked at me for a few inscrutable seconds, her hands on my chest, gently, not pushing just keeping me away. "Thomas…I'm sorry…I have to go."

She got into her car and started the engine, then lowered her window. I hadn't moved.

"You gonna stand there all night, you little dummy? See y'all tomorrow night?"

"That's a very nice offer, ma'am," I answered, affecting her drawl.

* * *

But I didn't see her the following night, nor any night the following week.

I imagined every possible scenario: auto accident; sudden travel; heavy work schedule; kidnapped, chained, and held for ransom. She had refused to surrender her phone number; wanted to keep her parents out of her personal life as much as possible, she explained. There was no phone at the condo for her to call, though she could have left a message at the club — and I checked nightly. I was embarrassed: the band, bartenders, management, club regulars, all were aware of my lovesickness.

"This bourbon's on me." Lee put his arm around my shoulder and guided me to the bar as we stepped off the stage from our last set of the week. Jeff was wiping the bar top, making exaggerated circles in the same spot, and singing softly "One for my baby, and one more for the road." Lee and Jeff looked at each other in agreement, then turned to me and sang, "We're drinking, my friend, to the end of a brief episode."

It was a kind joke. But I felt no better.

* * *

It was a Wednesday, the beginning of another week at Cousin Ned's, the eighth, ninth, maybe tenth week. I was, I confided in Lee, flat-out depressed. The whole world was draped in an ugly misshapen gray. For nearly two decades I'd chased the muse with little change in my lot. As employment, my meandering could hardly be classified as a job much less a career. As a life, mine was directionless, unsubstantial, and now so pointedly loveless.

I spent hours every day suppressing thoughts of Muriel. I was not likely to see her again. It was okay. I'd get over her. Maybe even block the sound of *Thomas* as she drew it out into something so mellifluous through three or four syllables. At least during these few hours every night, through these sets and songs, I could steal away from images of her and invest in my music. Performing was never, or never should be, rote; playing and singing with credible nuance and innovation required attention and focus. I'd wavered some in Muriel's absence, but this night, I was better, thoroughly into it. Adrift in the soothing reverie of song. Until halfway through the final set when Muriel arrived and made her way to the bar — the usual time, her usual spot. Band, bartenders, several regulars looked to me. I feigned indifference. Refused to look her way.

The night's last piece concluded, I replayed the changes of the final four measures as I thanked and wished the crowd goodnight. I rose from the piano and crossed the stage, muttering something to Hacksaw about how he'd played a certain passage in one of the set's songs.

"Man, that's pure dribble." He was packing away his tenor in its road-worn case. "Just go talk to her."

I returned to the piano, switched it on then off again, stepped down from the stage and paused a few more seconds. Then walked toward the bar.

"I know you. Let me think. Muriel, right?" But I couldn't help but be taken again by her beauty. Breathtaking. And tonight, apparently without makeup, a sprinkling of soft freckles underlining those eyes.

"Oh, Thomas, you silly boy."

Surely she had to be, must be…was aware of her paralyzing effect on me.

"I just got back in town and came right here to see y'all." She crossed a leg, anchored an elbow to her knee and rested her chin in her palm. "You gonna ask me to breakfast?"

"Where've you been?" I tried to sound emotionless, matter of fact.

"Chicago. Two whole weeks. So glad to be away from that cold. Don't know how or why folks live in such a place." No apology seemed imminent, and I wasn't about to press for an explanation.

Muriel would say nothing more about her absence, or her time in Chicago, or her failure to tell me she was going. An hour later we were in our usual Waffle House booth engaged in our usual small talk, Muriel explaining her ethical dilemma with an advertising campaign she was working on for a soft drink with several times the sugar and caffeine of Coca-Cola.

"I missed you," I broke in.

"I missed you too, Thomas." She reached across the table and stroked my hand. "I so enjoy being with you."

True to routine, the night ended at her car in Cousin Ned's parking lot. She slid her arms around my waist and pressed her breasts against my chest, leaning her head back to allow me to kiss her neck.

Again, she trembled in my embrace.

My days in agony had been pure misunderstanding. I reveled in the lingering taste and smell of her as I steered Blue toward the apartment.

* * *

"Man, you better wipe that smile from your face," Lee teased as I drove to the club the following evening. "Some cracker might take offense." He was quiet, spoke confidentially, his way with me.

"Careful." I thought Hacksaw, seated behind Lee on an overturned milk crate and leaning against Blue's sliding door, was referring to yet another Atlanta driver cutting us off, slipping in and out of lanes to gain a car length of time before I realized he too was talking about Muriel.

"In case you guys missed my birthday last week, I've hit the big four-O. I'll be an old man before I know it. This might be my shot at a normal life: a wife, maybe even kids."

"The danger zone," Walter, on the milk crate behind me, pronounced.

"Fe-els like the first time," I crooned the title line of the Foreigner hit.

"Oh man," Lee moaned, "this is truly tragic. Our little buddy's going pop on us."

Halfway through our final set Muriel made her entrance and took her corner barstool, cleared for her by Jeff, ensuring with a nod and wink and a perfectly tied bowtie that she was aware of his consideration.

With the completion of a final tune, Bob James' "Nautilus," a recent addition to the Metropole repertoire and one of the few arranged around my keyboard work, I powered off the Yamaha and joined Muriel.

"Muriel, let's skip the usual for a late-night jam." I'd learned of a club where some of Atlanta's better musicians were known to hang out after their paid work, usually society gigs where they had to play the latest pop hits and a few schlocky chestnuts.

* * *

The club was smaller and much darker than Cousin Ned's. I ordered bourbon, a cosmopolitan for Muriel.

The players were older and well schooled. They covered Miles' "Human Nature" and Dizzy's "A Night in Tunisia." I was particularly impressed with the trumpeter, who used the mute with effect and subtlety similar to Gillespie. I turned down an offer to sit in — one of the musicians recognized me from the stage as "the keyboard player from the New Orleans band playing Cousin Ned's" — even after Muriel encouraged it.

"I remember the first jam I went to," I began, Muriel attentive as always for my music-related recollections. "I was in Florida, and just starting to play with any bit of confidence. Those cats were so good, I was blown away. It was an every-night thing, so I went back like three nights in a row. Then one night one of the guys who'd seen me where I was playing asked me if I wanted to sit in. I just waved him off, paid my tab and got out of there as fast as I could. I had actually planned to sit in, but when the opportunity came I just couldn't. They were so much better than me."

"Can't imagine that," Muriel countered. I smiled and we sipped in unison.

"Anyway, the guy who asked me to sit in shows up at my gig a couple nights later with his girlfriend. They were really nice, telling me how good I sounded. 'Should've sat in with us,' he told me. I probably should have."

Another cosmopolitan for Muriel and a third bourbon for me. I leaned to her, mustering up a most determined expression. "Muriel, I love you."

There was no response, neither delight nor repugnance. Like she hadn't heard the words. The one certainty was she hadn't expected them.

"And I want to marry you."

Like the bourbons for me, the cosmopolitans had compromised Muriel. A tear slid down the gentle slope of her cheek.

"Oh, Thomas, I'm so sorry. I mean, I'm crazy for you, you know. You're good and kind and honest. So easy to be with. I love that about you. And when you kiss me…But as good as I feel with you, as good as we are together, it just will not do."

She was taken aback, clearly.

"Let's see. You're crazy about me. You think we're good together. I make you feel good. I'm stumped.

"What won't do?"

"It isn't that simple, Thomas."

Not simple enough to explain. But enough for me to understand that again there would be no explanation. We did not speak on the drive back to the parking lot; she got into her car, drove off without a word or a glance.

Gone this time for good. I knew it.

Why didn't I think before blurting those words? Should have saved them for a better time, a surer time. But I loved her and why shouldn't I tell her? Maybe if I'd just held off on the marriage proposal. I scared her. That was understandable. But I wanted to marry her. So had she been toying with me all these nights, whiling away her time with no real feelings for me? No, that wasn't it. She wasn't that kind of person. I knew she cared for me. I knew it in her embrace, in how she looked at me, in how she would squeeze my hand before sharing some intimate thought. But all this hypothesizing was useless. She was gone and that was that.

It all started innocently enough, a lazy Wednesday at Cousin Ned's and a generous offer to play a private party the following Sunday night.

"Major party, man. My house. Name your price."

"Well…" I could ask for what we were getting for one-nighters in New Orleans, but *name your price* had me thinking a few more bucks, a premium, so to speak.

"We'll have to break all this down and haul it there and back." I motioned to the stage full of Metropole gear, including the burdensome Yamaha. "Need at least two hundred a man."

"Shit, make it four." He handed me a napkin from the bar on which he'd neatly printed a name and address. "Come around nine and be ready to party hearty." His head danced right on *party* and left on *hearty*.

I figured the kid for about twenty, maybe younger. Nice looking, a clean shave and fresh haircut. Dressed casually, but shirt, pants, shoes all looked expensive.

"Can we get something up front?" I asked. "I mean, every musician's been burned by a private party that didn't pan out."

The kid pulled a money clip from his pocket and counted out ten one hundred dollar bills. "Pay you the rest if you show up."

"Touché," I consulted the napkin, "uh, Bobby. See ya Sunday at nine."

* * *

Lee, Hacksaw, and I could do little but gawk as Blue, trailed by Ricky's land yacht, followed the kid's directions through the mid-Atlanta neighborhood toward the address on the napkin.

"My God!" First Lee, then me, then both again as we passed each sprawling property.

"These aren't houses," Hacksaw craned his neck to peer around Lee through the passenger side window. "Mansions don't even cover it. That one looks like a fucking university."

"They sure ain't Pete Seeger's 'little boxes.'" I was having some difficulty negotiating curves and turns while taking in the scenery. "Man, how do so many people make so much money?" I didn't expect an answer.

"You don't *make* this kind of money," Hacksaw answered.

After several turns down several streets of similarly expansive estates and up a long, winding driveway, our two unbefitting vehicles stopped in front of a residence even more conspicuous than it had looked from the street.

"It's a wonder we didn't get stopped for casing the neighborhood," Ricky quipped, the six of us in the driveway staring up past three stories to a collage of flat and variously angled rooflines.

"They probably think we're here to rake leaves," Hacksaw added.

Mark nudged Lee. "Think we'll have to go in through the servants' entrance?"

A tall Black man in a starched white server's jacket answered the door, escorted us through a hallway and pointed to a corner in what looked like a parlor, something like Evan's but at least twice the size. Any furniture once in the room had been removed.

There was more than ample space for our usual setup: Ricky and his drums centering the band; Lee, Mark, me, our amps and the Yamaha, which only Lee was now willing to help me move, to Ricky's right; Walter and Hacksaw to his left; the PA speaker columns to either side. We unraveled and ran chords from instruments to amps, from microphones to mixer, from mixer to speakers.

Our host appeared wearing a blue blazer with gold buttons, a white golf shirt, seersucker Bermuda shorts, and flip-flops.

"Some kind of house, Bobby," I said as Lee and I hoisted the CP 70's harp and connected it to the keyboard.

Bobby handed me a folded pack of bills. "You guys want the nickel tour?"

The basement featured the biggest TV screen any of us had ever seen, 45 diagonal inches. Hacksaw was fascinated. "Not even in the stores yet," Bobby said, clapping Hacksaw on the shoulder. Two Barcaloungers aimed at the TV rested a couple of steps from a bar with shelves as stocked as I'd seen in some nightclubs. He walked us across the room and slid open a glass door to a stone patio and an Olympic-size swimming pool, the brightly lit water inviting even on a frigid February night.

He winked. "It's heated."

We returned to the main floor where Walter, who had not gone with us to the basement, stood behind a large wooden table crowded with mounds of sliced beef and ham and breads and bowls of various chips and sauces. I suspected Walter had violated the meat platters. But he wasn't eating; his back was to the table and he was examining a series of paintings hung side by side across the length of the wall. Each was covered by a glass-like box, the kind of enclosures you'd find in a museum.

"You gotta see this," Walter spoke without removing his gaze from one of the paintings. "That's Frida Kahlo!"

I came to look. "Artist or portrait?"

"Both. That's what she painted… herself. That painting's worth at least a hundred grand. And that's just the start. This is a Lee Krasner. Worth a million, easy. All these," he directed my gaze across the row, "are precious works, incredibly valuable.

"Hey, Bobby." Walter turned to address the host who was at the food table taking inventory. "The artwork. It's beyond overwhelming."

"Yeah, my old man's big into it. Got stacks of 'em in the basement he doesn't have any place to hang."

"Those are impenetrable enclosures right? Anchored and locked?"

Bobby nodded. "Alarmed too. If you're thinking of stealing one of those you'll have to take half the wall with you. And there'll be a driveway full of cops before you get through the front door."

I thought the remark a bit snide, but Walter didn't seem insulted. He was too taken by the artwork.

"If your dad's gonna be here tonight, I'd really like to meet him. I mean, I don't own any artwork, but I read about it a lot and go to museums whenever I can."

"He won't be here tonight. Off in Europe somewhere with his new wife."

* * *

It was nearly ten o'clock when we struck our first notes, and only a few guests had arrived. Nor were there more than ten or so couples milling about and making sliced beef and ham sandwiches by the time we'd finished our first set.

Eleven-thirty, then midnight.

We broke after a second set around twelve-thirty and I thought it time to call it a night. As I rose from the Yamaha to find our host, whom I'd not seen since the start of the first set, beams of headlamps began pouring through the windows. A parade of cars filled the driveway, then the street in front of the house, then onto the front lawn's slumbering Bermuda.

A torrent of twenty-somethings plunged through the front door. They wore lime green jerseys, the word "Grizzlies" embroidered across the front. They shed caked mud on the burnished hardwood floor and oriental rugs. A few wore shoes with metal cleats. They were thick and noisy, easily recognized as in the energetic stages of early drunkenness. As were the women, most wearing the team jerseys over unseasonably short shorts.

Bobby emerged from the basement, what appeared to be a fifth of gin or vodka in hand, to be greeted by universal hooting and hollering.

"Kicked some ass tonight, Bobaroo," the biggest, loudest Grizzly proclaimed.

I'd reached the basement stairs when the crowd had begun bursting through the front door. Bobby turned to me and yelled, "Par-tee, man, let's get it going." Then in confidence, "Tom, nobody's gonna give a shit what you guys play. Just play it loud." He threw his arms in the air and the team and their women cheered.

"Guess we've got another set. They want something loud, anything, just loud. So let's do 'Birdland.'"

"Again?" Ricky objected. "We..."

"Doesn't matter," I interrupted. "Those soccer players haven't heard it yet and according to Bobaroo they couldn't care less what we play as long as it's loud."

"Rugby," Hacksaw corrected me.

Hacksaw had just completed the series of chaotic descending lines in the arrangement's introduction when Bobby approached and yelled, "Louder, man. Turn it up!"

And so we did what we could. Played our Crusaders' tunes, Jeff Lorber's "Tune 88," even Chick Corea's "Spain" faster and louder than ever before. But not loud enough.

As we finished a tasteless rendition of "Blue Bossa," Mark leaned toward me and Lee and shouted, "Three-chord blues in E." To Ricky, "Hard and fast."

Mark's amp screamed at deafening volume, replete with screeching feedback and senselessly dissonant chords. Over and over, louder and louder, Mark's playing challenged the angriest of blues guitarists.

The rugby players and their dates, liquor bottles in hand, sometimes one in each hand, cavorted and jumped and ran in circles in front of the band. It quickly graduated to roughhousing, careening off each other, bouncing off walls and occasionally crashing to the floor. A few lumbered perilously close to the band. Lee moved to fend off any interlopers on his side of the drums as Hacksaw flanked Ricky on the left.

It was after two o'clock when I began my signoff. "Thanks, everybody. We're Metropole and it's been our pleasure to be here with you tonight. Please come and see us at Cousin Ned's where we play every…"

But by the time I got to "Cousin Ned's," half the crowd was booing.

"No fuckin' way, man. We're just startin'. You play till we're ready to stop." The grizzliest Grizzly stood in front of the bandstand, arms folded, behind him the affirmation of a roomful of missing teeth.

"Okay, guys, a couple more."

I wanted to appear in control, but the raucous crowd now owned the room. I looked around for Bobby and caught sight of him at the food table, a wry grin over a mouthful of sandwich, his silence consent to the mayhem. A thin, lanky redhead who could have been on assignment from a modeling agency stood next to him picking at the food.

We began again, more guitar-based blues, though not quite as loud or fast.

The Grizzlies and Grizzly girls lurched and leaned, pausing again and again to guzzle, many now struggling to remain afoot. Then one stumbled into the big man's date, and the two fell to the floor, him on top of her. The room sobered as the girl fought to free herself. The big man kicked the smaller man over on his back, pulled him up off the floor by his shirt, held him there for a couple of seconds as the smaller man grimaced in fear, then sent him sprawling with a right fist to the left side of his face.

"Hey, cut that shit." Another drunk grabbed the big man's arm and he too was sent reeling. Then the melee, fists and bodies flying; no sides taken, just punches thrown at the nearest person. Even the women were swinging at each other. One rugby player approached the band as if to share a confidence. When Lee bent over to listen he swung wildly, missing by a considerable margin.

Then his companion pulled a pistol from his shorts, waving it at Hacksaw.

"Get that fucking gun out of my face" — Hacksaw had been in enough confrontations as a teen in rural Alabama to know a real threat — "or I'll stick it in your mouth."

"Fuck you, old man." But the kid backed off, forcing a patronizing smile to save face.

I turned to Lee, shouting over the chaos. "You seen a phone anywhere?"

"Kitchen counter when we were coming in."

"Then find a way in there and call the police. This shit is way out of hand."

* * *

When the police came, they let everyone leave who appeared marginally able to drive. A few too drunk to stand unaided, including two naked couples pulled from the basement pool and wrapped in towels, were escorted to a police van. Some had to be carried. No one was cuffed.

"Let's get y'all home now, and you can come back tomorrow for your vehicles," one of the officers coaxed the capitulants into the van.

"Thanks, Ed." Bobby patted the back of the last of the policemen to leave the house. "We'll keep this between us? No need to concern the Senator."

The officer turned to say something, then stopped. "Looks like he'll have more 'n enough to concern him." He nodded past Bobby toward one of the paintings. Its impenetrable shield was shattered, a hunting knife buried squarely in the center of Frida Kahlo's nose.

Boo-hoo, boo-hoo,
Boo-hoo, Bobaroo.

As usual I was the first back on stage after a break, hovering over the song list, deciding on the first few tunes of the set, the third to this Saturday night's packed house.

"Tom." It was Jeff. He'd stepped out from behind the bar wiping his hands with a soiled towel. "Would you mind accompanying a female vocalist on a song or two to start off this set?"

It wasn't unusual for a Cousin Ned's bartender to relay a request from a patron for a particular song, or to let me know a horn man or guitar player wanted to sit in. But never to ask me to play something I hadn't rehearsed for a singer I didn't know. "I don't know, Jeff. We don't usually…"

"Her father's a friend of Mr. King's. And I've heard she's really good. Oh, and she says you'll know the songs she wants to sing."

"Still, I'm not sure…"

"I'll introduce her." He stepped on stage and behind Walter's microphone. "Ladies and gentlemen, we have a special guest with us tonight. Some of you know her, but probably not as a singer. Please put your hands together for Muriel Burns."

The song list slipped from my hands. I could only gape wide-eyed as Muriel took the stage. She cradled the microphone in both hands, looked out into the audience — not so much as a glance my way — and *sotto voce*, "Do you know 'Fine and Mellow,' Thomas?"

It couldn't be her. It had to be an apparition, something out of the ether. I shook my head to clear my vision.

"You might know it better as 'My Man Don't Love Me,'" teasing and turning to me with a smile that reminded me of that first "Can I buy you a drink?" and that I now took to mean "I couldn't stay away."

"Of course I know it," I finally answered into my microphone — for the audience the song, but for her that I understood the look.

Her bare shoulders glowed in the stage lights, and I wanted to scream, "God, you're beautiful!" but instead, teased back, "Billie's key?"

Sometimes things happen in a performance that capture an audience to the point of hypnosis. One by one, the crowd stopped talking and turned to the stage, like they were responding to some telepathic command. Her tone was sweet and sensuous, but more than her voice, it was her, furtive and seductive, glowing through those eyes.

The song is as unvarnished a blues tune as ever written, more about emotion than melody. Her singing was more breath than notes, the lyric inching its way through her pouting lips as she bemoaned "the lowest man" she'd ever seen. And crafty: her phrasing, sometimes anticipating, sometimes lagging and squeezing out meaning, drawing the crowd nearer, closer to the single honey blonde curl escaping the fold to drape the arresting blue eye.

At her final lament, the love that had "turned off and gone," I completed her performance with a single note at the bottom of the lowest register. That final note died in the stilled hush. Then the applause. It began in the back of the room and rolled like thunder toward the stage until, finally, those closest to us were jolted from their stunned silence and joined in, only quieting when, still focused on her audience, still caressing the microphone, she said, "Say, Curly, can you play 'All Of Me'?"

I caught my cue and answered, "What key, Big Eyes?"

I'm sure I sounded scripted, not as good at this banter as she. But I was as captivated as her audience, and as eager as they appeared to hear her sing again. She sang her encore with delight, light and bouncy, a counterpoint to her mournful blues, as if she'd spent a career in front of a band. Dancers swirled and beamed.

* * *

Back at the apartment, seated at the dining room table, we argued.

"We don't need a chick singer." Hacksaw was impolitic. He had not joined the band on stage to back Muriel on "All of Me," even as I'd signaled him when it was time for a solo. "Besides, we're a jazz funk band. That girl's pure pop. We don't need to throw ourselves in that ocean."

"But the crowd," I countered. "Did you see their faces? Spellbound. And the applause, more than we get for our best songs on our best night."

No one could dispute the point. Not Hacksaw's most innovative lines, nor Walter's circular breathing, nor Ricky's flights of counter rhythms, nor Lee's Wooten-like slap bass drew as much attention or appreciation. Not even my tender ballads that could bring women to tears.

"It's not like we've got a lot of extra dollars to share," Walter reasoned.

"I'll bet they'll kick in for her at the club. Besides, it won't be about the money. She doesn't need it. Her family's rolling in it."

"Yeah? Like yours," Hacksaw retorted. "I don't see you giving up any of your share."

"That's not fair, Hack. I don't get a nickel from my folks, and I don't take a nickel for getting these gigs. And you know it."

"No need to bicker," Hacksaw backed off. "I just don't see anything in it for us."

Still, he was vehemently opposed to allowing, as he saw it, this woman's hold on me to reshape Metropole.

"You're love struck, so maybe you think this is a way to keep her around. Or maybe it's something the two of you dreamed up during one of your late-night googly-eyed love fests. Or maybe she's been playing you all along."

I wanted to lash out at Hacksaw. But there was no gain in that. I stood and walked to the living room window looking out into the moonless night. It was so dark cars were indistinguishable against the blacktop of the parking lot.

"Yes, Hack, I'm in love. You guys all know that. And you're right. I'm thrilled to have her back. But I had no idea she was a singer. She never said a word about it."

Hacksaw bowed his head to scratch his balding pate. "I just don't want us reduced to a backup band, which, given what happened tonight, is more than a possibility. You're the one so damned determined to make Metropole a name band. We stick her out front and it'll be 'Muriel Burns and the Band Without Renown.' We'll be playing charts to 'Don't It Make Your Brown Eyes Blue.'"

"So what did the chick say about it?" Unlike others in the band, Ricky was never hesitant to oppose Hacksaw.

"She's in." My hopes rose on Ricky's intervention. "Loved singing with us."

There was a pause, enough to encourage me that the timing was right to propose the plan I'd crafted earlier.

"Let me talk to the club — just for the weekends. If I can't get some additional money for her and a raise for us to boot, I'll just tell her we can't do it."

"I'm not voting for this." Hacksaw was up, leaning on the table over his empty chair, and looking into our eyes from face to face. "It's not okay."

But it was for the club. Before the following night's first set, in an impromptu meeting in the club offices with the pock-faced manager we'd begun referring to as "Cousin Ted," it was agreed that Muriel brought something new and exciting to the stage.

The manager even offered to promote us on a local jazz radio station, said the club had some advertising dollars available. He assured me that Mr. King would approve the pay increase.

"They agreed to the raise," I announced as I mounted the bandstand. "They're even going to advertise."

Everyone seemed pleased with the news.

Except Hacksaw.

* * *

I remember thinking at the time that those days and weeks were the happiest in my life. Muriel would arrive in the evening, some days earlier when she could get away from her work at "Daddy's propaganda parlor." We'd pore over prospective material for her, and when we found common ground on a song, we'd spend an hour or two on it, familiarizing ourselves with its structure, then experimenting with how she would interpret the lyrics. Or we'd work a song she already knew: how to rephrase a line, spice up an ending, add nuance to enhance the arrangement.

On occasion Walter or Lee or Mark, even Ricky, would offer input or even participate in a rehearsal, though never Hacksaw. More often we developed the arrangements as we did most of our music, on the job.

One afternoon, Muriel told me how she'd conspired with Jeff the night of her surprise performance. "I knew I could talk him into it. He hasn't been exactly subtle about how he's gonna be around long after Metropole's gone."

She confessed to singing in choral groups and church choirs since elementary school, that her voice benefited from years of training from the best teachers Daddy's money could buy, and that, like me, she'd dreamed of one day performing with a band in front of an audience.

"I never said anything to you about it 'cause I didn't want it to sound like 'Hey, I can do that too.' You're a professional, making your living at music. I didn't want to disrespect that."

Nor did she explain why she'd left me heartbroken, or her reappearance. And just as I had not probed for details about her two weeks in Chicago, I didn't question what caused her to flee at the mention of my love for her, or even her assertion that our relationship "just will not do," as befuddled as I remained. I excused her actions and failure to talk about them as behavior I was inherently unable to comprehend. With six brothers and no sisters, how was I supposed to understand how women thought or why they did what they did?

Instead I'd show restraint, give her distance to keep her near. Through our rehearsals and post-performance meanderings to a diner or late-night club, I made no more mention of love, certainly not marriage. Even as our parting kisses grew increasingly passionate, I resisted the urge to utter words asking for commitment. And Muriel appeared content, happy to be together — without a hint of wanting anything more out of the relationship.

Until one evening, the two of us alone in the apartment, me sitting at the used Wurlitzer I'd bought as a portable practice piano. Muriel was studying a chart over my shoulder, humming the melody line at the opening of the bridge in "Somewhere Over the Rainbow." Her scent, some blend of sweetness and allure. I lifted my hand to touch her chin, to turn her head and kiss her cheek. She let my lips meet her face, then pulled away, and looked deep into my eyes. It was a look that so often had caused me to pause, to back off. But I did not. I held her chin and brought her mouth to mine, our lips barely touching. I was losing myself and struggling to regain control, her past rebukes so present and painful. Then a change in her, a long-held constraint abandoned, and we were standing, kissing more ardently, her arms locked around my neck.

"Thomas." She leaned back into my arms and cradled my face in her palms. "I want you to make love to me."

"You sure?" As I said it I realized how wrong it was, my words once again so awkward. But she only smiled.

And we fell to my room and into bed. And throughout I never stopped kissing her, nor she me.

* * *

Those who would be artists often invest in their art to the exclusion of all else. I had alienated my parents, misspent my education, scoffed at wealth, and ignored romance. But Muriel justified it all, made every decision a right one.

"I feel liberated," I told Lee as we leaned on the bar between sets. I wanted to share my euphoria with someone and Lee was always willing to listen. "I don't know from what, but I'm free and it feels great."

"I'm happy for you, little buddy." Lee threw his arm down around my shoulder and gave me a hug.

Whenever we were alone in the apartment, Muriel and I made love. If it was habit, it did not lack spontaneity. We'd be working on a tune or making dinner or watching television when the slightest sideways glance would send us tumbling to the bedroom.

Muriel gave me new perspective. In my loneliest hours I had only the past to dwell on, memories of Penny and what might have been had I stayed or returned. Now I had a future, happy and promising, with a beautiful, intelligent woman who loved me. And as if that were not enough, a woman who shared my passion for music, who not only respected my commitment to it but who understood what I'd achieved, what I knew.

"I'm not so sure about 'As Time Goes By,'" I might say. "It's a great tune, a standard everyone recognizes and likes. But I think people always think of Bogey and Bacall and Dooley Wilson tinkling an upright. It's a little out of character for you." And she'd defer.

She also understood why, mindful of Hacksaw's dire prediction of Metropole's diminished role, I restricted her weekend appearances at Cousin Ned's to a song or two a set. I was not so blinded by love to misunderstand Hacksaw's stature with the band, his persona even more essential to the fabric and continuity of the band than he who begets work.

So when management asked why Muriel was singing so little each set and not until the second set, I argued that it was best to feature her that way, reminding Cousin Ted, "Always leave them wanting more."

All was in balance.

I was a man in full.

* * *

"So what do her folks think about her singing in a bar? Come to think of it, what about her getting home at two or three in the morning ever since you met her?" It was another morning when Hacksaw and I were first up and talking over coffee and scrambled eggs.

"I guess they're okay with it."

"And what do they say about her dating a nightclub piano player?"

"Okay...I guess. She's never said otherwise." My inflection begged an end to the questioning.

"Don't you think it's a little odd you've never met them?" Hacksaw persisted. "Never been invited over for dinner with the parents? Or that they haven't come to the club to listen to her or us?"

"Why do you insist on finding something wrong with her, or with her and me? Isn't love supposed to be free of demands and suspicions?"

Returning to his plate of eggs, Hacksaw persisted. "So I guess your answer is that you don't think it's odd, that everything's okay as long as she's never said otherwise."

I went back to running a fork through my breakfast, but unlike Hacksaw, I corralled no egg.

"Time for Metropole to take a vacation." Cousin Ted — we knew him now as Carson, though were uncertain if that was his given or surname — laid a hand on my shoulder. "Your crowds have left their mark on the club. We need a deep cleaning and have to fix broken stuff and upgrade some of the equipment behind the bar. Plus, Mr. King wants to freshen up the décor and resurface the parking lot. I'm sure you noticed business is slow, what with more daylight and the end of the school year. He figures this is a good time to get things done. Shut down for June and plan a big Fourth of July re-opening."

"You mean starting next week? For an entire month?"

"Tom, Mr. King appreciates the work you've done here, and that a month might be tough on you fellas. Now, he can't pay your fee when there's nobody in here buying drinks, but he did say that he'd advance y'all some money, a hundred dollars a man, excuse me, a person, per week. You can work it off over time when we reopen." He smiled benevolently. "And you can stay in the apartment."

A hundred dollars a week? Despite making more than any of us had ever made playing music, no one was stashing away savings, except Ricky who was sending money home. Nor would we have saved anything had we been making five times as much. Only I had a bank account and Hibernia hadn't seen a deposit from me since the days of my dual employment at the Monteleone and A-Bar. A month off would surely have everyone scurrying for other work, or send us packing to New Orleans.

Another late night showdown at the apartment.

"Remember how you made fun of us for not having a contract at the A-Bar?" The layoff fueled Hacksaw's irascibility and I was a handy target. "What happened here, Mister Businessman?"

"Like we'd have the money to hire a lawyer and sue," Ricky checked in, "not to mention win."

"It's been a pretty good run. Served us well." As always, Walter accentuated the positive, leaving Hacksaw to counter, "As long as we served their purpose."

We spent another hour grumbling and squabbling before agreeing to return when Cousin Ned's reopened.

Meanwhile, Hacksaw would visit his mother, now in a nursing home just outside Florence, the town he'd grown up in. Ricky was pleased to have the time to return to New Orleans and spend an entire month with his wife — more pleased, Hacksaw suggested, than she might be. Walter would go to New Orleans to shack up with the Tipitina's waitress who one night had presented him several times with napkins on which she had scrawled her phone number until he could finally decipher one of them, who had instructed him through the gapped teeth in the unparalyzed side of her face to "be sure to look me up when you get back in town." Lee and Mark thought at first they could borrow a car from a pre-owned vehicle salesman who'd been hanging around Cousin Ned's, and drive into Tennessee for some cool mountain air. But conjuring the potential fate of two Black guys in a used Impala in the hills of Tennessee, they opted instead for Birmingham where there would be work with a couple of horn players they knew.

I was looking forward to catching up on some of the sleep I'd been losing as roommate to Hacksaw and his relentless snoring. And unfettered time with my beloved Muriel. But Hacksaw had other plans for me.

"You talk about new influences and improving your playing." He handed me a narrow, folded brochure. "This guy runs a weeklong summer jazz camp in Kentucky. Starts next Sunday and it's cheap. Why don't you take your girlfriend and go learn something?"

* * *

"So what do you think, Muriel? Can you stand a whole week with me – and all that jazz?"

She had just arrived from her day at the agency, stunning in a white lace sleeveless dress. Breaking the news and spilling the details of the trip and program without pausing to breathe, I danced her around the room to an unplayed melody.

Jazz camp would be a series of classes — theory, ear training, and lessons on an instrument, a "hands-on workshop," I read from Hacksaw's brochure as I waltzed her into the kitchen. "'Our uniquely comprehensive program is named for its founder, Jamey Aebersold, the University of Louisville professor who has achieved universal notoriety for his *Play-A-Long* books, and now, as the innovator of the summer jazz camp concept.'"

I could imagine nothing sweeter: the two of us hovering over lessons by day, cradled in each other's arms throughout the night. "Every one of five delicious nights," I crowed.

She stopped our dance, her lips pursed, and studied my face for a few agonizing seconds. She stroked my cheek with her fingertips. "I can't do it, Thomas. Daddy won't allow it."

I hadn't considered she wouldn't go. I felt so sure of her now, that she would be as enthusiastic about this getaway as I was. For a brief moment I couldn't think of anything to say, then just shook my head.

"You never cease to surprise me, my Muriel. A whole week together and learning more jazz. I thought you'd jump at the chance."

She laid her arms over my shoulders and tilted her head. "As long as I'm livin' at home, I'm playin' by their rules." As if I needed reminding.

"Then maybe it's time to leave. We could have our own place." Though in saying it, I knew the futility of it.

* * *

Readying Ol' Blue for the journey — she was about to travel her one hundred thousandth mile, well beyond her life expectancy — required two new front tires, retreads, and an alignment to cure a shimmy that had surfaced during Metropole's passage to Atlanta. But thanks to the fresh rubber and curative front-end work, a pile of eight-tracks and my experience with long drives, we negotiated the route in just eleven hours: Atlanta to Chattanooga, west to Nashville, and north to Louisville, alternating between stretches of completed interstate highway and various two- and four-lane roads once collectively known as the Dixie Highway as AAA Trip Tik'd the route to get Chicagoans all the way to Miami.

I shuddered as I pulled onto the Louisville campus, discomforted by recollections of my university days in Miami. Handmade signs pointed to a lot marked "Summer Jazz Student Parking Only" and an aching Ol' Blue rolled into an empty parking space. I dismounted like a cowboy in an old Western tying his snorting horse to a hitching rail after the long, dusty ride into town from the family ranch.

I entered the closest building where I joined thirty or forty in line at a table bearing a registration placard. From all the talk and jostling, it was clear many already knew each other. Almost all were teenagers.

"Jazz camp?" I asked a youngster in front of me.

"Yes sir," the boy responded.

Oh my.

Registered students were handed a packet of materials and sent to a theater off the registration lobby. Among the items in the packet was a test intended to determine the incoming student's familiarity with music theory. I breezed through the first few questions about time and key signatures, but my lack of formal training left me unfamiliar with terms like "perfect authentic cadence" and "rhythmic transformation."

Another sheet in the packet directed me to a practice room for an audition.

"I can tell you've been doing this for a while," noted the tall man with a tightly cropped afro and neatly trimmed mustache who conducted the audition.

"I've been playing professionally since college."

"Which was…?"

"Graduated in '66."

"Whew!" Then apologetically, "You don't look that old."

Point made. More than twenty years performing, and I was in school with a bunch of kids just learning to play.

But I was very wrong. These kids, most of them, played well beyond their years, often with flawless technique, many with an understanding of jazz nuance. I watched one kid who couldn't have been more than eighteen run a diminished scale the entire length of the keyboard bottom to top and back at breakneck speed with no change in tone or timing — with his left hand. The program was bloated with prodigies. Kid after kid played faster and cleaner and better lines than me.

And they knew it.

"Hey, man, you're kind of behind for your age, aren't you?" one of the kids, the drummer in the ensemble I was assigned to for the week, taunted me after a practice session. It was all the more cruel for its honesty. I had no comeback, though I did feel somewhat avenged days later when the kid was late for ensemble rehearsal. He was delayed in the infirmary with a bloody nose courtesy of another student not so easily humbled.

Worse were the nights as I lay in a dormitory bed missing Muriel.

But I pressed on, always the good student, and managed some benefit from the week's instruction. I learned to hear how certain lines were constructed and how those structures might fit into my solo work and was alerted to flaws in fingering that slowed me as well as compromised tone.

"More legato," insisted my mentor, identified only as Nate, even on the school faculty list posted on the bulletin board. "You can't play legato skipping across the keyboard like you're hunting and pecking on a typewriter."

Another demoralizing critique, though mitigated by encouragement and support, from an educator who understood how motivated a student of jazz must be to make even the slightest improvement.

"Chopin said fingering is a study for life." Folding his hands behind his head and looking skyward, the man brought back pleasant recollections of Artie Reardon and how he'd assume a similar pose as he was about to convey some well-vetted pearl of musical wisdom. "That's how complicated it is choosing which finger goes on which key."

He reached behind him, opened a desk drawer, pulled out a laminated page, the top of which read in all caps "RULES FOR FINGERING."

"There are three general rules." He waved the plastic at me. "The first is that if you're playing in stepwise motion, like a scale, you want to avoid putting your thumb on a black key. The reason is that the thumb is shorter than the other fingers, so if you use it on a black key you have to move your hand in and out as you go up the scale."

At least I wasn't in the habit of using a thumb on a black key. But I must have looked perplexed because he reached over, grabbed my right hand, and placed it on the keyboard.

"As they relate to the physical motion of playing, your hands move three ways: up and down, left to right, in and out." He moved my hand in each direction as he spoke. "The biggest problem most pianists have with fingering is that as children they were taught the 'thumb under' technique. Now, play a C-major scale."

I ran the scale, a little hesitantly but in my usual manner, thumb starting on C and then again at F, which is where the teacher stopped me.

"See how you did that? How you twisted your wrist to get your thumb under your hand to the F? That's unnecessary motion. Instead of twisting, move your whole hand over the keyboard and drop the thumb on F. That's rule number two: glide, don't twist. I know. It doesn't feel natural. It'll take time and practice."

Of that I was sure.

"The third rule is about the fourth finger. Put your palms together like you're praying and fold your fingers under so the knuckles in the middle of your finger touch. Now separate your thumbs. Okay, now your pinky fingers. Good. Now your first fingers. Okay, now your fourth fingers. Uh, uh, keep those knuckles together."

My fourth fingers wouldn't budge.

"Can't do it, can you? It's because your fourth finger is naturally weaker. So use your thumb and first two fingers as much as you can, and the fourth, and by association the fifth, as little as possible. Art Tatum famously relearned all his scales using just three fingers. You know Schumann?"

"The composer. Sure."

"Schumann built a mechanical device to strengthen his fourth and fifth fingers but the only thing he got out of it was a terrible case of carpal tunnel. He was going mad with syphilis at the time, a troubled soul…"

"I get the point," I interrupted.

Still, the week was dispiriting. What few things I picked up from the program would take months, maybe years to work their way into my playing. By week's end I was more worn than invigorated by my much-anticipated jazz camp experience. Descending from the auditorium concert stage following our ensemble's final performance, Nate pulled me aside and walked me to a practice room.

"Mr. Cliffe, I've enjoyed working with you. I hope you got something valuable out of your week."

I sat facing him, staring down at the gray tile floor, my hands dangling between my knees. "It was a bit demoralizing, sir. I've been at this for some time. These kids play rings around me."

"Most of the kids you're talking about have been studying piano since they could sit up. They're classically trained and have had the best instructors money can buy. They've got technique up the ying-yang." He leaned back and chuckled. "I guess you played less than half the notes they did in the 'Maiden Voyage' solos.

"But do you know the saying 'It's not what you play, it's what you don't play'? A lot of what we do with these kids is slow them down, get rid of the window-dressing, try to get them to realize every note should have purpose.

"That's where you're ahead of these kids. You play music, not just notes."

* * *

The return trip to Atlanta seemed much longer than the drive to Kentucky. It was Sunday and the only radio stations Ol' Blue could get broadcast either bellowed warnings of eternal damnation or nasally voices singing of glorious salvation.

I decided to proceed in silence and make mental notes of what I'd learned during the week, a list of things to work on when I got back. But mostly — a couple of times I got so distracted I allowed Ol' Blue to travel at speeds unwarranted by her ability to manage the curves and pitches of the mountain roads descending through Tennessee — I thought of Muriel, anticipating our reunion, reliving her embrace as we lay in bed, how she'd tremble ever so slightly as I slid my hand over her breasts and stomach, her skin all satin and silk, and down over her hip and inside her thigh.

I arrived at the apartment well after midnight, dropped into bed, and slept soundly until mid-morning. I awoke, surprised at the silence before remembering the rest of Metropole was away and would be gone the entire month. How delicious to have all this time alone with Muriel.

Rummaging through the refrigerator, I found one lonely egg in a carton, cracked it into too much butter in a frying pan, and made coffee. There would be a knock on the door soon and I'd open it to my Muriel.

But she did not come that morning, or afternoon, or at our usual evening hour. Nor the following day. I'd promised never to call her house, honoring her request by never asking for a phone number. I just had to wait.

I tried to practice, but concentration was as hard to come by as initiative. So I passed time watching television: a baseball game, though I didn't keep track of the score; old movies, though I did not follow the plots. I couldn't even lose myself in a book. A third day turned to night without Muriel. My sleep was now broken and restless. I arose Thursday morning deciding to wait no longer. It wasn't what I wanted to do, acting on information Hacksaw had finagled out of one of Muriel's blundering girlfriends at Cousin Ned's.

"So you two know each other well?"

"Grew up together."

[223]

"Really? That's cool. Here in Atlanta?"

"Yes, in Ansley Park."

"Oh yeah, I remember she mentioned that. I think she said on Baker Street; yes, I'm sure it was Baker Street."

"Nooo. It was Westminster Drive."

Nor did I want to admit to myself there might be substance to Hacksaw's suspicions. But it took no more than a walk to the 7-Eleven across the street from the apartment and opening an Atlanta phone book to find a Burns on Westminster Drive. I'd just ride by.

As expected, it was an imposing neighborhood. Long, sloping lawns climbed to stately two- and three-story homes suggesting generations of prominent residents. The Burns house was a sprawling red brick ranch perched atop at least an acre of elegant landscaping: groupings of azaleas and rhododendrons and rows of flowering blue and pink hydrangeas and towering cryptomeria.

I didn't see her Subaru in the driveway. The house looked quiet. Perhaps the family was on vacation.

I'd confirm the hunch with a drive by the agency, a modest office building in Atlanta's Midtown on one of the many streets with Peachtree in the name. I'd driven past the building before — Muriel had pointed it out. If her car wasn't in the lot behind the building, I'd assume she was indeed out of town, vacationing or perhaps meeting with a Burns & Associates client.

I wasn't scheming, I assured myself, but it was just before five o'clock, the hour she'd ordinarily leave work for the band apartment, when I just happened to pull into the parking lot. Her car was there.

Best to leave it at that, I knew.

But instead, I pulled into the empty spot next to her Subaru and turned off Ol' Blue's engine.

It was but a minute or two before she came out of the building. When she noticed Ol' Blue, she smiled broadly — and my heart surged. Then her smile faded. She turned to look behind her and quickened her pace.

"What are you doin' here?"

We were face-to-face through the open window. She'd cut her hair so that the longest part curled under her chin and the back was shorter, enough to reveal a flawless white neck each time she turned to look toward the building.

"I'm back." Of course, I'd made sure she knew the day I'd return. "Thought you'd want to see me. Thought I'd surprise you."

"Thomas, not here, you know not here." And she looked again over her shoulder. "I'll meet you later. At that bar in Decatur. We're havin' clients over for dinner so it won't be till around ten. Now please, get out of here before…

"Just go. Please!"

"Sure. Sure." But all I was certain of was my humiliation. Ol' Blue coughed a cloud of white oily smoke as we left the lot.

* * *

We sat staring into our drinks. She stirred two straws in a tall, thin glass filled with Coca-Cola. Those beautiful blue eyes teared up and she sniffled.

"I just can't see me in some rental house in New Orleans waitin' at night for you to come home from some bar. Or worse, from one of your road tours. Or worst of all, livin' some itinerant life. I want a man who goes to work in the mornin' and comes home at night to two beautiful children and a dinner I've cooked. I need a normal life, Thomas. And this life, our life together, would be anythin' but normal."

Examining my bourbon, I gave the glass a turn. For a moment, maybe less than a moment, I thought about how I could call Dad and see if he still wanted me to come run the factory.

"I've been less than forthcomin'." She remained focused on stirring, tears now streaming, her words in throttled bursts. "I'm engaged. Known him forever. Been together since high school. He's in Chicago. Finishin' law school."

Verdict delivered, she now appeared composed. I could only try to swallow.

"You made me think twice, Thomas," her eyes into mine. "A lot more than twice. I'm just a Southern girl who wants to be taken care of. That's the life I belong in." Then back to her Coca-Cola. "We're to be married this summer."

It was a few minutes before I could stand. I pulled a twenty from my wallet and dropped it on the table. I started toward the door then turned to look into those eyes, one more imploring gaze, but Muriel had wiped away her tears, those cerulean pools of lust and love suddenly cold and dry and distant as a cloudless sky.

"It's okay, Muriel. Come on. I'll walk you to your car."

I sat for a long moment staring at the keyboard, hands in lap. Some in Cousin Ned's crowd, arrested by the stillness, paused their conversation.

An initial pass of thick single notes, the melody of "Body and Soul" embellished only by an occasional passing note and an altered chord sometimes as open and empty as an octave. A second pass, erupting with a thunderous dissonant chord followed by a run of random-sounding notes landing at whole or even half-step intervals from the melody, a line heard by straining ears as torn and agonized.

At the bridge, each note, meticulously honoring the composition in tone and timing, and argued against in organized cacophony by two-handed chords of eight and nine notes. The concluding verse, correcting the dissonance with a melody different from but complementary to the original. A third time from the top, polychords galloping in double-time under arpeggiated scales and runs, a defiant freedom dance incorporating all eighty-eight keys, uninhibited through two verses, untempered at the bridge, unhinged through the final verse.

The closing four bars, mimicking the rubato of the first pass, retarding to a single, lugubrious final note.

Even as that last note still rang, even before the applause, I heard, "Man, who *was* she?" from a table near the stage.

[227]

My interpretation of "Body and Soul" had laid bare my misery. It had unleashed a new level of expression, innovative bordering on reckless. My unrestrained emotion had produced something organic and powerful, if painful.

Hacksaw stepped to his microphone and announced, "Tom Cliffe, ladies and gentlemen." The applause swelled.

* * *

Off stage, life reverted to an old pattern too familiar. We practiced little. Ricky, Mark, and Lee were willing when pressed but far from committed. Walter and Hacksaw were more concerned about their own regimens than band tunes; they'd rather challenge their skills at improvising and transposing, calling tunes on stage the band hadn't played and keys not found in fake book charts. Walter occasionally charted a new arrangement, but even then, rehearsals were uninspiring; not unusual for Ricky or Lee to arrive at Cousin Ned's after four o'clock for a two o'clock rehearsal.

I blamed myself. A stronger person would be a more inspiring leader. I pleaded instead.

New material arranged to capitalize on the strengths of each band member would distinguish us from a bunch of guys that often sounded like a pickup band!

Crafty arrangements, of which we are more than capable, could put us on a concert stage or in a recording studio!

But the others appeared congenitally unconcerned. Their idea of attending to their futures involved showing up for a gig and playing well enough to keep it.

The longer we held the Cousin Ned's job, the more lax we became. A nine o'clock start crept closer to nine-fifteen or later. Twenty minute breaks between sets extended past a half hour. Carson complained, but when I shared his complaints, it had little effect; they were as indifferent to directives as cats.

Our extended stay also allowed us plenty of time to make connections. Virtually every night, sometimes as early as our first break, any one of us might be in the parking lot smoking a joint or in a bathroom snorting coke.

"We play better high," Ricky insisted, but our play didn't validate the claim. An interesting idea might surface, but drugs created gaps: our groove got flimsy, horns sacrificed tone.

Lee in particular was susceptible to cocaine, out most nights, sleeping through most days, rarely ready to leave the apartment early enough for an on-time start.

One Saturday, as we mounted the stage for the night's final set, Lee was missing. A few minutes of random notes and tuning, and still no Lee. I jumped from the stage and made my way to the men's room. Not there.

"I guess we're going to have to do this set without a bass player," I announced upon my return.

"I'll cover," Mark said and went to work on Lee's bass.

Set over, instruments stowed, the last stragglers leaving Cousin Ned's, Carson rattling his ring of keys. Still no Lee.

"I have no idea where he is," Mark apologized to Hacksaw. "He was talking with a guy at the bar. Must've left with him."

"Let's head back to the apartment," Hacksaw said. "Sooner or later he's got to come there."

* * *

Lee entered the apartment at nearly four the following morning. I was up, unable to sleep, alternating between staring at as much of the building entrance as I could see from the living room window and trying to get some rest on the sagging living room sofa.

"Man, I'm sorry." His voice was unusually high-pitched. He wiped at his nose with his shirt sleeve. "We went to this guy's pad, and I couldn't get anybody to haul my ass back."

"So you've been there all night?"

"Man, more blow than I've ever seen. Four of us went through an eight-ball. I'm sorry man." Then with resignation, "I need to steer clear of those dudes."

"How'd you get back here?"

"Cab."

"Guess you didn't think of that to get back to the gig."

"Need to crash, little buddy. Later."

* * *

I knew I could only hold Metropole together by keeping us employed. But what continuity I provided served only to create apathy. Whatever enthusiasm about Cousin Ned's we'd first shared had vanished.

Ricky and Mark complained openly about Atlanta, citing, only partially in jest, Fats Domino's pronouncement that he would never again leave New Orleans because he couldn't stand the food anywhere else.

Club owners and managers know the warning signs: habitually late arrivals, arguments among players, a player missing a set, and worst, a perceptibly thinning crowd. These are the unmistakable indicators of a souring relationship between band and gig. The standard practice is to rid the club of the problem in its early stages and avoid an inevitably more troublesome separation.

On a night thick with the humid air of a blistering September heat wave, I was met as we arrived by an enormous man with no neck who, engulfing my hand in a meaty palm, introduced himself as "Ant'ny." In a thin, nasal voice belying his massive countenance, he asked me to join him at the bar before the band started.

"Mr. King believes a little change of music would be good for the club." He leaned over the bar and motioned to Jeff to bring us a couple of drinks.

"Really? I thought things were going pretty well. If it's about us getting started late some nights, we can fix that." But if Carson was good guy, Ant'ny was bad guy. No compromising, no time wasted on details.

"Mr. King appreciates your music. And he wants to keep you here. But our patrons also like R&B. We're going to mix in some blues bands."

Even if I thought it would make a difference, I had no argument. I understood that despite the redundancy inherent in blues music, interventions like long rock-style guitar solos were more appealing to young audiences than Hacksaw's and Walter's sophisticated flights.

"You want us to alternate sets with some blues guys?"

"Nights. You guys will play Tuesday through Thursday, the blues bands on the weekends. Starting tomorrow."

It was a shot to the gut.

Replaced.

Starting tomorrow night.

Metropole had opened for name acts, but we'd never taken a back seat to unknowns. And then, of course, the money "because you're only playing weeknights," Ant'ny explained. Not to mention the raise we'd already lost in light of Muriel's absence.

As we concluded the night's last set, I announced that, yet again, there was something to talk over back at the apartment.

"What do you think?" I asked.

"I think we're outta here," answered Ricky, who every week now was driving back to New Orleans on our days off.

"Maybe so, but we need some time. Let's stay for a few weeks while I see what we can get back in New Orleans or what else is going on. Maybe I can find us a weekend gig here. Atlanta might not be New Orleans but it's better than bouncing around Mississippi. They're not asking us to move out of the apartment — at least, not yet."

Reluctantly, all agreed to stay the course for two weeks. All except Lee who, by the time I retired at three a.m., had yet to return to the apartment.

Mid-morning. I awoke to Hacksaw rummaging in the kitchen. An oily substance of some sort spat from a frying pan set over a raging flame.

"What are you looking for, Hack?"

"The goddamn coffee pot. For Chrissake, it was here yesterday."

"It's right there."

"Where?"

"On the counter. Right there in front of you."

"Messy motherfuckers. Never put anything up."

"Think you should turn that flame down a bit?"

"Browning the butter. Have to get it hot to quick-fry the egg."

"Quick-fry?" I doubted the advisability of treating an egg like McDonald's does fries. "Looks more like flash fire."

"Yankee."

I never could tell whether Hacksaw was joking or actually irritated. I think he enjoyed keeping me guessing.

"Bet you never had a sunny side up over a Martha White under a ladle of sausage gravy either."

I hoisted myself onto a stool. "We're too good for this, Hack. There's got to be something better out there."

"You refuse to get it, don't you? It's jazz and there are only so many people who want to hear it."

I had learned it was better to ignore than argue Hacksaw's contrarian notions. "I don't even know where to start looking for other work here, but I hate to tuck tail and go back to New Orleans. I want to go back, but not with our heads hanging."

"Yeah, like ride in on a Mardi Gras float, the Metropole float, cheering crowds, dark-eyed Cajun ladies showering us with bouquets."

"Just with our heads up like we left New Orleans for something important. Like we shook Atlanta to its core. Something that'll get us creds, enough for, say, a spot in the Jazz Festival."

"We ain't gonna play Jazz Fest. Wouldn't matter what we did here. You have to be a name act."

"And we know what that takes."

"Original tunes, recordings," we mock-chanted in rhythmically tight, dissonant harmony. "And," I continued, "we know that ain't gonna happen."

"If you're so hell-bent on original tunes," Hacksaw poured me a cup from a full pot, "maybe you should dedicate some of the time you spend in front of that keyboard to working on one."

"I thought it would be better if we did it as a band. I've tried writing. Sometimes I can come up with what seems like a nice melody line or an interesting lyric but it never turns into a good song."

[234]

"What makes you think any of us could do any better? Or that combining all that lack of songwriting talent would produce something worthwhile? Even if we came up with something decent, chances are miniscule of somebody paying for us to record."

I refilled the cup and headed toward the living room sofa, its suspicious stains looming more graphic in the light of mid-morning Atlanta. I opted for an under-stuffed chair.

"Here's a thought." Hacksaw juggled his coffee as he plopped onto the sofa. "As long as they're letting us stay in this apartment, let's play out our weeknight gig and spend weekends in jam sessions. It'll be good for us, all of us, to hang with other players for a while. New influences. New ideas. You're big on that, right?"

Any kind of a plan was welcome.

* * *

It was past noon before Walter, Mark, then Ricky crawled out of their rooms.

"Lee still asleep?" I asked Ricky.

"Might be, but not in there."

"He's still not back?"

"It's those guys he's been running with. Free crack. They think it's cool hanging out with a jazz musician."

"Crack? How do you know?"

"I went with him one night, but that shit's too heavy for me. Ain't doin' him much good either."

"Well, at least we're not playing tonight. Not that he knows that."

Hacksaw had heard of a club where some of the city's best musicians came to jam, and we agreed to take our first night off and check it out, get the hang of the place and see if we could sit in. Lee came through the door as we were getting ready to leave. He was ravaged, eyes streaked red, nose so congested he was breathing through his mouth. The left sleeve of his shirt was stained with a telltale mixture of mucus and blood. He slumped, eyes downcast, his walk more of a lurch.

"I'll be ready in a minute. Just give me a minute."

"For what?" Walter asked.

"For the gig. Ready in a minute."

Ricky was on his way out for New Orleans but dropped his duffel bag to the floor with a bang and pushed to within inches of Lee, glaring into his dilated pupils. "You might be able to get onstage in your condition, but I wouldn't want to be up there with you."

"The good news is you don't have to worry about it," I interrupted. "We're not playing tonight. We're not working weekends anymore."

Lee paused in his progress toward his bedroom. "We're fired?"

Ricky remained fixed on Lee, a look not so much of anger but of disgust. "Yeah, and you being AWOL for the last set the other night is the reason."

Lee side-stepped Ricky's stare, then bent toward their shared bedroom. "Fuck you, man. That was no big deal."

"Yes, it was," I intervened. But it was useless, even mean, confronting him as he was, so wasted and worn. "Get some rest. We'll fill you in later."

* * *

THE MUSICIAN

Most of Atlanta's jazz musicians back then, at least the better ones, were Black. So some racial tension, more like territorial dispute, was not uncommon when white players showed up to jam with the local elite. Most often musical intimidation was the tactic; a frenetic pace or an arcane selection could send the fainthearted packing.

The place was named Club 66 in recognition of the year of its opening. A slender girl with soft black curls dangling in front of her narrow brown face was at the hostess stand. She was hovered over a paperback and didn't look up. "Five dollars…each."

We filed through a narrow hallway with framed drawings of Louis Armstrong and, just before it opened to the clubroom, a sign that read, "No guns or knives allowed. Weapons will be confiscated."

Square and conspicuously large, the room was packed. Across its expanse at the far wall, the biggest thing in it, the stage, featured a fiercely paced version of "St. Thomas" by a five-piece group comprised of three horns, bass, and drums. The drummer was perched behind a huge drum set, including a double bass and six or seven cymbals, and in front of two sets of chimes. The players' casual poses belied the intensity of their playing.

The stage itself was theater-like: elevated at least three feet, wide and deep enough to hold a small orchestra, and brilliantly lit. One spotlight beamed down on what appeared to be a Fender Rhodes, though I couldn't be sure from our distance. The keyboard was unattended.

A small rectangular dance floor separated the band from a section of cocktail tables and chairs and perhaps twenty rows of twenty or so chairs behind the tables, all facing the stage. It looked like every seat was occupied, as were the tables in a balcony circling the room except for the stage area, allowing the music to soar unimpeded to an acoustically accommodating ceiling.

In a corner at the back of the room, a man at a mixing board was busy balancing sound while a shapely figure in a bright floral dress worked the stage lighting, dimming and strobing and spotlighting the soloists. The clientele was almost exclusively Black, and everyone far better dressed than Mark, Walter, me, and especially Hacksaw, whose jeans were torn at both knees.

"What a place," I gaped. "What a crowd."

We huddled for several minutes where we'd entered, silent and a little intimidated, before Mark stopped a waitress who pointed to a man in a white linen suit, jacket buttoned over a dark blue shirt and white-striped, red tie, leaning on a corner of a bar that stretched the entire length of the club's street-side wall.

We moved pack-like behind Mark toward the man.

Mark set his guitar case on the floor and stuck out his hand. The man didn't take it, only gave a faint nod of his clean-shaven brown head. He did not recognize the name Metropole. Nor did Cousin Ned's make an impression.

He wrote each of our names on an index card. "Not a lot of the regular players here yet so be ready for a call sometime next set." And turned back to his conversation with a bartender.

We remained standing there, bunched together, the four of us. Had we been wearing fedoras, sunglasses, and nicer clothes, hanging on to those instrument cases as we were, we might have been taken for character actors from the set of a Prohibition-era gangster movie.

"This is awkward," Walter whispered.

THE MUSICIAN

As our host had suggested, it was only a minute or two into the set when we were called to the stage, not by name but as four players from a band called Metropolitan. "Would that be a city or the ice cream?" Hacksaw groused, but we made our way around the dance floor to the stage entrance.

* * *

The reception from the musicians, in particular for Hacksaw, Walter and me, was chilly.

"Call something," the bass player grunted at Mark who was plugging into an amp while Hacksaw and Walter fitted mouthpieces to their horns.

"How about 'Little Sunflower'?" Mark answered and began snapping his fingers to set the tempo.

I worked through several measures of the introduction with Mark, the bass player, and drummer before Walter and Hacksaw joined in to harmonize the head. Then Hacksaw stepped forward to take the first solo, and it wasn't but a few bars in that I saw the drummer and bass player grinning at each other, like adults surprised at a child's cleverness.

One by one, we played our way into acceptance, that comfort zone musicians fall into when they play collaboratively and well. I struggled some, due mainly to my lack of familiarity with the tunes being called, the more esoteric chestnuts of Hacksaw's didactic rants. But I played well enough to earn at least muted respect from the other musicians — a nod here and there at a well-chosen chord or a phrase well played — including the drummer, whose job it was to keep players rotating in some orderly flow and the combinations in some reasonable formulation, and, most essential to club management, get everyone in, which was no cake walk with four saxes, three trumpets and two trombones waiting a turn, and every solo starting from the top and exerting itself through the entire tune at least twice.

He kept Mark and me on stage through the night's stream of horn players, and as the final assemblage stepped off the stage, sent the two of us to the man in the white suit.

"We happen to be looking for a couple of players to fill out our rhythm section on the weekends."

"Sounds good." I looked at Mark who nodded in agreement. "How much does it pay?" I was back in my role as negotiator.

"How much do you need?" He seemed a bit annoyed with me.

"How about two hundred a night — apiece?"

"How about fifty."

It wasn't a question.

Well, this wasn't supposed to be about the money; it was a learning experience. "Okay with you Mark?" Mark shrugged. I shrugged.

We'd start the following night. In addition to the late-night jamming, we'd play two earlier sets — the drummer, bassist, Mark, and me the glue for, much like the jam sessions, a procession of makeshift collaborations.

I was honored to play in such a venue and with musicians of that caliber. I took it as recognition of some level of proficiency. But I was also challenged by my limited command of the literature, and spent the subsequent days and weeks riffling fake books, memorizing tunes from the nights before when I'd relied on Mark or the bass player to call the changes.

It proved, as Hacksaw had suggested, exposure of substantial educational value. The spontaneity required me to be at my most creative. I accompanied players I'd never worked with, and had to listen carefully to play the appropriate changes behind their solos. I was, at best, peripherally familiar with most tunes called; some, like Parker's "Bloomdido" or Powell's "Bouncing with Bud," I'd never heard and was expected to play some sort of intro, with or without the drummer.

Every so often a singer or horn man might hand me a chart for something they'd composed, count it off, and expect me to be on board from the first measure. I expected hectic tempos, but soloing at breakneck speeds, not to mention in unorthodox meters, was beyond challenging. No one would have confused me with Ahmad Jamal or Dave Brubek or Ellis Marsalis.

But I survived, even flourished as the weeks passed. I was applauded when my name as "house keyboardist" was announced to Club 66 audiences and occasionally as I completed a solo. At the end of a night, I'd drive home happy and sleep the tranquil slumber of the contented.

The times, as expected, were financially lean. My lease on the house in New Orleans was expiring and re-upping it defied logic. I called Evan from the 7-Eleven payphone.

"Good to hear your voice, Tom. How are things going in the big city?"

"Pretty good. I'm playing at this Black jazz club on weekends. Mark and I are part of the rhythm section. Working with killer players and learning lots of new tunes."

"What? There are good musicians in Atlanta?"

"Ev, I've come to realize they're everywhere. No shortage of gifted and skilled musicians in this world."

"Well, good to hear that things are going well for you."

"Music is going well, but we're only working three nights a week at Cousin Ned's and not making much at the jazz club. I hate it, but I'm going to have to give up the Lakeview house. I was wondering if you wouldn't mind getting the furniture out, and anything else that looks like it might be worth saving. Sorry to ask. I know it's an imposition, but…"

"*C'est très bien*. I'll call a friend with a truck, and we'll put everything in storage. Be here for you when you get back. You are coming home, eh?"

* * *

While Mark and I played Club 66 on the weekends, there was no other paid work beyond Cousin Ned's. Ricky was growing evermore restless and Lee was growing evermore disengaged. I thought to survey the musicians who came to jam at Club 66.

"Booking agents?" an incredulous trombonist posed. "Yeah, if you want to do society gigs."

I took the names and numbers, was able to get Hacksaw and Walter to share in the deposit to get a phone installed, and made, then waited for, calls. And so, for nights when we were neither at Cousin Ned's or Club 66, we began hiring out, sometimes two or three of us, but more often individually, playing with big bands for wedding receptions and corporate functions.

So-called society gigs were the purview of aging bandleaders with passé arrangements of clichéd tunes. The music was mostly languorous and dull, charts that could turn a three-hour assignment into an interminable slog. The direst of evenings required uniforms: a jacket perspired in on previous nights but not dry cleaned; or an outfit that had to be purchased at a price of more than the job paid, excused by a promise that it would be dollar-cost-averaged over future similarly dismal engagements.

As satisfying as playing jazz with accomplished musicians was, society gigs were unfulfilling, humiliating. Coming off stage from a wedding set, I was glad to comply with protocol, stepping outside, weather permitting, or at least somewhere away from the society. Hacksaw was less willing to stay on the society wagon, falling off one night with a growling yackety-sax blowtorch through his solo on "Goodnight My Love," the evening's slow-dance finale, and another night, a clarinet squeal through an entire verse of "On the Sunny Side of the Street" broken only by quick gasps for more puffy-cheeked air.

"If it smells it sells," Walter waved off a particularly nauseous evening of syrupy melodies.

Still, a wedding or bar mitzvah might pay as much as a hundred dollars a man or more, and through the better part of the fall, despite grumbling all around, we got and took the calls. And now, with Christmas just weeks away, holiday parties and sodden celebrators were in full swing.

"Some place north of town, in the Blue Ridge foothills, this Sunday." Hacksaw took the call on a Friday afternoon. "Needs sax and keys. And we don't have to lug the beast."

* * *

No matter how episodic and desultory their lives, there is one constant for most musicians: their instruments. Notwithstanding a horn or drum set pawned to resolve some economic crisis, the relationship between musician and musical instrument is more steadfast than most marriages, their marriages at least.

Except for pianist and piano. The promise of a quality instrument recently tuned, if not a lie, is typically perfunctory. It is a persistent professional annoyance for which there is no known solution. Booked where you haven't been, and can't get there beforehand to check it out, you can only pray the keys will not stick, the hammers will attack the strings with some degree of accuracy, and the strings will vibrate according to their designated frequencies.

Hacksaw and I jostled along in the back of a 1958 Mercury Monterey, the driver, an elderly, blanched drummer who decades before had nicknamed himself Stix, negotiating S-curves into the North Georgia mountains. Passing Dalton, dubbed The Carpet Capital of The World as nearly all carpet made in the USA is manufactured within a fifty-mile radius, the Monterey lumbered through Rocky Face, a rural bedroom community but for a neighborhood of opulent homes lining a world-class golf course contracted by and for flooring industry executives made wealthy by the nation's post-World War II obsession with wall-to-wall carpet.

Gas fumes pervaded the Monterey's interior, so traveling with windows up was not an option. Hacksaw and I, at opposite windows in the back seat, shivered uncontrollably. The bassist between us — seventy-five if a day — rode silent, spread-eagled, seemingly unaffected by cold, his acoustic instrument between his legs, the neck in front of Hacksaw's face and through the open window. We shimmied up an increasingly steep crawl the last few torturous miles: beyond Rocky Face, climbing the Blue Ridge foothills into dense forest, up an unpaved winding road under darkening skies. Swerving through a final curve, the Monterey's working headlight aimed a shallow beam at a wooden structure shakily aloft with alternating wooden and cinder block piers.

"What the fuck," Hacksaw said, taking in the ramshackle building.

We five musicians, including a Jack LaLanne look-alike trumpeter, unloaded in the pebbled parking lot and began hauling our gear into the building and across a floor that sagged with each step. We were greeted by the bandleader, a fidgety, skeletal, eighty-something survivor of the Big Band era who'd secured our commitment with an offer of fifty dollars per man, plus tips, which would be substantial, he promised, if revelers were sufficiently moved.

The building, more accurately, the shed, was separated into two squares by a paneled wall. Sounds of clinking glass and high-pitched cackles indicated a number of couples on one side of the wall. We were directed to a corner of the open space on the other side, catty-cornered to where a bulky, unshaven man in a soiled apron was examining the inventory of a portable bar.

I scanned the room. "Where's the piano?"

Our leader followed my eyes, shrugged, and left. I looked to Hacksaw who also shrugged. "What the fuck," he restated his earlier observation. In less than a minute, the leader was back and pointing at a door on the far side of the room opening to an outdoor porch.

The piano was an ancient spinet, though not of antique quality. And the porch, even wobblier than the rest of the building, was where it was stored. In their limited grasp of the principles of instrument preservation, the owners of this inelegant facility had sought to protect it from the whimsical mountain weather by sealing the top shut with duct tape.

I turned to the leader in disgust.

He lifted his arms in that way which feigns ignorance. "They told me it was just tuned."

Hacksaw and I dragged the piano inside and shoved it across the floor and into our corner. A first strike, one finger to a middle C. As the key moved, two or three keys to its left and right leaned with it — and addressed their hammers and strings as well, if not as boldly. An octave higher, a similar collaboration. Wherever I sought to play a single note, the keys surrounding that note played along inharmoniously.

"Better tune that...fast," the leader snipped. "Baton up in ten minutes."

"Tune?" I decided against arguing the semantics, and Hacksaw and I started at the duct tape. But it had clung there so long, it had become one with the façade. A paring knife borrowed from the beefy bartender proved more effective in freeing the lid, and what we discovered was even more foreboding than the external condition of the maltreated spinet: green slime, hardened by age, pervaded the strings and bound the hammers.

"Five minutes, boys. First tune, 'String of Pearls.' B flat. Consult your charts."

We decided the fallback was to work the knife to separate the hammers and unclog the related strings. We might have time to free the midrange.

The party of forty or so couples began lumbering into the room, men not of the cloth of carpet moguls, women as worn as the mutated piano so long ignored on the cold and precarious porch.

"A little party music," one man slurred.

"Mind if I take your honey for a spin?" Another grabbed the arm of a reluctant wife.

Hacksaw and I exchanged glances, tacitly agreeing to suspend all gentility. He hoisted the weapon and aimed it at the fungus uniting middle C and C-sharp. The blow was struck and the targeted blob burst, spewing a cloud of pent up, slime-textured spores into Hacksaw's face in a shower of muck. He reeled, then vomited.

I pulled the tool from the congested hammers and continued to work, quickly but gingerly, one arm raised in protection before my face, freeing nearly an octave and a half of notes in time to strike up the introductory bars to the Glenn Miller classic.

The condensed arrangement for piano, bass, brushes, and two horns completed — Hacksaw had recovered sufficiently to join in at the bridge — the leader was counting down the prescribed rhythm for a cheerful rendition of "Tangerine" when one of the mountain men approached and brayed, "How 'bout playin' that 'Hound Dog' song? Or that song about 'All My Rowdy Friends'? We need some party music, boys."

"We perform the standards," our offended leader responded, pointy chin thrust over a scraggly bowtie and frayed tuxedo shirt, "the greatest music of our greatest generation," and raised his baton to begin the beguine.

Then the unmistakable sound of beer bottle ricocheting off knotty pine…and another. I looked up from the battered spinet at a still sickly pale Hacksaw. The ugly potential of such an angry rural gathering was obvious: a cowering if well-conditioned trumpeter, four nonathletic musicians, and one indignant elder with a baton were no match for a roomful of beery mountain men. This was generally understood. Our baffled leader scurried toward the exit, amazingly spry, in particular in regaining his balance after slipping on Hacksaw's vomit as the rest of us vigorously stuffed instruments into cases.

Recognizing the band's intent to depart without even trying to muster up an Elvis medley or a Hank Jr. ballad, the party participants elevated the dispute with a chorus of colorful epithets, some of which I was hearing for the first time. Leaderless, the frantic five of us bolted from the building to the Monterey, and amid a barrage of increasingly depraved execrations, and an occasional beer bottle, somehow escaped.

At the bottom of a harrowing freefall where the road spilled back into civilization near I-75, the Monterey choked to a unanimously agreed upon intermission at a Jimmy's MiniMart for a twelve-pack of Bud Light, a three-dollar bottle of wine, and two dollars each in gas.

We were giddy over our getaway.

"I think they stepped back when you flexed, Bill," Stix teased to the trumpeter's amusement. "But stopping to check yourself in the mirror on the way out was a little risky."

"Looking wasn't so bad," the bassist, seemingly invigorated by the evening's events, chimed in. "It was the time you took combing your hair that made me nervous." Despite his age and corpulence, he had spirited his unwieldy instrument out of the lodge and rather deftly into the back seat of the Mercury and its place between his thighs as I was helping Stix fling cymbals, stands, and drum cases into the trunk.

An hour later, not yet back in Atlanta, the wine and twelve-pack consumed, quiet settled over us. No fifty bucks, no tips, and the sober realization that a flying beer bottle, or worse, could have inflicted real pain.

A sullen Stix retraced his earlier course, dropping each player at his residence, Hacksaw and me last.

"Sometimes when they call," Hacksaw mused, "just say no."

* * *

The late-night December chill was harsh, and the evening's musical miscarriage shed a sickly light on our broader circumstance. Our playing at Cousin Ned's was habitually uninspired and work with society bands demoralizing. And while our nights at Club 66 were rejuvenating, it was still not enough to offset my sense of drudgery and dissatisfaction. Ricky and Mark were increasingly inclined to reminisce about New Orleans and had called friends there asking about work.

The amenable and pliable Walter added that he "might prefer to be in New Orleans, maybe, if it's cool with everybody else," and went around the apartment humming, *sotto voce*, the melody to "Do You Know What It Means to Miss New Orleans." Lee, lacking the will, or more now the ability to disengage himself from his addict cohorts, could be saved only by flight. A morose Hacksaw declared his playing had grown stale and that he would take a day job repairing clarinets.

Nor could I recapture whatever made my post-Muriel version of "Body and Soul" so substantial. Must I be struck by emotional tragedy to play that well, find that freedom, that intensity? Like a baseball player seeing the seams of a curveball, I too had been in the zone, playing with uncanny ease and certainty, instinctively. But also like that baseball player in a slump, I couldn't will it back. Couldn't design it. Couldn't decipher it. Couldn't intellectualize it.

My frustration was the subject of conversation with a guitarist named James Bean following a Saturday night Club 66 jam. Bean was in his seventies with more than fifty years vacillating between struggle and success, from traveling blues bands to recording sessions with Ella Fitzgerald.

Encouraged to talk openly, and flattered by his interest, I covered a litany of exasperations: not enough recognition, unsatisfactory gigs, no recording offers, never enough money, no wife or family. He was attentive, pensively stroking his goatee with thumb and forefinger.

"You might be shittin' in the wrong stall, man." Bean looked a bit like James Earl Jones and his voice had the same timbre. "That is, if you want dough, a pad, a girl like the one you talk about, rug rats. It happens for some guys, but it's just that, brother, happenstance.

"It's not what you're choosing if you choose music. If you're a player, playing is *numero uno*.

"You play well enough, man. That's a rare thing, so dig it. Lots of folks'd sell their souls to do what you can do. You might not be getting rich, but you're getting by in a world only a few people would even try to make it in. Be happy with that, and anything else comes your way is, well, you're from New Orleans, right? Anything else is lagniappe, baby."

It was a version of a talk I'd had with myself. Still, time on the road, the work I put into my music, lack of status, all argued against Bean's life view. There was something about it that didn't apply to me, that I couldn't accept.

The disassociation of players so long associated was quick and bloodless: no financial obligations to resolve, no contractual agreements to dispense with, no joint assets to dispose of. At the end of another Cousin Ned's short week, Ricky and Mark packed Ricky's Cadillac, readying for the drive to New Orleans. They had a job the following night, and it sounded like more than a pick-up gig.

"I'm sure we'll play with you cats again." Ricky's nonchalance betrayed his perception of Metropole as starkly contrasted with my notion of the band as close-knit and enduring.

Despite the lull, I still believed in Metropole, had been committed to keeping us together. Our combination of jazz and funk, not to mention the individual talents, had proved broadly appealing. A decade together had provided what only time can: instinctive communication where even in the most spontaneous flights everyone knows where you're headed and how you're going to get back. My own development was rooted in Metropole's content.

I was tied to this music and by the music to these players. I was crestfallen.

[252]

Hacksaw seemed relieved.

"Hey, man, time to move on." He, Walter, and I were conducting the post-mortem, sipping Hacksaw's daily blend at the dining room table in the suddenly spacious apartment. The television droned on at low volume, cameras panning a near-empty baseball stadium, zooming in on Dale Murphy waggling lumber in anticipation of an under-powered preseason fastball in an early inning of an Atlanta Braves spring training game.

"But all the time we've invested." I was bent over the table, left elbow anchored, thumb and forefinger stroking my forehead. "All those tunes. All the gigs and places we've played. All the people who come to listen."

"I might remind you that we're playing three weeknights in a blues club at less than half the money we were making a year ago." Hacksaw bit into a slice of white bread supporting a huge glob of raspberry jam and chased it with the rest of his coffee.

"It's my fault," still massaging my forehead. "Should have called Star or somebody and gotten us another road gig. I let it go too long."

"The best you could have done is drag it out." Hacksaw stepped back into the kitchen for a refill. "It's been over for a while." He was addressing the coffee pot. "This ain't IBM. We're just six guys playing funk."

"We gigged pretty steady for a long time, almost ten years." Walter had been reading *The Power of Positive Thinking*. "Not bad for a jazz band."

"And you're a better player for it," Hacksaw garbled at me through another mouthful of jam. "Now, you can take what you've learned and move on somewhere else where you'll learn something new, your next musicological adventure. It's time. Time for you, time for Walter and me, and Ricky and Mark knew it was time for them."

Which left Lee, who at that moment emerged from the bedroom he'd shared with Ricky. His nose was running blood and he was dabbing at it with the front of his tee shirt.

He nodded to us. "Where's Ricky… and Mark?"

"Gone."

Working his way back from another crack-driven all-nighter, dimly aware, Lee still grasped the finality in my answer. "What happened?"

"Our work here is done." Hacksaw grinned broadly.

"Nah…c'mon." But it was becoming clear, we could see it in his face: the significance of the situation, what it spelled for Metropole, what it meant for him and the cocaine train he'd been riding.

"Doom for you and yours," Hacksaw confirmed.

Lee sank into the couch. "So we pick up a couple other guys."

"No, Lee, we're done." But there was reluctance in Hacksaw's voice, almost melancholy. Even he couldn't completely dismiss the loss. We wouldn't verbalize it, but we understood — anyone who does this understands — there is little more personal than what happens among players when they're playing.

"But…"

But there was no *but*.

For a few moments, the room was silent except for the prattling of television announcers attempting to keep viewers entertained while pitchers pawed the mound and batters stepped out of the batter's box to adjust their gloves.

Hacksaw broke in. "I've been talking to my buddy Wellmore in Pensacola. He's working with some serious players. He says they're a hot commodity on the Gulf Coast. Spring and summer on the beach, and they're working it. He's asked me to come down. I'm going."

As with Mark and Ricky, there was no counter. It would violate band culture to begrudge a player his independence, to question his decision to play with someone else elsewhere. It was that inalienable right.

Walter rose and turned off the television. The room was so quiet I could hear the living room wall clock ticking off-time. *So that's why that clock is always wrong.*

* * *

Lee left for a shower and Hacksaw pulled a chair closer to me at the table and sat.

"Hey, Walter's coming, and you're invited. I told Wellmore about you and he wants you to come. We just can't take Lee. Nothing there for Lee. It's sorry, but that's the way it is."

I was reminded of Muriel's declaration: "This life, your life, is anything but normal."

So much uncomfortable and uncertain about what would come next. I had to tell Mr. King or at least Carson that Metropole wouldn't be returning Tuesday night as scheduled, which would likely be answered with a discourse on how unreliable musicians are — despite their failure to give us notice before shutting us down or cutting us back. I'd be moving where I'd been just once and for only two weeks, not counting the Saenger Theater debacle, where I knew no one or even where I'd stay. Nor did I know when I'd work again, or for what kind of money, or if the money I had would last until a next gig.

[255]

And how would I break the news to Lee? Kind, good-natured Lee, whose broad smile welcomed me to Metropole. Who always talked to me with that endearing air of confidentiality. Whose greatest weakness was not to be judgmental enough to save himself.

* * *

"I don't know what else to do," I tried to explain. It was later that afternoon, Hacksaw and Walter out of the apartment, leaving me to break the news to Lee.

"Hack was already thinking about splitting, but when Ricky and Mark decided to go, that sealed it. And I guess they've got a spot for a piano, or maybe that Wellmore guy's taking me just to get Hack and Walter. I don't know. But I can't stay here and I'm not ready to go back to New Orleans without the band."

"It's okay." Lee sat, legs akimbo, head in hands, sagging with the old, weary couch, staring at the crushed and matted fibers of the orange shag carpet. "Hey, you're gonna dig it down there. Plenty of good players to work with. And those beaches. Flip-flops and bikinis. Yeah, little buddy, you're gonna dig it."

But his heart wasn't in it. And even with his face buried in those huge brown hands, I could see his tears.

Told his buddy he was gettin' him to
South Alabam
He said, "I'll tell you what, there's some
wildlife down there
So bring back a trophy or two
To hang on the wall."
He stopped in a roadhouse for a
drink or two
His eyes lit up, what would his
friend do
If he saw the wildlife hanging
out on the line?
So he took out his camera,
started shooting souvenirs
Of the size and shape and color
of braziers
"Caught me a two-legged deer
Man, you gotta see
the wildlife down here."

Elaine Petty
"Wildlife"

The Gulf, languid, crawled timidly to shore then backed off, the quiet disturbed only by two gulls overhead arguing over an unsuspecting night fish. A full moon directed its narrow beam across the argentate stillness to where I stood and moved with me as I stepped along the shoreline, its celestial spotlight a stark contrast to the hurrying headlights and clamorous streets of Atlanta's nightly confusion of hustle and hurry.

In this summertime Gulf Coast existence, I recognized my life as counterpoint. I was forty-two, an age when many of my college contemporaries had already raised children and were compounding their retirement fortunes, buying second homes in these Florida beach towns to while away their ample free time with golf and fine wines and white tablecloth dinners with their wives, or second wives.

There were no recording executives here, no talent scouts, few places even for live music outside the beach bars. Hardly somewhere to be discovered, it was more a place to get lost. At this stage of my life and career, did I have time to waste? True to Hacksaw's depiction of Artis Wellmore, the man was schooled, practiced, a virtuoso. His playing was reminiscent of the revered Jaco Pastorius, technically unparalleled, melodious, and funky, and dead at thirty-five from a massive brain hemorrhage inflicted by a Ft. Lauderdale nightclub bouncer who served just four months in jail, an eclipsed sentence from a reduced charge.

Like Pastorius, Wellmore's playing was heavily laden with Afro-Cuban rhythms. His funk was comfortable bedding for Hacksaw's lines, similar to how Lee could solidify a Jeff Lorber or Crusaders tune, but more educated and inventive. On the heels of my years with Metropole, I fit in okay, complementing the escapades of Wellmore and

Hacksaw, and the ebb and flow of others who came to test their skills with these best-of-local musicians. Even here, in this small beach community, on this unsophisticated Gulf Coast, there were fine players.

Less true was Wellmore's assertion that work was plentiful. The beach was inundated with sound, but a far piece from jazz. By day, kids strummed simplified chords for already simple Jimmy Buffett songs for beer-guzzling college jocks and string-bikinied co-eds. By night, youngsters who would graduate to jobs as plumbers and carpenters and insurance salesmen relied on three and four chords in bars inside the aging hotels of Ft. Walton Beach, overbuilt Pensacola Beach, and deteriorating Panama City.

Hotel gigs no longer held any appeal for me. To surrender my jazz perch would be a huge step backward. So Hacksaw, Walter, and I made do with a couple of nights a week in the few downtown Pensacola bars catering to a handful of local jazz devotees.

The combination of infrequent work and scant pay had us sharing a tiny, long-disregarded cottage, a broken building behind a grassless yard and rutted gravel driveway bordered by U.S. Highway 98 and speeding commercial traffic moving east and west well away from the beaches. We were living the most meager of existences.

Disillusion found its way to my stomach. Alternating home-cooked meals of iceberg lettuce and canned spaghetti with fast foods brought on bouts of painful cramps and diarrhea, which were becoming harder to combat even by the deadening effects of chugged Pepto-Bismol.

* * *

Work was harder to find with each passing gig. A slumping economy was doing what it usually does, hitting the least wealthy hardest, requiring a Southern middle-class — poorer by national standards — to use most discretionary income to meet mortgages and dress kids for school. Gulf beaches were less crowded than usual, and bar owners and restaurateurs, party boat operators and tee shirt shop proprietors, all the Gulf Coast business owners and workers who gathered their acorns during the weeks between Memorial and Labor Days, grew increasingly nervous over the slovenly season.

In better times, there had been plenty of work for good musicians: jazz and big band nights in Pensacola's hotels and dinner clubs. But those were the venues hardest hit. Bereft of options, Wellmore turned to an old friend from his Auburn University days to beg work for his dependents.

The club was the Flora-Bama; the owner, an uncommon Joe who revered musicians; his mantra: "Musicians are as underappreciated as they are underpaid."

Joe's regard, incredulous to other Gulf Coast club owners who limited their interactions with players to laying down rules and begrudgingly parting with a night's pay, won him the abiding deference of an interminable procession of players eager to work for him, and usually granted the opportunity.

The essential Flora-Bama entertainer was a guitar-strumming country singer mixing current hits with his or her own songs and a few enduring country classics. The nature of their music was reflected in the titles in their repertoires, the likes of "Did I Shave My Legs for This?" and "Tequila Makes Her Clothes Fall Off," and one that for a while claimed a top spot on country charts, "You're Out

Doing What I'm Here Doing Without." Some performers grew so fond of the place they penned songs about it, such poetic articulations as "Making Love in the Flora-Bama Parking Lot" and "I Saw Your Bra Hanging in the Flora-Bama."

Joe's fondness for the country singer-songwriter had the Flora-Bama playing Betty Ford Clinic to a host of pickers down on their luck and worn as the wheel bearings on their '67 F100s. Joe provided a place to play, a few direly needed dollars, and often housing, from beach condos to a trailer park to couches in his home.

His care and feeding also made the Flora-Bama the respite and developmental center for several Nashville headliners, if during their in-between years. He spoke most often and proudly of Mickey Newbury, best known for his "American Trilogy" pastiche recorded by Elvis Presley, who had made Flora-Bama something of a second home.

Originally a package liquor store on an otherwise deserted section of hurricane-prone beach property at the Florida-Alabama border, the Flora-Bama campus had been extended by a series of decks erected in sequence and aimed at the lapping waves of the Gulf of Mexico. Three, four, five stages rotated country singers, R&B bands, and now even this loose assembly of jazz musicians. With bands and solo acts performing throughout the day and night, often simultaneously, it was no stretch for Joe to find four or five slots a week for us.

This was hardly a jazz venue. Still, the atmosphere was so convivial and tropical that even our jazz was well received. "It is," Wellmore explained, "a culture by design, intended to show appreciation and respect for those who dedicate their lives to making music."

The music, the beach, the incidents and events, including an annual competition where participants see how far they can throw slime-coated mullet (the fish not the haircut) combined for a brand that made the Flora-Bama a destination for an unlikely blend of humanity united by a single inclination: to party as heartily as possible.

"Mostly college students this time of year," Joe answered while Hacksaw and I slid the CP70 onto the stage on the deck closest to the Gulf, "from Alabama and Florida, but also Mississippi, Louisiana and some from the Midwest. We don't get a lot of locals, but we take good care of the ones who do come, because they pay bar tabs year-round." There were also young professionals, recent graduates who returned to the beach to renew university relationships. And more than a few snowbirds, even Canadians, drawn to sun, water, and sugary sand.

Among this mix and mingle were myriad sub-cultures, "from bikers to bankers" as coined by Ken Stabler, the Crimson Tide then Oakland Raiders quarterback who grew up in nearby Foley, Alabama, and who reportedly had professed, "There's nothing wrong with studying the playbook by the light of the Flora-Bama jukebox."

This day Wellmore had assembled six players for a three-hour, late-afternoon slot. The crowd was small but impressive. Staggering beauties lingered conspicuously in bikinis, ordering multi-liquor cocktails in tall, frosty glasses, some braving the infamous Flora-Bama Bushwacker, a prefabricated concoction of various shades of rum, the recipe unknown even to the bartenders.

Standing at the bar was a quartet of subtly muscular and overtly handsome young men, pointed out by Joe as members of the Blue Angels squad of daredevil pilots operating out of the nearby naval air station.

"Those guys make me feel smaller than I am," I whispered to Hacksaw.

"In oh-so-many ways," he agreed.

At a table next to the stage, two men were thoroughly engaged. One sweated through a three-piece dark blue suit and held a tall, clear drink in a lily-white hand sporting a gleaming gold wedding band. The other, in jeans with butt-length hair not quite hiding a Harley Davidson logo on the back of a worn leather jacket, wrapped huge, hairy knuckles around a Coors beer can.

"There was this old guy who used to come in here all the time when the bar first opened," Hell's Angel explained to Banker. "He was about eighty then. Been in World War I. Remember him talkin' one night about how bad it was. The worst thing, he said, was the lice. Couldn't get rid of 'em. He said they'd get so bad he and his buddy would go out in the demilitarized zone late at night lookin' for bodies dead at least three days but not more 'n a week. Then they'd strip and switch out long-johns with 'em, because after three days the lice would be dead and before seven the body wouldn't be too decayed to get the long-johns off."

* * *

"I'll be damned. Tom Cliffe. My eyes didn't deceive me. It was you up there."

"Jim Stecky?" It had been twenty years since I'd seen my college classmate, one of the few I'd gotten to know even marginally and only because he was something of a regular at the Village. He was standing at the open doorway

[263]

between the main bar and first deck, a cold Bud sweating in his right hand. "My God. What are you doing here?"

"What does anybody do here? Escape for a couple of weeks. Get drunk. Chase pussy." He looked around. "And just look at all that pussy!"

I tried to elevate the conversation. "Hard to beat — summertime, college girls, the beach."

Stecky took a long pull from his Budweiser and, apparently impervious to my discomfort, pointed it at the stage. "Bet you get fresh pussy every night."

"Jim, I'm as old as you, remember? Class of '66? They don't even see me."

I had nearly shouted, intent on distancing myself from his crassness for anyone within earshot.

Stecky, in a crisp Hawaiian shirt and pleated white khakis that broke perfectly over tassels of brown leather loafers, had played baseball at Immaculata and still had an athletic build. He was an inch or two taller than six feet and his full head of aspirin-white hair had him looking more distinguished than old. Back in college, I'd admired Stecky's aggressiveness, his self-confidence, one of those students whose picture in the senior yearbook looks just right captioned "Most Likely to Succeed."

A Cindy Crawford look-alike, breasts and bottom hardly concealed by a string bikini, passed us on her way to the inside bar. She grinned up at Stecky, and he down at her.

"So what are you up to these days, Jim? Still single?"

"Not exactly. You remember Nicki? The two of you did a couple of gigs together after that folk joint cratered."

"Sure, I remember Nicki. Good singer. Pretty girl."

"That summer after college, she got pregnant…and we got married."

There was bitterness in his tone, maybe even a bit of regret. But I wasn't about to pry.

"Ah, a family man, eh? Raised a houseful of kids, I bet."

"Yep. Three girls. Two are still in college; the oldest works at Hallmark Cards and is getting married in a couple of weeks."

Wife and kids. The older I got the more jealous I was of lucky bastards like Stecky. "And business? Your dad was a real estate tycoon, correct?"

"Yes, I worked with him for a while, then took over when he retired."

"And made a mint?"

"Kansas City grew like crazy. Right place, right time. Sold a lot of land and a shitload of houses."

"That's great. Sounds like life's been good, Jim."

"'Into each life…'" He guzzled the last half of his Bud, belched, then stopped a waitress. "A refill, honey."

We might have been three steps from the bar and a bartender standing behind it, and the look we got from the waitress suggested she was busy with people not so conveniently located. Still, she nodded and took his empty.

"The bitch divorced me."

How attentively he watched the waitress as she headed toward the bar made me think for a split second that he meant her. But of course the bitch was Nicki.

"One, little, insignificant piece of ass," he grumbled. "Between the divorce and the alimony, the bitch is taking about everything I made, make, and will make." He seemed more indignant now than distressed. "Whatever's left goes to the girls' tuition. I'm already in hock up to my neck for this wedding.

"And you know, Tom, all four of 'em hate my guts."

"Sorry. I really am sorry." Maybe sorrier for the wife and kids than for the asshole who'd screwed up their lives.

The supermodel-like cutie paraded back before us, returning from the bar with a drink sporting an umbrella and short straw. As she passed, caressing the straw with her goldilocks lips, she turned her head to glance coquettishly at Stecky. He returned a big smile, raised an eyebrow and, keeping vigil as she sashayed to the beach, nudged me. "Some of that'd make your day, eh?"

I led him away from the crowd in the main bar to a table on the first deck.

Stecky settled in, stretched his legs, and took a long draw on a fresh Budweiser. "You're one smart fucker, Tom. You bailed. Look at you, never had to work a day in your life. Hanging out in bars. Playing music. Free as the wind. No silent desperation for you."

I remembered Stecky too had been an English major at Immaculata, but apparently not quite as accomplished at literature as baseball.

"Oh, I've got plenty of *quiet* desperation," I corrected on both counts. "Spent all these years working on my music, trying to be an artist. Chasing opportunities. Coming up short. Wife? Kids? A business? Never had any of it."

I ordered bourbon, a double.

"And another Bud," Stecky yelled after the waitress, then turned back and waved dismissively at me. "Artist, schmartist," he scoffed, eyes narrowing. "That's bullshit. Your kind checks out because you can't handle real life. Three kids, vengeful wife, mortgage, car payments, tuition, keeping 'em fed and clothed. Can't quit. Can't start over."

"Jim, let me ask you this. You're here a week, maybe two weeks?"

"Five days."

"Then where are you going?"

"Back home."

"Back home. Yeah, back home. I'm here for another week, two weeks, maybe longer if Joe will keep us on. Then where do you think I go, huh? Ain't no back home."

I thought about throwing bourbon in his face. But Stecky was probably just venting more out of frustration than scorn, more discontented with his own situation than disdainful of mine. And he might have chosen his words more carefully, not been so brash, had he not been on his fifth Budweiser.

But he was on his fifth Budweiser, leaning in a little and sneering. "A little dose of reality, Cliffe. While you were out strumming your guitar the rest of us took on life. We were drafted or enlisted, and when we got out of the service we went to work. Got married. Raised a family."

I ordered another double. "Exactly. We were the sons of Depression-era parents. They thought a job, a house and kids and food on the table and enough money for summer vacations and a new car every few years — that was a successful life. You could die with a smile on your face if you accomplished nothing more. They thought so highly of it, they wanted the same for us, and worked hard for us to have a chance at it. It just wasn't enough for me."

Stecky's dismissive tone had advanced to contempt. "You and your beatnik, drop-out friends."

"It wasn't dropping out. It was tuning in. We thought living like our parents was accepting average. And average was the worst thing we could think of being. Don't you remember, Jim…or did you *have* to forget?"

I downed my bourbon in one tilt. Stecky gulped another Budweiser.

[267]

"Truth ish…I might have turned out to be just that, fucking average." Stecky, the table, the people behind us moving in and out of the main bar — everything was starting to jiggle and blur. "But I took a chance, a chance on something different, something unconventional. And I bet my life on it."

I anchored myself to the table with an elbow. Stecky was looking around for a waitress.

"I might not be star quality, but I'm good enough to work. That's a big accomplishment in this biz-nish, and sometimes, my old college buddy, sometimes I'm damned good. Sometimes, the music I make reaches into people's guts and they feel…something…maybe as much as they can ever feel."

I stood up, wavered for a couple of seconds — was it me or the rest of the Flora-Bama spinning? I took a few uncertain steps away from the table, then came back and leaned into Stecky's face. "That ain't dropping out, pal; that's a lot of work for a fucking lot of years."

Stecky shook his head and waved both hands at me in a gesture I read as "Go to hell." But I wasn't through.

"Never worked a day in my life, eh? You have no idea how much practicing I do, how hard I have to work just to hold my own with these players. Free as the wind, eh? When's the last time you moved from town to town, week after week, to new job after new job, not sure where you'll be next? 'Freedom's just another word,' baby….Even when I'm lucky enough to settle someplace for a while, I'm still an itinerant, a regular frickin' gypsy.

"And here's another thing, mister real estate mogul: No matter where I am, I have to be on every night, have to prove my-schelf all over again every time I get up there."

I pointed in the general direction of our stage, then dropped back into my chair. "Can't just close the office door and put my feet up on the desk when I'm not feeling up to it.

"How many years you been in your bish-nish, in the same freekin' office, Steck, ol' pal? Try keeping a band together, even a really smokin' band. But I wouldn't expect you'd under-schtand 'cause you never strayed outside the lines. Had everything set for you from birth. James R. Stecky, strolling through life in Daddy's foot-schteps."

Stecky stood and walked around the table so that he was looking straight down into my face. I had to squint into the sun to look up at him.

"Thanks for the lecture. But frankly, you're boring me. I came here to drink beer and get laid."

Then, much more steadily than I could have, he started toward the back bar and the elevated deck that overlooked the relentless afternoon waves.

I came to appreciate the Flora-Bama songwriters. It wasn't my music; I couldn't sing those songs convincingly. But the stories and their tellers, they were real, carved from the circumstance of Southern lore: a mix of humor and pain, forbidden relationships, tragic loss, and outright foolishness. In some ways the country songs of the Flora-Bama were like the folk songs of the Village: the picking and strumming, the simple chord structures and sing-song melodies, the lyrics paramount. Just the stories and accents differed.

Most of the sessions Wellmore got for us were afternoon or early evening slots, before the crowds were unruly enough to just want to hoop, holler, and stomp. In no hurry to return to our dismal accommodations, I'd capitalize on the freebie drink and fried shrimp that followed our sets, then stick around for a few more drinks, most on my own tab though occasionally sent over by an appreciative patron. I was often there late, joining Joe and his Coors at a table in the main bar for a picker's last set.

I made friends with a few of them, the pickers. At first they'd kept their distance. I guess they thought I'd be critical of their country songs and ways. But I spotted a few from time to time on our deck during our sets. One, a kid wearing wire-rimmed spectacles over a long, sharp nose, and with a

[270]

beard he'd somehow knotted on either side of his jaw, told me he admired how we played "so many notes without seemin' to repeat a one of 'em."

One night, I spied a replica of my old Goya on the stage in the main bar. I was a little full of myself, given the white-hot set we'd closed with that afternoon. I thought it good timing to test my theory of the cosmic connection between folk and country.

Too many years from my guitars and calluses, no way I'd pick up a D-14 or the like. But I thought I could still get through an old Hartwell and Cliffe tune on that wide fret board with the nylon strings. I asked its owner, who chuckled and turned to look at his guitar like it couldn't possibly be what I was referring to, then seeing I was serious, waved his approval, surely wondering what in the hell this jazz pianist was going to do with a six-string.

> *Don't ask why of me*
> *Don't ask how*
> *Don't say forever*
> *Love me, love me now*

It had been a long time since I'd sung that ballad, that staple back at the Village and those years on the road and in New Orleans, then in Atlanta where Muriel changed the meaning of it for me forever. But the instrument was as comfortable in my lap as a stirring spoon in a chef's palm. And I could still summon Silvertone.

The applause was noisy. Some stood. I heard "fabulous," "beautiful," and one "yeah, baby, that's what I'm talkin' 'bout."

One of the voices rang familiar. I shaded my eyes and ducked to look out under the stage lights, but couldn't find the face that went with the voice. Then there he was.

"*Mon ami*, how you do?"

"I can't believe you're here." I led Evan to a table on the deck just outside the main bar. "How cool is this!"

"Not that long a drive to hear *la bonne musique*. And what a kick, to walk in when you're playing your old favorite. I don't guess you've given up the piano?"

"Yep. Decided to go country, too."

"Like the Pope is Buddhist."

"We play early, usually hang around. Not much else to do…and you might have noticed the scenery ain't so bad." The main bar was swimming with short shorts and tank tops. "Just saw that guitar up there. Reminded me of the axe I learned on back in college. Got the urge."

"After that reception, you might be tempted to return to your old ways." Evan, as always, complimenting and encouraging. How pleasant to be in his company again.

"Wait'll you hear these guys I'm playing with. Hack and Walter are here, you know. And our leader, a killer bass player, guy named Wellmore. Other than that, it's a different cast every day. Sometimes we have four or five guys on sax and trumpet, even trombone. We hold the groove. They take turns blowing. It's a fucking horn contest."

"Sounds like you're enjoying it."

"I'm hearing something new all the time. I'm picking up about as much here as I have anywhere. New ideas, Evan, new ideas. You know how I love that. Hey, how long can you stay?"

"Long as I want."

But his voice lacked the usual exuberance, and as he spoke he looked past me toward the Gulf. "Hey, this big shot New Orleans lawyer should buy this poverty-stricken musician a drink, eh? They got Sazerac up here?"

He was trying to be his cheery self again but it was just posturing. So evident. Still, I didn't want to probe, not yet.

"Sure. Got anything you want. You should try a Bushwacker. House drink. Kind of like a Hurricane is to Pat O'Brien's."

"Two Bushwackers." Evan signaled a waitress poised on a barstool.

"So how's Elaine and her family?"

"Elaine's fine. And Pearl, she's a little terror. Runs around the house as fast as she can go bouncing off everything like a *poulet ivre*. From the kitchen to the parlor, she'll waddle along, then run headlong into the couch. Then she turns and laughs as if you thought she'd hurt herself. And if you don't act concerned, she'll cry like she did."

"Elaine and her husband don't have their own place yet?"

"Bastard's gone. The more he drank, the meaner he got. He hit her one night. I was there. When I realized what he'd done, I kicked his fat ass to the street. I don't think Elaine would've run him off on her own. She was mad at me at first, but she's okay with it now; worthless son of a bitch hasn't even called her."

"I don't get it. How could somebody with a little kid *not* do everything he could to be around, whatever it takes?"

"He's just a useless coonass. Probably glad to off the responsibility. Elaine'll never see a dime of support. But that's okay by me. Just happy to be rid of him."

[273]

I remembered how giddy she was about getting married and having a baby, how she was following in the steps of the mother she idolized, and I felt sorry for her.

"And Eunice?"

Evan looked down at our table, which now held two Bushwackers. "What a pussy looking drink, like some kid left his chocolate milk on the bar."

He raised his eyes and again looked past me out at the Gulf. I turned to look with him. The night was moonless, so dark I couldn't see a horizon. Waters churned and a wave attacked the beach with an angry crack.

We stared into the darkness for several minutes before I turned back and pointed a finger at his Bushwacker.

"A couple of those will change your tune." I paused, then, "Tell me, Evan. What's up with Eunice?"

He winced. It was an awful look that put a lump in my throat. "Pancreatic cancer."

"No. No...not Eunice. It isn't right." I had to force each word. "Is she getting, like, chemotherapy or..." I couldn't think of what else to say.

Evan raised a hand to stop me, even though I wasn't saying anything. "There's not going to be a lot of pain, but she's not going to get well."

I stared at the table for another long minute, then up at Evan. "Can I come see her? Will she be okay with that?"

"She'll love it, Tom. She's got a mother's love for you. Hated to see you move away. Talks about you a lot. Still thinks you should have stayed right there in New Awlins and right there at home with us."

She was likely right about both.

Cocaine was broadly available at the Flora-Bama, snorting rampant in bathrooms and hallways and only slightly more covert on the decks. The '80s had seen cocaine replace marijuana as the preferred recreational drug, bankers and accountants as likely to be packing blow as bartenders and prostitutes. Anyone with a hundred dollars could score a gram. Evan and I had been well ahead of the times. I recoiled at the familiar knee tap.

"I can't, Ev. Does me no good."

"Well, if you don't want to share my last baggie ever, that's cool, *mon ami*," and he headed toward a bathroom inside the main bar, pausing on his way to talk with people at three different tables. How easily he engaged others never ceased to amaze me — already at home in this bar and on this Gulf Coast where he'd been for maybe an hour.

Coke. I had to admit it. The draw was still there, the high. I could almost feel that first jolt. I congratulated myself on being able to turn it down.

"Maybe we can find some jazz somewhere, eh?" Evan had stopped on his way back to re-engage with one of the couples he'd spoken with earlier.

[275]

"Ain't happenin'. In this neighborhood, nothing but country, and this time of night, not much of that."

"Ain't New Awlins, is it?"

Evan had reserved a hotel room in Pensacola. A drink later, and a little afraid I might give in to the old seduction, I called it a night. Evan said he might "hang here for a while," but promised to return the next day for our afternoon performance. With three days off before our next Flora-Bama session, I would go to New Orleans with Evan for the break.

I looked forward to the trip, catching up with him, then spending time with all the Fontenots — Evan, Elaine, little Pearl for the first time, and Eunice — poor, dear Eunice.

The next morning, Hacksaw, Walter, and I had coffee and eggs, the most nutritious meal of our day every day, then I retreated to my room to pack clothes and that Dopp kit I'd had since boarding the bus for Kansas City and my college freshman year. It was still the nicest thing I owned, and other than my instruments and Ol' Blue, probably the most valuable. We left for our afternoon gig, Ol' Blue clunking and creaking over the back and beach roads, and upon arrival I entrusted Hacksaw with the keys to the complaining but ever-faithful vehicle.

I would leave the Yamaha as well, on the deck where it had lived for several weeks. Considering the humidity and the salt and sand, even though I covered it with a U-Haul blanket after each day's final set, it wasn't the best environment. But I was tiring of the bulky instrument and its demands, including daily tuning, and increasingly less meticulous about its care. Despite lack of ready cash, a newer generation keyboard was in the wings.

* * *

Evan eschewed Interstate 10 for the more scenic and historic U.S. Route 90, also named Beach Highway, where the road hugs the Gulf shoreline. He guided the Mercedes away from the Flora-Bama and deliberately along the mostly two-lane road, summer sun glancing brilliant and blinding off stark-white sand.

In bright daylight, I was struck by changes in Evan since we were last together in New Orleans. Receding hairline, advanced. Eyes bracketed by web-footed wrinkles, narrower and deeper set, their warmth compromised. Face narrowed, not yet gaunt but more serious, teetering on grim. In fact, his entire countenance was thinner, and he appeared the less jolly for it.

Even the scenic route at an unhurried pace should have required no more than four hours, but Evan was extending the trip with stops at gas stations and fast-food restaurants, ostensibly to use the bathrooms. Each time he returned to the car he appeared more agitated, eyes blinking like he couldn't focus, nose twitching uncontrollably, hands less and less willing to settle on the steering wheel. I had little trouble guessing the cause. He wasn't foisting coke on me — out of respect, I assumed, for my declaration of abstinence the night before — but his secrecy about his own use suggested a new distance between us, and a creeping paranoia, a reaction to the drug I knew well but had never seen in Evan.

Yet another stop. Evan returned to the car and I was in the driver's seat.

"If you want to get high, that's cool. I'll drive."

"Yeah, you drive." He got in on the passenger side. "But you are wrong, *mon ami naïve*. I'm not snorting to get high.

[277]

Last night you said it messes with you too much. I'm a mess without it."

I recalled his claim that the previous night's baggie had been his last. I thought of Lee, addicted and helpless. I was scared for Evan.

"Does Eunice know about this?"

I drove maybe twenty miles before he responded. Then, as if there had been no time between question and answer, "Everyone knows now."

Another long silence.

"Have you been arrested?"

"Caught is more like it."

I kept my eyes on the road, gripped the steering wheel a little more tightly, and waited.

"Sometimes the drug has you a little overconfident, you know? I made one too many visits to the john one day during a long trial. What I was doing was obvious enough that the judge, he had one of the court deputies follow me. I guess he heard me snorting because when I came out of the stall he was standing there, shaking his head, a little sorry for me, I think. There was no denying what I'd been doing."

"So what happened?"

"*Naturellement*, I was separated from my client, escorted out of the courtroom. A week later I was suspended by the disciplinary board."

"Are you disbarred?"

"Not yet. But there's not much tolerance in the code of ethics for snorting coke while arguing a case."

Evan slept. I was alone at breakfast with Eunice who had waited up to greet us as we arrived late the previous night, hugging me fiercely then sending me to "your room."

Of course she wanted to know "ev'ry little t'ing" I'd done since leaving New Orleans. My version was selective and condensed, noting that Metropole did well in Atlanta until the club decided to bring in blues bands, which left us half-employed and ultimately to disband. And that the club on the Gulf Coast where Hacksaw, Walter, and I had been playing was better known for country music and our work there would surely be over by Labor Day.

"Then you're coming home?"

Since leaving Atlanta I'd considered returning to New Orleans and trying again to put a band together, this time with musicians serious enough to rehearse, write music, do what was needed to advance our careers and improve our opportunities. But *coming home*? I was reminded of my inebriated argument with Jim Stecky. I hadn't thought of any place as home. Not Kansas City or Florida or Atlanta.

Not even New Orleans.

"Eunice, you make it sound so right. Like New Orleans is home."

"And we are your family. I'd like you to feel that way, Tom. It would make me so happy to know you think of us as family, 'specially now."

The *now* stung — so abrupt. There was nothing to say.

"Tom," Eunice interrupted the silence. "I know Evan tol' you about my cancer. When he called to say you're coming home with him, I asked him did he tell you."

"I'm so sorry, Eunice. It's just not…" I was tearing up.

She reached across the table and covered my hand with hers, swollen and rough with so many years of housekeeping and meal making and dishwashing. "It's okay. I'm fine with it all. I've had me a wonderful life. As good as anyone deserves. I'm ready."

I desperately searched for words that would express how sad I was, how much I wished the cancer wasn't there, how arbitrary and unfair that it should happen to Eunice, but couldn't think of anything helpful or appropriate.

Perhaps there were no words.

"You know, Tom, when you come to my age and you got a disease, the thought of dying, it's not so scary." She rose from the table, stepped to the stove, and leaned over it, bracing herself with both hands, her back to me. "I'm more scared for what I'm leaving behind. Tom, would you do me one really big favor?"

"Of course. Anything."

"I'm so worried for Evan." She turned and looked at me, her eyes narrowed with intensity. "He swears he's done with that dope. And he's agreed to go get him some treatment. But I know it's hard to quit, and a lot of people, they never do. Just tell me you'll help him. Help them make him stop. That you won't let him die of it."

* * *

"Mirror, mirror." I leaned in after shaving, up early this morning to accompany Evan to his appointment at the venerable Touro Infirmary's drug rehab clinic. Perhaps it was the lighting, a lot better than I was used to, but the signs of aging were clear: gray creeping through my hair, crow's feet at corners of my eyes, the beginnings of the dreaded double chin. My days on the beach were done: the summer, the bikinis, the jazz to a setting Gulf sun, the ramshackle house we shared, even decrepit Ol' Blue and the deteriorating Yamaha.

Everything, the good and the bad of it, Metropole and my lovely Muriel, irretrievably past. The present and foreseeable future was here with Evan and Eunice, Elaine and little Pearl, and the adversity dismantling their lives.

Was it coming home, or just here for a time to help a friend? I couldn't know. I simply will stay, I told the mirror. At least for now. Until Evan was on better ground.

Until Eunice…

* * *

As Evan drove, I shared my plan. I'd call the Flora-Bama when we got back home and leave a message for Hacksaw that I would be staying in New Orleans for a while.

"You don't have to stay on my account." But there was no energy behind his protest.

"It's not just on your account."

"*Mon ami, mon ami, mon ami.*" Evan reached across the front seat and tousled my hair. "I'm proud to have such a friend as you."

At a stoplight, Evan pulled a small, amber-colored glass vial from his shirt pocket and unscrewed the cap to which a tiny spoon was attached by a short chain. He dipped the spoon into the bottle twice, one to each nostril. "It's my going-away party. Wanna join me?"

I ignored the extended hand and bottle. "You know, you look terrible, like you haven't slept in days."

"Not far from wrong, *mon ami.*"

We turned into Touro. Evan pulled the Mercedes to the back of the parking lot where he finished off the contents of the vial. He inhaled the last scoop then reached across me and opened the glove compartment. He tossed the vial in and extracted what looked like a cordless phone but without a base, and held it out.

"You want to call Pensacola, use this."

Concerned it might be fragile, I accepted it gingerly, then realized what it was, this gadget with the name Motorola at the bottom. I'd used a wireless phone once, Joe's at the Flora-Bama. It was in a case in his car, huge and awkward compared to what Evan handed me.

"Go ahead, call," Evan said.

With some additional instruction, I was able to make the call. But I heard no ringing, nothing.

Evan sighed. "That's the problem with these things. It's hard to find places they work. We can try it again later."

Evan tossed the phone back into the glove compartment. "Part of Touro's instructions," he explained while we walked toward the hospital entrance. "'Patients must check their cellular phones at the reception desk.'" Perhaps Touro had already come to realize the value of a portable phone to an addict.

I flipped through waiting room magazines for more than two hours before Evan appeared. The equilibrium he had been trying to maintain with the drug was gone, and he was visibly anxious, scratching at his chest and arms through his shirt and alternately swiping the back of his hand across a runny nose.

"They're admitting me. Want me here now." He fidgeted, scratched, then steadied and smiled at me. Far from his mischievous grin, or *espièglerie* as Evan preferred, suggesting another drink or accompanying a tap on the knee, it was a smile of surrender.

It was my turn to speak. "I'll take the Mercedes back to the house and tell Eunice. We'll bring you some clothes and…well…whatever you want."

Evan took hold of me by my shoulders. "Tom, as an attorney I've always had to look into people's heads and ignore what's in their hearts. But you, I never once got past your heart. It's what's best about you, what makes for such good music. For sure it's all you need. Everything else doesn't matter."

The door from which Evan had emerged remained open. A large, stoic-looking man in white scrubs stood sentry. Evan reentered; the man pulled the door closed behind him.

A lock clicked.

At home, Eunice was pleased Touro had admitted her Evan, her hopes tied to this abiding institution that had cared for New Orleanians for more than a hundred years through yellow fever epidemics, the Civil War, Jim Crow laws and integration, and two world wars.

* * *

"Hey man, haven't you been getting my messages?" I'd been calling for almost two weeks, leaving messages at the Flora-Bama for Hacksaw that I wasn't going to get back in time for this week's gigs, then several more, each more detailed, including the Fontenot house phone number.

"Yeah, yeah. Everything's cool. How's your buddy?"

"He's currently the guest of an old, revered institution here, doing a couple of weeks of inpatient rehab. Don't know what after that."

"Terrible drug. I talked to Lee, and he's hooked up with one of the blues bands playing Cousin Ned's. They do some road gigs, too."

"He can put a bottom under anything. He'll make any band better."

"He sounds rough. Worse than when we left him."

"Damn. I thought when you said he's working that, maybe, he'd cleaned up his act."

"Blues guys? Slim chance."

"Listen, Hack, I'm staying in New Orleans for a bit. Gonna hang here with Evan's family. They're going through all kinds of shit. Probably see if I can get some piano bar work here for a while."

Hacksaw did not reply, as if to say *no explanation required*.

I asked, "You plan on coming back to New Orleans anytime soon? Not much going on at the beach after Labor Day was what I understood."

"I've been talking to Walter. He left two days after you and he's there, living with this girl in Metairie. A teacher. They've got a pad in the basement with its own bath that they're going to rent out. Says I can have it, so I guess I'll take him up on it."

"Cool, maybe we could get a bass player and drummer and pick up a night here and there." Thinking about the possibility made me smile.

"There you go. Never say die. Me, I might lay low for a while. Like Walter. He's playing the Sunday jazz brunch at the Sonesta, but that's it. Got a day job with a pest control company. Sounds like he's being dragged off the bandstand and marched to the altar."

"Pest control? Well, you gotta admit there's a lot of security in that. Always be rats in New Orleans. Hey, when you come, would you mind bringing my stuff with you? You can drive the van. Ol' Blue should have one more road trip in her."

"Sure. Except for the Yamaha. The beast is dead. Couldn't hold a tune past eight bars. We buried her in the back of one of Joe's storage barns."

"It's not surprising when someone suffering from a dopamine deficiency self-medicates to feel better," a small man in a gray lab coat with "Touro" embroidered in large letters above the left pocket explained to Eunice, Elaine, and me. Evan's dependency was controllable with medication, he assured us, but Evan would need counseling, too, though for now he'd remain in an inpatient wing.

Evan's confinement coupled with Eunice's cancer left a fragile Elaine virtually helpless. If only by elimination, I was now responsible for many of the family's daily activities. I drove Eunice to her oncologist appointments, took Eunice and Elaine to visit Evan, even went to Schwegmann's to "make groceries." None of it was drudgery.

I hadn't played a piano or sung a note in weeks or talked to anyone about work until one Saturday afternoon.

"Can you play tonight?" It was Ricky, though he didn't identify himself. "Some good players. At Tip's."

"Ricky, is that you?"

"Can you play? The guy who called me, Jack Rush, said he remembered you from Metropole. Said it would be cool if you could make it."

"I'm a bit rusty. Haven't seen a piano in a blue moon."

"Well, come and reacquaint yourself — on Fess' keys."

Tipitina's and good players. Eunice would want me to. I might even be able to get her and Elaine out for a night.

"Okay. Wish I could get a few practice licks in though."

"Warm up with your solo act. Do a first set. They'll be cool with that."

"Can I get paid for it? I'm kind of broke with not playing all these weeks."

"They'll cover you. It's Tip's, man."

New Orleans always seemed, and maybe would forever seem, on the brink of economic collapse. But in the years since my departure, times had become particularly tough. The '84 World's Fair, which was supposed to rejuvenate the local economy, furthered the decline kick-started by an early '80s oil glut and the devaluation of Louisiana's most precious natural resource. I'd heard that musicians were suffering in kind.

"It's bullshit," Ricky rebutted as we set up for the night. "If you can play, there's plenty of work." He talked as he tuned, rapping a drumstick sharply on the head of each drum.

"Some of the old clubs shut down. But places like Tip's, they'll always draw. And there's new life in other neighborhoods. Like the Marigny. Frenchman Street's the new Bourbon. And clubs in Bywater and the Upper Ninth Ward and even a couple opening in the Warehouse District."

In fact, live music remained abundant in New Orleans. Breakfast restaurants hired players to bang out tunes on uprights while families waited for eggs and ham. In every quarter, bars filled to accompaniment: from a singer with a guitar in a dark corner of a West Bank dive to the Neville Brothers on stage in Jackson Square; from bluegrass to blues, zydeco to Dixieland.

No matter how poor or distressed, the people of New Orleans were least willing to give up their music. And of all the venues, Tipitina's reigned — the players, the crowds, the cachet. So long away, I didn't realize how much I'd missed the city, and was grateful to be here and part of it again.

Ricky's promise was honored. I worked through some awkwardness in the opening selection of an arrangement of "One Note Samba" as patrons funneled through the entrance, the first thirty or so to ante up the ten-dollar cover charge claiming the seats in front of the bandstand. But I was soon comfortable, the companionship of keyboard and voice through an arrangement of Ellington's "Don't Get Around Much Anymore" with a Fats Waller-style stride accompaniment in the bridge. Reminded of the pleasure of playing music well, I tested myself with my take on Steely Dan's "Deacon Blues." A concluding song, my song:

> *We'll make a place in the lives*
> *that we planned*
> *And here we'll stay until it's time*
> *for you to go*

THE MUSICIAN

As I struck the final chord, Jack Rush was onstage, picking up on my ending note, extending it on tenor sax into an introductory line to "Little Sunflower," that Metropole staple, Rush's gesture of respect to Ricky and me. One by one, players joined in, a bass player, then Ricky, then three young, energetic players — soprano sax, trumpet, and trombone — mounted the stage and soloed from the edge, introducing themselves to band and audience.

Rush was admirable in how he controlled the night. The sets were well planned, starting with modest tempos and building in intensity, from the predictable "Blue Bossa" to more arcane selections, including Wayne Shorter's nearly impossible — at least for me — "Endangered Species." My turn to stretch came in a break from the quickening pace, a fifteen-minute version of "When Sunny Gets Blue," including several sung verses and a series of arpeggios McCoy Tyner would have approved of.

The mix was eclectic: the funk, capitalizing on the Metropole feel; the straight-ahead pieces, Miles' lingering "So What" and something from Coltrane's perplexing "Love Supreme," to demonstrate the considerable virtuosity on stage this night; and in honor of the ever-present spirit of the Professor, a freelance on a couple of iconic Longhair tunes, ending the set with "Big Chief" to a standing ovation.

My time away from a keyboard, brief as it had been, left me more fresh than rusty, and immersion in the disarray of the Fontenot household, efforts to assuage some of the anguish and distress, infused my playing with new insight, a kind of maturity. How comfortable, and shielded, here behind this piano and microphone. How appreciative of the opportunity to make music: the association of players; our tacit, intimate communication; the solos from tender to edgy to violent; and the pulse. Fulfillment unlike any other.

It was nearly two o'clock when we packed up, congratulated each other on our playing, and parted, exhausted with our night's work and the exuberant Tipitina's crowd.

Ambling through Uptown to find Evan's car, I hummed "Big Chief," and was still relishing the night's highlights when I pulled into the driveway and walked through the front door. I had started up the stairs when Elaine burst from her bedroom.

She clutched a sleepy-eyed Pearl to her breast. "Eunice. A stroke. The ambulance just carried her to Touro. We got to go. You got to help us."

Little was said on the way. Pearl sniveled and Elaine held her close. I was scared, considering the stroke, the possibility Eunice might never again be herself, our *Mère* Fontenot.

* * *

The reception area was sterile, silent. We sat in hard metal chairs. I was up and down, pacing the white tile floor.

It was more than an hour after we'd arrived and checked in that a bushy-haired man in surgical gown and mask came through a door behind the receptionist's desk. He approached and lowered his mask; it was Eunice's oncologist. Elaine rose to stand at my shoulder, Pearl at her side attached by two fists full of Elaine's dress. The physician, expressionless.

"We have her on a ventilator." His voice was flat and professional though not uncaring. "She's not responding to external stimuli."

"But she's gonna be okay, right?"

"I'm sorry, Elaine. It's the cancer. I'm so sorry. She's," he paused, maybe to find better words, "not coming back."

Elaine, eyes filling with tears, stood in stunned silence, surely mustering all the lectures she'd received from Eunice about handling this inevitable misery, this most damnable of things that she couldn't undo.

I watched her, my eyes welling, too, and Pearl, her face buried in her mother's dress.

"Evan, we need Evan," I appealed to the doctor. "Does Evan know? Has anybody told Evan?"

The doctor was puzzled. "I thought he would be with you."

"No," Elaine corrected. "He's here at Touro, in the rehab center."

"Oh. No," the physician uttered painstakingly slow as yet another episode in this hapless drama unfolded. He eased Elaine into a chair and sat by her. "Evan was released yesterday. Said he wanted to spend a few days with Eunice. His doctor and I agreed it would be good for them both."

* * *

In accordance with the living will Eunice had Evan draw up as soon as she'd learned of her cancer, and with Elaine and me bedside, the ventilator was turned off.

I arranged the funeral for St. Francis of Assisi Catholic Church, leaving Elaine to her heartbreak and Pearl, her sole diversion. The Thursday mid-morning service consisted of a brief mass and a few vacuous platitudes from a priest who'd never met Eunice. Few attended, fewer than Eunice might feed in a single night at her table. The altar was adorned by a single floral arrangement sent by Evan's office. And Elaine, Pearl, and I shivered through the November drizzle, alone with the priest at the burial plot, also bought and paid for in advance by Eunice.

No one Elaine or I called — friends, neighbors, bartenders — had seen or heard from Evan. And without Evan to make drinks and Eunice to cook, the Fontenot home stayed eerily quiet.

Even hangers-on would have been welcome.

Drained and dejected, I lost all initiative. For weeks, I can't recall how many, I spent the days alone, at the used Fender Rhodes I'd purchased from the same Werlein's clerk who'd sold me the CP70 all those years before. But I hardly practiced, sometimes sitting for hours without striking a key. I might wander out in the evenings, but only for something to eat, a po' boy from a nearby bar, but never into the Quarter to Brennan's or the Nap House, or anyplace else someone might ask about Evan.

I turned to reflection. My efforts had accomplished nothing for Evan, nor for Eunice, and I could do nothing to console Elaine or Pearl. Even Dropsy was disconsolate. It served as metaphor for my life, from folk house to piano bar to jazz club, an existence decided for me by indifferent agents, fickle bar owners, and purposeless band members, all shaped by waves of disinterest. I had little money, few possessions, and fewer friends. I agonized over Evan: had I misjudged him so thoroughly as not to see that he could abandon his family and our friendship when he was most needed?

THE MUSICIAN

At Evan's insistence, ownership of the Fontenot home had been transferred to Elaine at the announcement of her pregnancy and impending marriage, then protected by prenup from what proved an ugly dispute with a boorish, indolent husband. But without Evan's support, Elaine fell quickly and hopelessly behind on the mortgage. The shotgun had to be sold.

A young couple, a lawyer and her CPA husband, bought it for the asking price two days after it was listed. I moved Elaine into a two-bedroom apartment near a public school Pearl would attend in a couple of years, and I rented a six hundred square-foot flat deep in the French Quarter, on Burgundy near Barracks, reclaiming from storage the furniture Evan had removed from the Lakeview house.

"Anything yet from Evan or anyone who knows where he is?" I was in Evan's law office. His secretary was at her desk, though it was evident she had nothing to do. Blonde curls dancing at her shoulders reminded me of Muriel.

"Good to see ya, Tom. Been awhile."

"Been layin' low. But it's time to get back into the fray. Confront the demons. Starting here."

"You playing somewhere?"

"I need to. About out of money. There are three or four places I've been thinking about. Couple of good rooms in the Quarter. Maybe one of them."

"Be sure to let me know. I'll get the girls together for your opening night."

"Thanks, Jill. So, about Evan?"

"Nothing. Completely disappeared. You're not the only one looking for him. He has so many friends, Tom. And his clients — even though the partners have taken over his cases, they always ask first if Evan is back when they call or come in." She looked across her desk at the phone like she expected it to ring.

"What a bum he turned out to be," I muttered, mostly to myself, and turned to go. Next demon: the Nap House.

I made the familiar walk, pushed open the door and, not ready yet for familiar faces, went directly to the table by the window that looked out on St. Louis Street. It was early afternoon and, with the exception of the clatter of cutlery being arranged over white tablecloths in the connecting restaurant, three tourist couples at a table near the bathrooms consulting their city guides, and a few locals bent over their drinks at the bar, the place was quiet.

I sat mindlessly staring at my bourbon, stirring it with a straw. I'd stirred long enough to melt the ice when a tap on the table alerted me to a man in blue jeans and a white sleeveless tee shirt standing at my chair.

"I know you got troubles, you, over your friend, Evan. Maybe a little angry too. Like he done let his family down, let you down, got caught up in them drugs, put you in a bad spot."

Coal-colored eyes and heavy black eyebrows governed his rugged face. He was young, probably early thirties, with bulging forearms and biceps, the arms of a man who does heavy labor. He spoke with a heavy accent, the southern part of the state but not New Orleans. He rested a hand on my shoulder in a consoling gesture, then pulled a chair from the table and sat down. He waved to a waiter. "Bring me mine," and pointed to my bourbon, "and one for this man."

"Excuse me, Mr...?"

"Cormier, Adam Cormier. Of Lafayette."

There was that brand of self-assurance in his approach that reminded me of the people who consider it their mission in life to go around spreading hope among the disillusioned — the last thing I needed.

"Are you from a church, or the hospital, or some religious group? Who sent you here?"

"Nobody done sent me. Evan's secretary, she tol' me where I'd likely find you. Jill and I go way back. Me and Evan, too. I tol' her, call me if you come by. 'Cause I want a talk wit' you."

"Well, let me make this quick and easy. Right now, I don't much give a shit about Evan. He deserted his family when things got tough. Drugs or no drugs, there's no excuse for that."

The man emptied his glass and, ignoring my snub, waved at our waiter for another round.

"Evan said what good friends you were, and you, such a good singer and piano player."

"So?" I downed the first of the three drinks that sat in front of me and picked up a second.

"I thought I might tell you somet'ing make you feel better 'bout Evan."

I thought to end this conversation, rid myself of this intrusion. "Evan lied to the doctors to get out of the hospital, to escape any responsibility, any obligation. Eunice is dead, and he wasn't there for her. Nothing you can tell me changes any of that."

"Lemme tell you a little story 'bout Evan and what he done for this dumb coonass."

He was showing no signs of giving up on me, and the bourbons were slowing my resistance.

"When I came back from Vietnam I started USL in Lafayette on that GI Bill. I went for t'ree semesters, but I was no good at it, me, so I quit. My uncle, he got me this offshore oilfield job, in the patch, a roustabout wit' Schlumberger. Then I got me a job wit' a driller operating a crane. A big deal going from hourly to salaried. Third week on the job, I fall off a access ladder on the rig. Rung give way, and smack, I hit the deck about twenty feet down, flat on my back, me.

"I was disabled, on what they call 'maintenance and cure.' The company has to pay that. It's the law. Seventeen dollar a day and medical expenses."

Again Cormier signaled the waiter for drinks. "A few months in, I get me a letter from the company sayin' I had 'maximum medical cure.' No more payments. Their roomful of lawyers dug up some records on a ten-year-old back injury. It wasn't even no injury, just a strain. I was takin' a muscle relaxer and treatments between trips to the patch. Never missed an hour of work. But they figured that was enough to get 'em off the hook.

"My uncle tol' me 'bout a lawyer he knew that took rig workers' cases. I didn't care much for lawyers, specially then, but funny how that changes when you need you one, eh? So I come to New Awlins to talk wit' Evan, and I know right away I can trust him."

"Yeah. I trusted him too. Never knew anybody I trusted so much." I was on my third or maybe it was a fourth bourbon; I didn't know and surely don't remember now. Anyway between the booze and the sentiment, I was growing more despondent than angry.

"First t'ing, Evan sends the company a letter sayin' to start up my payments again. I'll never forget how Evan read it when he got their answer: 'Your request is denied without further discussion or negotiation.' Well, I thought, that was that. Thanks for tryin'.

"Then Evan files suit in Lafayette. And what do you t'ink? They was in cahoots with the judges there, pro'bly in each others' pockets, 'cause no matter how many times Evan tries to get us a hearing, they're puttin' us off.

"It went on so long, I got real depressed." Cormier paused, but only to guzzle another of the dark drinks, darker and taller than mine.

"Then I got addicted to pain meds. This quack in Lafayette was writin' scrips anytime I wanted. I was t'inkin' crazy. Started blamin' Evan for my problems. I'd show up at the law firm and yell at him, right there in front of Jill and his partners — they was about to call the cops a couple times — 'bout how he wasn't doin' me no good, that I should get me another lawyer. And he'd take me into his office, sit there and listen to me go on, and calm me down. Sometime we'd talk a couple hours."

"I can see him doing that." Now I was the one motioning for more drinks. "Yeah, I can see him doing that."

"Finally, Evan gets the case moved to New Awlins. He sets it up with a judge where a court reporter is gonna take my deposition. I drive in the night before and Evan, he puts me up in a really nice hotel here in the French Quarter near his office. But I get so fucked up on meds I miss the deposition. Don't wake up, me, till Evan come to the hotel bangin' on my door."

I remembered how Evan, no matter how reckless our ramblings, was always able to negotiate the madness and bring a night to a calm, reasonable conclusion.

"Now you might t'ink that's about as much as any lawyer would put up with for some low-life client," Cormier continued. "But not Evan. No, no. He takes me to his house. That room you was in. He takes my pills and stays with me the whole night, me screamin' at him, then threat'nin' him,

[298]

then beggin' for my dope. And he keeps tellin' me I got to do this, and he wasn't goin' to let me do it alone.

"Next morning, we come down for breakfast, and that sweet Eunice puts me a big plate of eggs and grits on the table and pats me on the head like I'm some lost puppy they done took in."

Cormier chugged another tall drink and waved a finger at me. "That very day Evan introduces me to a former client of his who's now a drug counselor for the VA. Been drug-free and sober ever since, me."

I was reeling from all the bourbon, but couldn't help but question his assertion. I pointed to his latest drink, at least his fifth or sixth.

"Black tea, cold but no ice."

I buried my face in my hands.

"By the way, we won that case and I'm gettin' a lot more than that seventeen dollar a day they tried to weasel outta. But more'n that, I got me a friend for life. So when Jill tol' me you was likely here, I thought I'd be a real bastard not at least to let you know my story so maybe you won't be so mad wit' Evan, and maybe you give him another chance when you see him."

"*If* I see him again."

Adam Cormier stood, reached across the table, lowered an eyebrow over a black eyeball, and patted me on the arm, then he stopped at the bar on the way out to pay the tab. I stayed, stirring and drinking, looking out on St. Louis Street at the tourists gawking in every direction, filled with wonder, so taken by New Orleans.

"Tom, you need to go home now."

It was Evan's favorite waiter. "Camille, right?"

"That's me, Tom. You right. Come on now, let's get you to the cab."

"Thanks, but I didn't call a cab, did I?" I tried to stand but dropped back into the chair.

"Come on, Tom, let's get you home." Camille helped me out of the chair then into the back seat of a cab at the Nap House door. I gave the driver an address, then passed out as he pulled from the curb.

I awoke to the driver shaking me by the shoulders. "You're home."

We were in the driveway of Evan's old house.

A rented three-room flat in the French Quarter. Evan and Eunice had wanted me to think of New Orleans as home; this was just the place for someone without a home.

I thought often of Evan. If I saw him at my door I'd forgive all. And Muriel — would her life unfold as she'd mapped it out, she and her children welcoming a proud father from a diligent day's work to an elegant home?

One afternoon from my studio, the converted living room, I picked up the phone from the TV tray next to the Fender Rhodes and dialed a number so easy to recall even though it had been more than a decade.

"Hello, Tommy. What a nice surprise." The voices of grown children argued in the background.

"Sorry to bother you. Sounds like you have company."

"Not company. We all live here, five of us in this two-bedroom apartment."

I didn't know what to ask first — who, when, or why? "Cousins? Nephews? Ah, I got it. Your friend and her kids?"

"My husband and his. Two boys, two and three years older than Janice. They're both tall for their age, and blond. Janice adores them."

"So how long…?"

"Just since June. It's why we're still here. They moved from Salina. Ed was teaching at Wesleyan, now at UMKC."

What did I expect? That she'd still be single and pining for me twenty years since I'd seen her?

"I'm happy for you, Penny — and for Janice."

"So how are you? How's your music? Still traveling town to town?"

"No. Got off the road and settled in New Orleans. Great place to be a musician. Lots of good rooms to play, and great audiences, and…well…honestly, Penny, things aren't all that great. Not so great at all. I remembered how you could always put things in perspective. Make me feel better about things…"

I immediately regretted saying it, come crying to a girl I hadn't seen or talked to in so long, and who, really, I'd barely known — and who's married.

"Tommy, I'm glad you felt that way about me. And if you're ever back in Kansas City you should look us up. We'll all go out for dinner somewhere."

I hadn't talked to anyone in my family for a long time either. Didn't have phone numbers for any of my brothers, and had only called the folks once or twice since Dad retired and sold the company and they moved to Sarasota.

"Thomas, it's you. Are you okay?" She never ceased being the worrier.

"I'm fine, Mom. How's everybody?"

"I'm fine." A sigh. "Don't know about your brothers. Like you, who calls? Oh, it's so good to hear from you, dear. So...what? You have news? Like a job or a girl?"

"I have a job, Mom. Just thought I'd call. How's Dad?"

"He's taking his afternoon nap. And you know — well, you probably don't know — his instructions are not to wake him unless someone has died or the house is on fire."

"Just thought I'd say hello."

"Honey, he's not doing so well. He's tired all the time and just grouses about how he spent his life working to raise seven kids and nobody respected what he did enough to follow in his footsteps, and blah, blah, blah. He'd just grumble about how you squandered the education he paid for. When he's up later, I'll tell him you called and we had a nice chat."

Next up, Artie Reardon. He'd surely be glad to hear about how I'm playing, all I learned since those early sessions with him. But the number I had for him was no longer in service. Probably still at the El Dorado. He said he'd be playing there till he was fired or got in the way of a Mafia bullet one night. I called Information for Miami, then got the front desk at the Fontainebleau.

"Hello, can you tell me if Artie Reardon is still playing in the lounge?"

"Hold please."

"El Dorado. This is Chris."

"Chris, this is Tom Cliffe. I used to sing there many years ago. Trying to reach Artie Reardon. He still the house pianist?"

"Artie's gone."

"Do you know where he's playing? Or how I could get in touch with him?"

"I mean he's dead. Been several years now. Had a stroke one night here at the piano. Some drunk lady at the piano bar screeching into the microphone," he scoffed. "Thought he was kidding and was yelling at him to get up so she could finish her song. Ugly scene. By the time the paramedics got here, it was just too late. A really nice guy. Too bad."

I replaced the handset. Yeah, too bad, the whole thing. All of it.

* * *

Almost immediately the phone rang.

"Tom, this is Woodrow Tyler." The caller paused as if he expected to be recognized.

I was still preoccupied with thoughts of my old friend and mentor, parents, first love, and always, always when feeling sorriest for myself, Muriel.

I finally broke what had been at least thirty seconds of dead air.

"Can I help you?"

"You don't know who I am?"

"I'm sorry, no."

"I'm your dream come true."

Great timing for a scam. Free cruise to the Caribbean; just give him the numbers on the credit card I don't have. I considered hanging up, but instead, vented. "Ah-h-h, finally, your call has come. The annuity that guarantees a lifetime of financial security."

"Could be. If you're as good on record as you are in person."

I wasn't so distraught that "record" didn't command attention, even if I'd long ago given up hope of ever recording anything but a demo.

This time the caller broke the silence.

"Tom, I'm a producer, independent record producer. I work with local talent. A few have done pretty well for themselves. You might have heard of Irma Thomas? Ernie K-Doe?" He paused to allow time for the awe those names inspired to take hold. "I was in Tip's a while back, the night you played with Jack Rush."

I was grappling with too many images, having a hard time fighting through unconnected thoughts: of recording, of the luminaries he'd named, of the Tipitina's performance the night Eunice died, of those disheartening phone conversations I'd just had, of whether this guy was a producer or a prankster.

"I heard your warm-up set. Think you have a unique voice that might play well on vinyl."

Even if the guy was for real, there was *the* problem.

"Mr. Tyler, thanks. I've thought so for a long time, and dreamed of a chance to prove it. But I don't have anything to record. No originals. I just do other people's songs."

"Not an issue." Tyler's response was quick and firm. "How about you and I meet for coffee at Café du Monde tomorrow morning?"

* * *

I arrived at Café du Monde early enough to finish off two cups of Chock full o'Nuts, *au lait,* and a sack of beignets as an antidote to the seething intestinal distress that drinking the acidic blend straight had once inflicted upon me. About an hour and a half in, Woodrow Tyler was more than a half hour late. "Should I stay or should I go?" the punk lyric teased. Fat chance I'd be going.

"Sorry. Couldn't get out of the lawyer's office." Tyler was tall, imposing, maybe five or so years older than me, with a strong, square chin, and thick gray hair combed straight back to expose a deeply furrowed forehead. Most conspicuous were his glasses, coke-bottle thick lenses in a fat black frame. "Once some of you guys get a little taste of success, signing you for a second album gets sticky. Suddenly you want all kinds of guarantees."

Second album? I'd sell my soul to have a single getting occasional play on a local jazz station.

"I'll tell you, Tom, straight out. I get my best results when we can have an open and trusting relationship."

Relationship? Really? If references to second albums and guarantees were designed to get me salivating, it was working. I'd try to remain cautiously skeptical, but I was excited — and jacked up by the Chock full 'o Nuts.

"Mr. Tyler, I've spent damn near twenty years trying to get to a meeting like this. So I won't be quibbling over a few dollars. I just want to get into a studio and come away with something people will want to hear."

Tyler studied me for a moment, perhaps gauging my sincerity, maybe, I hoped, appreciating my maturity.

"I've come into a couple of songs that I think would be just right for you. Ballads. Nice lyrics. Pretty melodies."

That was it. The answer. I didn't need my own originals.

"The way it works is we get the basic tracks laid, then shop them to the labels. When we get a bite, we go back into the studio for the finishing touches. Any label that buys us will want an album's worth of cuts, and that's where your other stuff comes in, your arrangements, like the ones you played that night at Tip's."

"Mr. Tyler."

"Woody."

"Woody. One more thing. I'd like to know what you saw, what you heard that made you want to record me."

"Certainly not what I saw," he laughed an engaging laugh. "Not even what I heard. It was what I felt."

Tyler got it. It wasn't about technical prowess or range or even voice quality, but how I connected with my audience, what I'd been best at throughout my not-so-illustrious career.

"So are you in?" He didn't have to ask and I didn't need to answer. I simply reached across the table and shook his hand. "Good then." Tyler stood to leave. "I'll drop by your place in the morning with the songwriters and a contract."

* * *

"Mr. Cliffe, it's an honor to meet you." When was the last time anyone had addressed me as Mr. Cliffe? "In high school, my buddies and I, all of us jazz freaks, used to hang out outside the music bars in the Quarter. Our favorite was the Old Absinthe Bar when Metropole played it."

Woodrow Tyler had introduced the songwriter as Eddie Cobb, "a fine young fellow from the Ninth Ward, with promise." You could read admiration in the boy's eyes from across the street. It was a little embarrassing. What if I hated his tune?

In fact, "My World of Broken Dreams" was quite good, I thought, as Eddie Cobb sat at my piano and played through it. The singer's heart had been broken by a woman who loved him but was "tied to another for my life." I could play the part with conviction.

The other songwriter was less gregarious, more like surly, a kid with an attitude. His song, "A Stone's Throw from Your Heart," was country in lyrics and melody, simple and redundant, but "with a gumbo blues feel…if you can do that," he challenged.

"I'll leave you guys to your work." Tyler excused himself, then stopping on his way out at the piano, handed me a single sheet of paper. "Says I own you to the tune of twenty percent for these two songs and anything that comes of them. If you're okay with it, just sign and I'll get it next time I see you."

I would be absolutely fine with it.

Learning original songs was a peculiar experience, making music out of songs that had never been recorded or performed. I had no reference to how they were supposed to sound. And no matter how I sang them, it wasn't what Eddie, who grew less awestruck as the afternoon progressed, or the other songwriter, I'd already forgotten his name, had in mind.

Worse, they didn't know what they wanted, just that, "You don't get it."

None of which could dampen my spirits. They might be too young, too new to this to be humbled by the opportunity, but I'd waited too long to be anything but delighted and determined.

I recalled Tyler's explanation of what he liked about me.

"Guys, I am who I am. I sing how I sing. I know they're your songs, but I have to sing them 'My Way.'" I sang the Sinatra lyric in jest to a quizzical look from both.

But they got the point. At least Eddie said he understood.

"It's going to be great. Don't worry," I said, letting them out of my flat onto a dark and musty Burgundy Street.

It was a week. Then two. I thought to call Tyler but then thought better of it. Don't want to appear needy. If I'd learned anything about the business side of music, it was that no one accommodated the needy.

A third week. I decided to call. I could keep myself above needy.

"Mr. Tyler, what's up? Haven't heard anything in weeks." Damn. I definitely sounded needy.

"Woody, Tom. Sorry about not being in touch but there's lots to get done on the production end, mainly scheduling — musicians, engineers, the studio. Hang in. I'll let you know as things progress."

"How are they progressing so far?" But Tyler had already hung up.

Two weeks later came Tyler's call. "How's the sixteenth for you?"

He could have asked for the twelfth of never.

* * *

I'd been playing cocktail hour sets at the Bienville House, just a few blocks from my flat, and spending the rest of my days and nights on the two originals, poring over every phrase, every bar, refining, improving. I worked three straight days with an arranger sent to learn how I was interpreting the songs so he could write charts "for the studio cats." I grew as comfortable with these originals as a rat in a French Quarter dumpster.

The session was to start at midnight. I hailed a cab outside my front door and gave the driver the studio address. The neighborhood was one of the few areas of the Warehouse District that hadn't been revitalized in anticipation of the Louisiana World Exposition, and none of the mostly dilapidated warehouses had posted addresses. We drove the street, four or five blocks worth, back and forth several times, stopping and pointing and shaking our heads, disagreeing and agreeing in very different languages, before settling on the most likely location. I hurried through an open security gate and across a broken concrete floor, up a set of wooden stairs and through, I discovered upon entering, the back door of the studio control room.

I was greeted with disapproving glares from Woody, another man sitting behind a soundboard, apparently the engineer, and both songwriters.

"Thrilled you could join us," the kid with the attitude snarled.

"We only have a couple hours, Tom," Tyler scolded. "Let's get busy."

I descended to the studio floor, to an area enclosed on three sides by floor-to-ceiling panels. A microphone dangled from a boom stand large enough to double as a construction crane. A drummer, enclosed in a small, separate room, sat motionless. A bass player leaned against the closed door of the drum room, his hands crossed over the strings of his Fender, eyes closed. A third studio cat sat cross-legged at a shiny black grand studying a chart and cracking his knuckles.

I leaned into the microphone and looked up through the control room window. "Woody? Can you hear me?"

Tyler bent over the engineer's shoulder into the control room microphone. "Yes, Tom, what is it?"

"I thought I'd be at the piano."

"We're going to lay a rhythm track with your vocals tonight. You don't need to focus on anything but singing. Headsets, everybody," Tyler barked. "Let's get this show on the road."

An introduction to "My World of Broken Dreams" was nowhere near what I'd been practicing, faster and set to some sort of syncopated Latin rhythm. A first take was awkward, like the studio musicians were playing a different song than I'd learned. A second take was better; I even recognized some of what the arranger and I had decided on. A third seemed quite good. I'd been doing vocal calisthenics all afternoon and my tone and control were at their best.

I looked up through the control room window and saw Eddie and Woody conferring, the songwriter animated. Then Woody was back on the control room mic.

"I thought that was pretty good. We'll save that cut, but let's do it again."

I stopped halfway through a fourth take, stumbling over a phrase in the bridge, again early in a fifth, then managed to get through a sixth take but less convincingly. I was trying to evoke the image of Muriel in tears, but she wasn't cooperating: it sounded more like work than music. Eddie threw his arms in the air in exasperation, then Woody leaned over the engineer again.

"Let's take a few minutes, then try 'Stone's Throw.'"

The musicians pulled off their headsets. The bass player lit a cigarette. I stayed in place. No one spoke.

We experimented with a couple of verses of "A Stone's Throw from Your Heart," trying unsuccessfully for a working blend of country and blues genres. Again, the studio musicians and I were at odds. The engineer called for a second take, but before we could begin, Woody was on the studio floor, talking first with the pianist, then the drummer.

He came to me. His eyes appeared to bulge and blur through those glasses.

"The writer wants a peppier tempo. We're going to pick it up a bit and go harder on the downbeat. See if you can get a feel for it."

The *feel* was distinctly country, and what I distinctly never was was country. We made a couple of passes at it, and while the instrumentalists seemed able to pick up on it, I couldn't.

Two hours and no usable tape. The musicians packed and departed. The songwriters followed in a huff. The engineer was preparing for a next session. I moved to the piano, admiring the long and slender grand, sat sideways on the bench and fingered a few keys.

Woody's voice once more from the control room: "Gotta go, Tom. Our next session's on the way in."

I climbed the stairs, stood for a moment, and without a word or glance from Woody or the engineer, left through the back door. Crossing the crumbling concrete, I passed five teenagers in dashikis strutting toward the studio. At the street, I turned toward the Quarter.

My phone rang early the following morning, too early for anyone with good news.

"The songwriters are out." Woody never identified himself when I picked up the phone, just blurted out whatever he had to say.

"The songwriters?" I was perplexed.

"Sorry."

"But you're the producer. It's your project, right? You're the one making the decisions."

"It's their money. The studio, the musicians, the engineer, the arranger – and me. Eddie liked the way you did 'Broken Dreams' but they're in this together. They decided it'd go smoother, you know, quicker, with someone more comfortable in a studio."

"Okay, look. I should have been more assertive. I should have insisted on doing the piano, doing these songs the way I practiced them. I worked on these tunes for weeks. Made them mine. That's why you signed me, right?" I was begging, and hating myself for it.

"The contract ties us together if we make money." Tyler sounded irritated. "Nowhere does it say I have to back a loser. Sorry, but I promised I'd be straight with you. You had your shot. You blew it."

Something was balling up in my stomach. Surely this could be fixed.

"Okay, so I'm new to studio work. You said Eddie liked me for 'Broken Dreams.' Maybe we can talk them into one more try."

"No second chances in this business. Maybe if you were twenty years younger…"

I spent the rest of the morning in bed, but not sleeping. I got up sometime around noon and despite the ache in my gut, thought I should eat something. I started on a baloney and cheese sandwich, but the last two slices of bread were covered with mold. Too old. I made coffee and sat at the table near the kitchen, staring for what must have been hours at the scars that spread across its cardboard surface. I couldn't keep myself from an occasional glance at the Rhodes, the innocent bystander in the middle of the flat, nor could I stand the sight of it.

So I opted for the distraction of noisy French Quarter streets. I wandered aimlessly into the sultry New Orleans evening among wide-eyed tourists and harried locals, past brawling threats and raucous laughter spilling out of barroom doors, passing swank establishments of fine dining and side-street oyster bars, negotiating narrow aisles of the Central Grocery, skirting the lineup of mule-drawn carriages on Decatur Street.

Without plan or purpose, and changing direction from time to time to avoid a familiar face, I followed the course of so many afternoons and evenings, from Brennan's and the Monteleone, toward the River and Chart House, a few blocks to the Napoleon House. I stopped to take in the attempts of a few of the lingering late-night portrait painters and street players in Jackson Square, then turned back, past Johnny White's and Cosimo's, walking and churning till nearly midnight before finding myself where I was likely headed all along, the Burgundy Street bar of no name and the Quarter's stiffest drinks and cheapest prices, a place not to see or be seen, just to get drunk. And I got as drunk as I'd ever been, as drunk as I could get myself, drunk enough that sometime near dawn I picked up a steel chair and hurled it across the room.

When it hit the French doors it held firm and the doors gave way, their splintered wood mullions and shards of glass parting a couple staggering by in the pre-dawn darkness over the broken concrete slabs of the Toulouse Street sidewalk. Two boys locked in embrace in a back corner of the room leered at me, then hugged defiantly — like I'd give a shit. At the bar, the resident hooker held fast, working the crotch of a drunk and drooping senior citizen who rolled his head toward the shattered panes then back over his drink. The bartender, a lumbering mound, unshaven, drinker's nose and slit-eyed, approached my table sneering and toting a small wooden nightstick. I stood weaving, my head bowed over my newest double.

"What's wit' you, *compagnon*?" He loosened his grip on the club and tucked it into his belt behind his back. "Never took you for no violent type."

Raised my head, tears welling, anger pent up no longer. "Just leave me the fuck alone, Basile."

"No can do, *mon amie*. Somebody do what you just done," he patted the nightstick, "we got to get involved."

"I've had it!" I should've understood, had been in there enough to know, but some ill-conceived fight in me welcomed the confrontation. "I've just fucking had it!"

"Whatever *it* is," Basile was growing impatient, "got to take it somewheres else after you done pay for them doors."

"Well, lots of luck, Basile." He'd triggered another sore spot. "Just one more thing my brilliant career has left me without — money." Of course it wasn't about money. I'd given up on that long ago. "Yeah, yeah, I'll pay for it. Don't worry about it. I'll get you the fucking money."

But I don't think Basile in his capacity put much faith in the future, at least as foretold by me.

"It ain't about gettin'; it's about payin'...now. Le's say two hundred bucks. Nah, le's make it t'ree." He smirked, obviously pleased with his delivery, liberated of any compassion he might have had a few minutes earlier.

"What do I look like? A fucking pimp?" Now the hooker paused in her work to cast a menacing look my way. "Like I'd have three hundred bucks in my pocket."

"There's the ATM, right over there next to that door you done blew. You got you a bank account?"

"Not with three hundred in it."

Basile pulled the bat from his belt and mumbled, "Now you actin' like one *méchant homme*, you."

"Now hold on." I was not so drunk that I didn't know it was time to temper my bravado. "I said I'd get you the money, Basile. I'll get you the money."

I turned to leave. Just wanted out of there. Then Basile grabbed me by the back of my shirt and slammed the nightstick into the side of my head. I dropped to the floor, felt blood trickle across my nose and watched it drop onto the red concrete.

Later — I wasn't sure how much later — I came to on the sidewalk lying in the shattered glass, the ache in my head far worse than the pain from the cuts on my arms and face. I struggled to my feet only to be blinded by a menacing morning sun that found me over a French Quarter roof. I leaned toward my flat and wobbled through a crowd of early office goers scrubbed and fresh and taking little notice of me.

A life given to music. Everything in exchange for the harmonies of a fine tune expertly played, the interplay of skilled musicians, the approval of an enthusiastic audience. I thought back through the cold Midwest to the sunny Florida coastlines. To Artie Reardon's dining room and the lyrical playing of Bill Evans. To the finger-snapping adulation of Village crowds, even to the standing ovation at my college stage debut. To the night I played "Body and Soul" so tenderly and powerfully, to everyone's amazement, including my own. To the respect I'd won from Atlanta jazzmen. To Metropole and the players I missed as much as the playing.

Did it really matter that I'd spent so many years in anonymity from town to town and bar to bar, my gain at each stop a small check and another long drive? That even in New Orleans where I craved it most, I'd won little recognition? That my closest friend deserted me and the woman I loved found me inconvenient? That my parents considered me a bum? That my college buddy called me a coward, and a record producer called me a loser?

I sat at the Rhodes and fingered a melodic line over changes marked by close harmonies, then modified the line for the next four-bar phrase. Something reminiscent about that line. Kind of Gershwinian. Like "I've Got Rhythm."

What if…

What if I played "I've Got Rhythm" over a polyrhythm…use that line to start the solo…did the bridge in three-four? Neat. Nice.

No matter how far you travel, something new and necessary lies ahead. You will never run out of things to learn.

I smiled.

Epilogue

From William Belli
Contributing Editor, *The Times-Picayune*

These days, Tom Cliffe plays solo five nights a week at a small club several blocks into the French Quarter from Canal on the corner of Toulouse and Chartres. His photo is in a corner of the window at the entrance, under cursive lettering, "Tom Cliffe Appearing Nightly," the words painted, suggesting permanence, like the "Sale" signs in the windows of the Royal Street antique shops. The club is a converted warehouse, maybe twenty-five round-top tables over a concrete floor under a ceiling of exposed pipes. From time to time other musicians drop in to jam, including a brilliant if churlish saxophonist who calls himself Hacksaw and a trumpeter with a toothbrush sticking out of his dress shirt pocket.

But most nights it's Tom alone who fills the room beyond the New Orleans Fire Department's posted limits.

Occasionally there's a tourist, guided there by a hotel concierge, but most at the tables are locals partial to jazz who know the club as a place where the music and the musicians playing it are good.

Very good.

Many researchers have tried to determine the number of people in the United States who make their living playing music. One pre-pandemic Bureau of Labor Statistics count estimated 173,000 employed and another 70,000 self-employed professional musicians.

Organizations that represent composers and songwriters claim as many as a half million registrants. The American Federation of Musicians and other unions count in the neighborhood of 90,000 music-producing members.

But as all who have tried agree, there is no reliable way to measure the actual size of the population. The difficulty in quantifying the profession, in particular performing musicians, is understandable. Much of the work is night-to-night in different venues, and for cash, so players are hard to track: no W-2s or 1099s, often not even a bank account.

Like athletes, most musicians — songwriters and studio instrumentalists as well as club and concert performers — don't become stars or make much money. (The 2018 Music Industry Research Association's survey of 1,227 working U.S. musicians revealed an average annual income from performing of $21,500.)

Players can have their moments — work with a popular band, back a touring star, play a prestigious hall — and be appreciated enough to draw audiences, or minimally, accommodate them, and therefore continue to work. Many are extremely talented; virtually every town has a collection of folks strumming, blowing, beating, plucking, and singing impressively.

For the hundreds of thousands who call music their career, life can be frustrating: a commitment to a dream that doesn't pan out. And for those of us who enjoy their music, who applaud their talent, and who have our own unfulfilled fantasies and passions, their efforts mirror our own odysseys and how we ourselves have fallen short.

Acknowledgements

I want first to acknowledge **Linda**, my wife, who will not read this book because she believes it's about me and what I might have done or been before we met. For so much more, and that as well, there is no luckier man than me for having met her and convinced her to marry me.

The Musician is fiction. The truth is not so much in who the characters are or what they say and do but in the experience that generated them and their actions. The fictional musicians in Metropole were inspired by five guys I was fortunate enough to work with—all great players and even better people. Evan Fontenot, in particular his good nature and *laissez les bons temps rouler* attitude, was inspired by my closest friend of more than 40 years. I apologize to all of you for the deeds I ascribe to those characters in my attempt to portray a life that isn't always pretty.

I am grateful to the members of my Atlanta Writers Club critique group who listened to every paragraph of every chapter, twice, over the four years of its writing and refining, and whose input is on every page, especially **George Weinstein, Kathy Nichols, Chuck Storia, Marty**

Aftewicz, **April Dilbeck**, and **Kim Conrey**, who were there for the whole ride.

Thanks too, to my first editor, the brilliant author **Mary Rakow**, and my first agent and encourager, **Bonnie Daneker**. And to my early readers who contributed so much to the evolution of my story: **Bill Nahill**, who advised me to expand my original manuscript; my boyhood friend, **Bill Hayes**, who I learned only recently is also a career writer; **Mary Lynne Thompson**, who convinced me to add some early spice; and especially **Simeon Smith**, the award-winning documentarian, who was intensely supportive and contributed so much to shaping my earliest versions. I cannot fail to mention Atlanta Advertising Hall of Famer **Ken Bowes**, who on a drizzly February afternoon in 2015 at lunch at the bar at McKendrick's steakhouse commanded, "Write the book!"

Not a few of the stories within the story came from the great jazz pianist **Kevin Bales**, who not only shared several experiences that made their way into *The Musician*, but provided the knowledge reflected in many of the sections about how music, in particular jazz, is played.

Kevin continues to help me progress in my life's endeavor to play better jazz piano.

Jazz is a powerful and permanent affliction. To play it well you need not only more than the average person's share of creativity, but an understanding of the most complex relationships between notes and chords. As my character Artie Reardon noted — I take the opportunity to include the observation twice in *The Musician* — "No matter how far you travel, something new and necessary lies ahead. You will never run out of things to learn."

Getting an agent or a publisher for a first novel is a herculean task. Agents and publishers are pestered by literally millions with their stories, many quite good. Taking a chance on one is a leap of faith and a risky investment.

Which is why I am most grateful to my publisher and the pickiest editor anyone could ask for, **Angela K. Durden**. Not only has Angela spent countless hours putting my feet to the fire over timeframes, sensitivities, phrasing, and more, she also has my protagonist Tom Cliffe whispering in my ear that there is more of his story that needs to be told.

Mike Shaw is a writer and musician. He spent twenty years — the last five in New Orleans — performing in nightclubs and on concert stages as a singer-pianist, both as a solo artist and with jazz combos.

As a writer, he counts more than 15,000 published articles, from investigative pieces adapted by *60 Minutes* on CBS and ABC's *20/20* to ghostwritten articles, white papers, blogs, and two book-length documentaries for corporate clients. Mike's *Understanding Economic Equilibrium*, which he co-authored with Federal Reserve System Chief Economist Dr. Thomas J. Cunningham, was published by Business Expert Press in 2021 almost simultaneously with *The Musician*.

Mike has worked in radio, founded and edited city and trade magazines, and presided over three Atlanta-based marketing agencies.

"Until It's Time For You To Go" lyric print permission applied for from HalLeonard.com on March 22, 2021.

THE MUSICIAN
MIKE SHAW
BLUEROOMBOOKS.COM
978-1-950729-09-8

THE MUSICIAN

MIKE SHAW

Made in the USA
Columbia, SC
06 July 2021